The *Second Alcibiades*

PLATONICA MINORA, DUBIA ET SPURIA

THE UNKNOWN PLATO: Shorter, Dubious, and Spurious Works in the Platonic Corpus

Series Editor: Richard McKirahan

THE *SECOND ALCIBIADES*

A Platonist Dialogue on Prayer and on Ignorance

Harold Tarrant

PARMENIDES PUBLISHING
Las Vegas | Zurich | Athens

PARMENIDES PUBLISHING
Las Vegas | Zurich | Athens

This edition published in 2023 by Parmenides Publishing
in the United States of America
ISBN soft cover: 978-1-7335357-8-6
ISBN e-Book: 978-1-7335357-9-3

Library of Congress Cataloging-in-Publication Data

Names: Tarrant, Harold, author.
Title: The Second Alcibiades : a Platonist dialogue on prayer and on ignorance / Harold Tarrant.
Description: First edition. | Las Vegas : Parmenides Publishing, 2023. | Series: Platonica minora, dubia et spuria. The unknown Plato. Shorter, dubious, and spurious works in the Platonic corpus | Includes bibliographical references and index. | Summary: "This work provides a challenging new interpretation of the Second Alcibiades from the Platonic corpus, seeing it not only as a work of philosophic ethics, but also as one steeped in ancient literature, particularly Euripidean tragedy. The dialogue's philosophy is underpinned by an epistemology paying special attention to one's personal viewpoint, as its language shows. Dramatically, it presents a Socrates who falls into a similar trap from the one he steers Alcibiades away from, facing the dangers of a tragic character thanks to their mutual attraction. Understood in this way the dialogue, here re-translated to bring out such features, is revealed as the work of an author with linguistic and literary gifts who is deeply conscious of the human condition. While reminiscent of the Academic Skeptic picture of Plato, it is the work of somebody still moving cautiously in that direction"-- Provided by publisher.
Identifiers: LCCN 2022037451 (print) | LCCN 2022037452 (ebook) | ISBN 9781733535786 (soft cover) | ISBN 9781733535793 (e-Book)
Subjects: LCSH: Alcibiades 2. | Philosophy, Ancient. | Philosophy and religion. | Prayer. | Self-knowledge, Theory of.
Classification: LCC B391.A53 T37 2023 (print) | LCC B391.A53 (ebook) | DDC 184--dc23/eng/20221007
LC record available at https://lccn.loc.gov/2022037451
LC ebook record available at https://lccn.loc.gov/2022037452

Typeset in Monotype Bembo

Printed digitally by Integrated Books International (IBI), Chicago, IL

1-888-PARMENIDES
www.parmenides.com

For Judith,
who has endured Greek philosophy
for half a century

Table of Contents

List of Illustrations

Tables

Figures

Preface

It would be wonderful to think one could offer the last word on any dialogue either written by or ascribed to Plato. I would rather nobody ever imagined that I had this intention. My principal reason for writing is that I believe the *Alcibiades II* to be more interesting than most have believed, and from several perspectives: dramatic, philosophic, and historical. I also suspect that this text offers us important insights into the years leading up to Arcesilaus' headship of the Academy, and into the kind of epistemological theses that were of interest to Academics during this time. I think it not impossible that it was, in its final form, the work of Crantor of Soli or of the young Arcesilaus to whom Crantor had been very close, both as mentor and more personally. But thinking something "not impossible" is palpably different from claiming it to be so.

For this study I have not wanted simply to produce a new translation of the work, or to write the kind of commentary that is committed to addressing all points of relevance to the interpretation of the text. Rather, I have tried to offer my thoughts on the content and language of each section of the dialogue in turn, and to explain how those sections interrelate. I have been particularly concerned to tackle the dialogue's epistemological themes, since I want to extract everything of relevance to the possible connection with Arcesilaus—whom we know almost exclusively as a contributor to epistemological debates. However, I have tried not to take too strong a view of Arcesilaus, since most of our evidence comes from two or more centuries later and/or from opponents rather than from those sympathetic to his position. In the end I believe we have a slightly better candidate than Arcesilaus for the dialogue's authorship, but one closely connected with him.

While I have taken note at several points of other dialogues of doubtful authenticity or acknowledged spuriousness, there is much more that can be done in this area. Hopefully this book will be just one small step forward.

Acknowledgments

I have been indebted to numerous scholars across the world for details and thoughts that have contributed towards this book. Among them François Renaud, my collaborator on *The Platonic Alcibiades I: The Dialogue and its Ancient Reception* (Cambridge, 2015), has continued to offer helpful suggestions about my ideas and the relevant literature. My colleague Elizabeth Baynham has been of particular service regarding elements of Macedonian history. Will Altman read a draft and made some very helpful comments. John Dillon provided his typically constructive comments, and Richard McKirahan made many helpful suggestions regarding my translation. Various scholars, including Rick Benitez, Marco Donato, and Pietro Bertocchini, have kept me informed of their important work on the *Axiochus*, *Eryxias*, and *Cleitophon* respectively. My work on topics related to the *Alcibiades II* has also been published recently in a volume edited by Alessandro Stavru and Christopher Moore and in another edited by Andrew German and James Ambury. I have tried to heed all their comments, as well as points made by Christopher when we met recently. I have also been helped by the opportunity to present my work on the difference between the *Alcibiades* dialogues at a conference held at the Faculty of Classics, Cambridge University, in September 2018, organized by Ellisif Wasmuth, Frisbee Sheffield, M. M. McCabe, and Pauliina Remes. My late thoughts on authorship have been responded to by Christoph Helmig and discussed more generally at an international workshop on Crantor organized by Pia de Simone, Christian Vassallo, and Kilian Fleischer in Milan (January 9–10, 2020). To them, and to any whom I may have forgotten, I offer my sincere thanks.

Abbreviations

A = Aeschylus
Acad. = Academica or Academicus
adv. Math. = Against the Mathematicians
Ag. = Agamemnon
Alc. I = Alcibiades I
Alc. II = Alcibiades II
Alc. [Plutarch] = Life of Alcibiades
Alex. = Alexander
Amat. = Lovers (Erastae)
Anab. = Anabasis
Anth. Pal. = Anthologia Palatina
Ap. = Apology
Ar. = Aristophanes
Arist. = Aristotle
Ba. = Bacchae
Chrm. = Charmides
Crat. = Cratylus
Cyrop. = Cyropedia
D. L. = Diogenes Laertius
de An. Proc.= De Animae Procreatione
E. = Euripides
Ebr. = De Ebrietate
EE = Eudemian Ethics
EN = Nicomachian Ethics
Euthd. = Euthydemus
Euthphr. = Euthyphro
FHG = Fragmenta Historicorum Graecorum
Gorg. = Gorgias
HA = Historia Animalium
Hist. Plant = Historia Plantarum
Hp. Ma. = Hippias Major
Hp. Mi. =Hippias Minor
in Alc. = On Plato's First Alcibiades
in Eucl. = On Euclid book I
in Grg. = On Plato's Gorgias
in Parm. = On Plato's Parmenides
in Phil. = On Plato's Philebus
in Remp. = On Plato's Republic
in Tht. = On Plato's Theaetetus
Intr. Arithm. = Introduction to Arithmetic
La. = Laches
LSJ = Liddell-Scott-Jones
Lys. = Lysias
Lxx = Septuagint
Mem. = Memorabilia
Mor. = Moralia
Nic. = Nicias
Nicom. = Nicomachus
Nub. = Clouds (Nubes)
OC = Oedipus at Colonus
Od. = Odyssey
OT = Oedipus the King
Per. = Pericles
PH = Outlines of Pyrrhonism
Ph. = Phoenissae
PHerc = Herculaneum Papyri
Phd. = Phaedo
Phlb. = Philebus
Pl. = Plato
Plt. = Statesman (Politicus)
Plut. = Plutarch
Pol. = Politics
Prot. = Protagoras
Rep. = Republic
S. = Sophocles
Sep. = Seven against Thebes (Septem)
SVF = Stoicorum Veterum Fragmenta
Symp. = Symposium
Th. = Thucydides
Tht. = Theaetetus
TLG = Thesaurus Linguae Graecae
Tr. = Trachiniae
Tro. = Troades
VH = Varia Historia
Xen. = Xenophon

Introduction:
On Prayer—A Second Alcibiades

A Platonist Theory of Prayer

The *Alcibiades II* is a dramatized philosophical discussion of "prayer." Platonic dialogues regularly blend more than one principal theme, but this dialogue at least seems clearly to identify the topic of prayer as its *raison d'être*. Some readers, on hearing the word "prayer," may quickly decide this discussion will have little relevance to them. Perhaps they do not pray and are simply not of a religious disposition. Perhaps they merely recite prayers specified by a religious organization to which they belong. We may not believe there is any room for a change in our attitudes towards prayer. "Prayer" can be non-negotiable. Perhaps we should think again. After reading a book on Platonist theories of prayer of which I had promised a review,[1] I came away thinking that perhaps I did "pray" after all, if not as a vocal act as the Greek word usually implied. The range of things that seemed to qualify as "prayer" for ancient Platonists was wider than I had imagined. Perhaps we all "pray" in some sense. And as for this dialogue, it is *relevant* to anybody who simply has wishes. If we have ever made a wish when stirring the Christmas cake mixture, splitting the wishbone of a chicken, or tossing a coin into a wishing well, then it might just be that we have prayed. If we have ever bought a lottery ticket in the hope of acquiring a particular prize then the same might apply. Perhaps even the genuine exchange of marriage vows constitutes a kind of prayer. And perhaps these are all things that we really ought not to be doing, since they're neither wholly compatible with religious skepticism that respects only

1 Dillon and Timotin 2016; for my review see Tarrant 2017.

what the sciences can teach us, nor in many cases compatible with the teachings of our religion.

Therefore, if we are to obtain the best possible value from a reading of this dialogue, we should try as far as we are able to forget the associations the word has today, particularly for the adherents of any modern world religion, and to think of prayer rather in its ancient Greek context. The word *eukhê* ("prayer") and its associated verb *eukhomai* ("I pray") do not signify an act that only spiritual persons would perform, nor even an internal religious act, but something done aloud and outwardly which seeks to obtain outcomes in one's own interests, or those of the wider community. In effect one is petitioning the god concerned, and for the most part what the Greeks practiced is known as "petitionary prayer." Ordinarily one might pray for something for oneself, one's family, or one's city; one might be alone, with a few others, or part of a large communal gathering. Most commonly one would pray to divinities with whom one had established, or was trying to establish, a relationship: some god one conceived as being interested in one's own well-being. One did not have to be religious to initiate or participate in an act of prayer; one merely had to have some conception of supernatural power that could be persuaded to support one's wishes: whether because they were conceived as having looked after one's city or family for a long time, or because one either had offered, or was about to offer, gifts that were conceived as honoring the divinity. The more one wanted something, perhaps, the more likely one was to be praying for it: just in case prayer worked in the way that tradition said it did. Alcibiades wanted personal glory and wanted it badly, and in such circumstances it is not surprising he should have resorted to every means possible to secure some advantage in obtaining it.

Platonism found a good deal to object to in the normal Greek attitude towards prayer.[2] It had been typical of Socrates to call into question many of the suppositions that underpinned Greek life. Apart from his critical examination of the Athenian democracy on which most of his fellow citizens prided themselves, he is best known for wanting to re-examine and redefine the virtues—among which holiness (*hosiotês*) or piety (*eusebeia*) was often numbered, whether as an independent virtue in its own right, or as that part of justice that dealt with one's relationship with gods rather than men. The *Euthyphro* is

2 See Timotin 2017 for a continuous account of prayer in Plato and Platonism.

given over to an attempt to define, or at least explain, this concept, and in it some of the most cutting satire is reserved for the notion that it is some kind of science of prayer and sacrifice—or a science of getting from and giving to the gods as Socrates rebrands it. Ultimately, though, it is hard to see why the gods would need anything from us, and far from easy to explain why they should even appreciate anything from us. Conventional piety is built upon such notions, modeled on the way that fairness operates between human beings. We are in effect trading with the gods, either giving them something that we hope will lead to their repaying us in some way, or promising to give something if they grant what we wish. But what would the gods want from us that could encourage them to give us in return something that they would not give us if we abstained from such giving? What kind of trading would this be?

The *Euthyphro* asks penetrating questions, and in their very asking the ridiculousness of some fairly standard Athenian assumptions is unmasked. The fact is that piety of Euthyphro's kind does not exist. It does not exist because gods as Euthyphro conceives them, along with their squabbling, intrigue, and mutual violence, do not exist either. Platonism was committed to the idea that anything properly called a god or goddess behaves in accordance with what is best. That behavior does not alter no matter what we humans might want. We have no role in deciding on the gods' behalf what best practice involves. They decide what is best, because their knowledge is superior to any human knowledge.

So do our prayers have no consequence at all then? Will nothing we can do influence the gods? If we assent to such a proposition then we are coming close to another heresy: either the heresy that the gods care nothing for us, or the heresy that they have no power to intervene in our affairs. Platonic gods may only act in accordance with what is best in a given situation. Our actions can change what is good in that situation, for what is good in situations that affect us will depend upon our deserts. Our prayers, like our actions, may affect what we deserve.

For Plato, then, it was one thing to challenge people's perception of prayer, and another to argue against the wisdom or efficacy of prayer altogether. The very fact that prayer was deeply embedded within Greek life, and in the lives of all other peoples that the Greeks were aware of, could serve as an indication that there was something in it. Even the most respected speakers in Platonic dialogues could recite a prayer within them. Socrates offers a prayer to "Pan and all other divinities here" after his inspired conversation in the countryside with Phaedrus (*Phdr.* 279b–c):

> . . . grant me to become beautiful on the inside; and let all that I possess on the outside be in harmony with what is within. May I regard the wise man as rich; and as for gold let me have only as much as the moderate man could wear or carry.

This prayer is beautifully nonspecific, but expresses concern for one's internal (psychic) qualities over and above one's external (physical) attributes. It sees true wealth as being found in wisdom rather than gold. This is most unlikely to have been the type of prayer that the common man would favor, but is largely in tune with Greek philosophical ethics. Whereas in the *Phaedrus* the prayer is at the close of a discussion, the chief speaker of the *Timaeus* begins his undertaking with a prayer. It is as if Timaeus appreciates that only with divine support can a human being like himself expect to carry out what he has undertaken. One might regard this as akin to the address to the Muses that so often began an ancient poetic project, and this in turn may be viewed as an act of self-preparation. One must be ready to receive some higher inspiration.

Both of these prayers are far from being public acts, with only two and four persons being present in the *Phaedrus* and *Timaeus* respectively. Yet neither of these are silent prayers that confine the act of supplication to the individual. They are a little more than expressions of hope, suggesting also a consciousness that we are only human beings and not everything that we attempt will turn out right. Again, they are ways of trying to seek the approval of others present, including but not limited to supposedly divine beings, for the goals that we seek. But above all they are restatements of our goals and priorities for our own benefit, trying to keep us upon the kind of path that we identify as the correct one. Therefore they have an obvious connection with philosophy more widely, and with moral philosophy in particular.

It would be highly unusual for any dialogue by Plato or a close imitator to be exclusively devoted to a single subject. Plato loved to interweave themes, and his concept of philosophy was not one of a plurality of compartmentalized subjects. Everything interlocked. Hence we shall see that the *Alcibiades II* also has findings that may influence far more than our prayers. While (i) the dialogue arises out of Alcibiades' intention to pray, and (ii) there are two monologic sections of the dialogue (141c9–143a3, 148b9–150b3) in which the emphasis is firmly on prayer, and on what must be said and done when entreating the gods, the wider dialogical discussion concerns more than ritual practice, since the same issues arise when deciding what to pray for and in deciding what to strive for and what to avoid. The whole of the human endeavor is at stake. A dialogue in the Socratic tradition is expected to intertwine ethics with a concern for knowledge. It was so in the *Alcibiades I*, where the path to self-knowledge is emphasized and Alcibiades' self-ignorance, including his erroneous assessment of what he knows, is decried.

The *Alcibiades II* moves in a different direction. It is concerned to separate the kind of knowledge that may prove harmful for some human beings and in some situations from the kind that is always beneficial, so that this latter actually ensures the usefulness of the former kind. Placed at the center of the dialogue it is not a peripheral distinction, and it tells us what the author thinks philosophy should be all about. The fundamental requirement for a flourishing human life is seen to be knowledge of what is best, without which all other knowledge can easily prove harmful. To neglect the need to acquire and to act in accordance with such knowledge is considered crazy. And such crazy behavior is very important both at the beginning and at the end of our dialogue.

The Drama and Tension of a Relationship

The relative neglect of the *Second Alcibiades* is not the result of the dialogue's lack of interest. To begin with it involves a conversation between Socrates, the standard protagonist in the dialogues of Plato and many others, in conversation with one of the most controversial public figures of late fifth-century Athens—and Athens did not lack for controversial public figures. Alcibiades' flamboyant behavior that transgressed accepted norms was noticed as early as Aristophanes' *Acharnians*; and after his alleged involvement in the twin religious scandals of 415 BCE (the mutilation of the Hermae and the profanation of the Mysteries) he was prepared to turn traitor not once but twice, associating both with the Lacedaemonians and with the Persians. Indeed, the belief that Socrates' friendship was partly responsible for the way Alcibiades turned out may have been—if we can believe Xenophon (*Memorabilia* 1.2.12)—the source of much later antagonism towards the older man. And certainly Socrates, too, was highly unconventional in his own way, so we see in this dialogue a youth with some highly ambitious plans encountering a mentor with some very challenging ideas.

The *First Alcibiades* picks a dramatic moment in these same two characters' personal lives and builds up a certain tension because the reader hopes for a good outcome against the odds—indeed, against the facts of history. So too, here in the *Second* dialogue, we meet an Alcibiades on the point of trying to secure some god's cooperation in his ill-thought-out plans for enormous political power, allowing Socrates the opportunity to give him a timely warning and strive again for a better outcome. These plans have direct consequences for the city as a whole, even reaching far beyond the city, so that the drama extends beyond the personal situation. Strictly speaking, the *Alcibiades I* had done nothing to persuade Alcibiades against attempting to gain political power; indeed Socrates might rather have seemed to be offering himself as an ally in that endeavor—when the time came. In fact, Socrates uses Alcibiades' very ambitions in an attempt to persuade him that he is the right man to team up with. He might have persuaded Alcibiades that being fair and sensible were key requirements if he was going to achieve his aim of dominating the Athenian political scene, but he did nothing to alter Alcibiades' underlying ambitions. He simply encouraged more of the qualities that would be needed for the latter's ambitions to be achieved. The Socrates of the *Alcibiades I* might still be charged with being an accessory to the crimes of Alcibiades. While Xenophon can suggest Socrates might properly have been praised for making both Alcibiades and Critias sensible rather than for encouraging their foolish and incontinent traits (*Memorabilia* 1.2.26), what neither Xenophon nor Plato could claim is that Socrates had in any way undermined the determination of these prominent citizens to achieve their ultimate goals.

That, I believe, is why we needed a *Second Alcibiades*: because the *First* establishes that Socrates had influence over Alcibiades, without ever showing him doing anything to rein in the young man's ultimate aspirations. We need another dramatic moment, in a more public setting and with far-reaching public consequences, when Socrates can attempt to make Alcibiades reflect on the wisdom of the goals that he was hoping to achieve. We are not told that this is the first time since he met Socrates that Alcibiades has gone to a temple to pray for assistance, but we can reasonably suppose it is intended to be implied. If one has read the *First Alcibiades* it is easy to imagine that some providential divinity had actually caused Socrates to be there, though presumably not his famous *daimonion* (or "divine guide"), which never leads him on but only holds him back.[3] At any rate the dialogue does not encourage us to believe chance is at work on occasions like this.[4] Socrates appears in the nick of time, just as Alcibiades is about to pray for something that is likely to do him great harm; this is what Socrates himself senses. The need for his intervention is soon underscored by the reference to the unwise prayer uttered by Oedipus, the consequence of which had been the disastrous outcome of the war fought between his two sons (138b–c). And a little later it is revealed how Socrates suspects that Alcibiades is intending to ask for power from the god whom he is entreating (141a–b). Socrates is keen to stop him from doing so, warning him of the catastrophic consequences that despotic power or even high democratic office has had for many others (141d–142a). Not only for the sake of the speakers but for that of Athens the readers want Socrates to succeed. But what exactly do they want Socrates to succeed in? Are we willing him to successfully restrain Alcibiades or do we want him to emerge as a successful lover, at least in such terms as he recognized? And could it be that we are intended to view these two outcomes as being interlinked: an outcome for Athens and for Socrates at the same time?

Because it presents another crucial moment in Alcibiades' career, the *Second Alcibiades*, as I argue, presents us with a situation full of dramatic potential, and the success or otherwise of Socrates' intervention may be seen to have important consequences reaching far beyond the individuals themselves. I do not claim the author has extracted the full potential from this dramatic opportunity, but perhaps he has resisted doing so for good reason. Perhaps he wants to make an impact not so much through the situation that prevailed at the *start* of the dialogue, a

3 See *Theages* 128d, *Apology* 40a–b; this tradition is evidently followed at *Alc. I* 103a–b.

4 Tarrant 2015.

situation that we always suspected Socrates would be able to handle, but rather through the situation we are left with at the end.

There had been earlier talk of how most people cannot resist certain kinds of gifts, even when harm follows from them they eventually wish they had never acquired them (142c–d). Alcibiades has indeed given up his intention of going to pray, but the outcome has been an offer of the wreath, which had been earmarked for the god, to Socrates instead. Socrates agrees, not only accepting the crown but also affirming that he would gladly accept anything else that came from Alcibiades (151b4–5).[5] Would he then accept from him political office, or even tyranny, just because of where it comes from? Had not the dialogue warned against the hasty acceptance of any such offers? In tragedy, too, the unwitting acceptance of deadly "gifts" went far beyond that of the wooden horse, and included Pentheus' agreeing to receive from Dionysus the bacchant's garb that was his undoing, and Deianeira's taking from the dying Nessus a poison she took to be a love-charm, ultimately bringing about the death of her husband Heracles.[6] And all the evidence confirms we are meant to be thinking of Greek tragedy as we read this dialogue, from Oedipus' dreadful curse mentioned almost at the beginning (138b9–c3), recalling Euripides' *Phoenissae* 66–68,[7] to the quotation from the same play at the close. Matthew Sharpe (2012: 137) has written of the entire dialogue that it

---

5 Proclus, who accepts that the dialogue is genuine and is a great admirer of Socrates, has noticed the ending of the book, and claims that Socrates does not feel anything problematic in accepting and putting on such wreaths.

6 E. *Ba.* 821–838; S. *Tr.* 672–692, 1114–1145.

7 For the emphasis on this play compare Neuhausen 2010, 32. Several other passages in the *Phoenissae* also refer to the curse (475, 765, 876–880, 1051–1054). This may not have been the only play the author had in mind, as the Platonic text substitutes a different metal, "bronze," for Euripides' "whetted iron" (referring to the sword), and chooses a more prosaic verb διελέσθαι for Euripides' διαλαχεῖν (cf. A. *Sep.* 788–789, σιδαρονόμωι διὰ χερί ποτε λαχεῖν); indeed, while Carlini (1963, 185; 1964, 258) takes this as tragic echo, others assume that the allusion is from the lost epic *Thebaid* (Cooper: 1997, 597). However, accounts in the *Thebaid* are not known to have key details. Other tragic sources for the curse might include A. *Sep.* 785–789 and S. *OC* 1383–1389. The following points are in favor of seeing Euripides' play as an important source here: (i) both texts make Oedipus' mistake follow on from other woes (*Ph.* 66, πρὸς . . . τῆς τύχης; *Alc. II* 138c2, πρὸς τῶν παρόντων κακῶν); (ii) Alcibiades' reaction was that Oedipus was crazy, or not in a healthy condition (c7, ὑγιαίνων), whereas *Ph.* 66 talks of Oedipus being ill (*nosôn*) as a result of the blows of fortune; the echo in the phrase for unholy curses (*aras . . . anosiôtatas*, 67) serves to connect the act of impiety directly with the sickness.

"is filled with an atmosphere of darkness and tragic foreboding." This is much more accurate than Brisson's discovery of greater optimism here than in the ending of the *Alcibiades I*.[8] Euripides in particular also surfaces in the middle of the dialogue, with 146a making use of the same scene of his fragmentary *Antiope* as Callicles had done in Plato's *Gorgias* (especially 484a).

What had Socrates been thinking when he accepted the wreath? He knows the situation is extremely difficult, and it is underscored by a reference to the wreath of victory referred to by Euripides at *Phoenissae* 858–859. He quotes two lines from Kreon's words, which mistakenly interpret the prophet Teiresias' wreath, received for his services to Athens, as a good omen at a time of crisis (literally "stormy swell") both for him and for his own city. Yet in the play Teiresias' impending prophecies spell disaster *either* on the public level for the city or on a private level for Kreon and his son Menoeceus, who must be sacrificed if the defeat of Thebes is ever to be avoided. Kreon had made a dreadful mistake about what the wreath signifies.[9] Might Socrates not be making a similar mistake? He says outright he is taking the honor of the wreath as an omen since he believes that he too is in a crisis, adding that his wish is to become victorious over Alcibiades' lovers.[10] The dialogue closes with what is, in effect, his own prayer for victory in love—whatever kind of love and lovers he might here be imagining. And if this wish could qualify as a prayer, then would it not be a rash one, comparable with the ones that Alcibiades was warned of? Socrates is at a moment of crisis. Like Creon, he will take an optimistic view of

8 See Brisson 2014, 396n88: "Dans le premier *Alcibiade*, Socrate accepte d'aider Alcibiade, mais se montre pessimiste sur les résultats (135e); ici, Socrate est optimiste." The character Socrates may plausibly be described as an optimist, but only if Socrates still represents the ideal philosopher does this make the ending itself optimistic. And Socrates is quite conscious here that storm clouds are gathering.

9 Something of the complicated nature of this ending is appreciated by Johnson 2003, xx, though not the possibility that Socrates might be bringing disaster on himself.

10 If one acknowledges that the dramatic situation is supposed to follow that of the *Alcibiades I* then one may find it odd that Socrates should be craving victory over Alcibiades' lovers, who are all by that time supposed to have disappeared (103b, 131d); but victory may simply mean that he has more success than they had had, not that he is vanquishing any current rivals. Johnson (xx) believes that the lovers could be referring to the people of Athens, but they are feared as Alcibiades' object of love, not as his lovers, at *Alc. I* 132a. Socrates may be grasping his opportunity to wear this crown as a symbol of a victory that he hopes is complete, though in that case it is somewhat difficult to understand his fears concerning the present situation.

the meaning of a wreath held before him. But what would accepting it actually mean for him?

The dialogue can too easily be read as concluding with a claim of victory, but in reality it ends, at best, in studied ambiguity. Not only is it likely that Socrates, or some Socrates, is not here aiming at the correct goal, he may also have given religious offense and invited retribution—assuming the god to whom Alcibiades had intended to pray is indeed capable of responding to human conduct and rewarding both piety and impiety appropriately. He has accepted a present that was about to be given to the god. What can this wreath symbolize, victory over lovers or (dare one say it?) victory over a god? If the latter, then wearing it would be a case of that blind folly the Greeks called *Atê*, positively inviting divine retribution. But whatever one thinks, Alcibiades has now taken the safer course (151a5–6), while Socrates finds himself still facing a storm-surge (151c1) rather like the captain-less ship referred to at 147a. When one thinks of characters in tragedy who have accepted gifts honoring them above their proper status, one cannot ignore the case of Agamemnon, who against his own better judgment accepted the offer to walk upon a luxurious red carpet spread before him at his wife's request.[11] Agamemnon had previously offended by forcibly taking the virgin prophetess Cassandra, to whom even Apollo had shown a degree of respect.[12] Has Socrates somehow usurped the place of the god as far as Alcibiades is concerned, and if so what will the consequences of this action be? The dialogue is not intended to answer such a question; the very uncertainty that readers should feel here is enough to show that Socrates himself is not invulnerable.

We have said enough to show that the dialogue has dramatic merits, and to suggest that the earlier tension concerning Alcibiades' prayers is released only to introduce hitherto unexpected fears about the consequences of Socrates' choices. Such switches of tension are characteristic of Greek tragedy. The second drama in a trilogy could resolve one tension only to terminate in a different one, and hence Aeschylus' *Choephoroi* began with worries about the physical safety of Orestes in his just quest for revenge, and ends with one source of danger removed and a second even more horrifying threat to him emerging.

11 A. *Ag.* 908–957. The consequence is Agamemnon's murder, plotted by his wife and her lover.

12 E. *Tro.* 41–44. The rape of Cassandra by the younger Aias at the altar of Athena had earlier earned Athena's deadly enmity against the Greeks in general (E. *Tro.* 69–86).

The same might be said of the partnership of Orestes and Electra in Euripides' *Electra.* The personal disaster that can follow a long-awaited rescue is more than hinted at in Euripides' *Heracles*; it is actually staged. Aeschylus' *Suppliant Women* likewise achieves something for Danaus and his daughters as a result of their supplications, but the audience knows that the success will lead only to further unpleasant consequences. Indeed, Greek tragedies frequently depict prayers or supplication at the beginning, averting the immediate problem but promising greater trouble over time. Even in Sophocles' *Oedipus at Colonus* the initial prayers of Oedipus may be answered, leading to an almost transcendent release for Oedipus himself, but the audience will not forget that his actions have insured the future collapse of the family he has left behind. All this reminds one that the very stories that for centuries had captured the imagination of Greece, especially those of the houses of Cadmus and Atreus, were full of apparent victories with tragic consequences—including the very tale of the Trojan War in which the triumph of the Greeks was full of forebodings so brilliantly captured by Euripides in the *Troades.*

The strange thing about the failures foreshadowed in the *Alcibiades II* is that the lesson that Socrates had successfully communicated about what one should hope and pray for, though appreciated by Alcibiades, will eventually be heeded neither by pupil nor by master. The forces of desire for popular adulation are too much for the former, those of a different kind of desire, Eros, are too much for the latter. In spite of their combined talent, nothing that either has learned will be sufficient to control their lives for the better without the elusive knowledge of the good to act as a pilot. This is where the dramatic force of the dialogue unites with its philosophic message. Not even the much-lauded philosophic ability of Socrates, impressive though it might be, will guarantee that his choices lead in the best direction; even he needed to evaluate his choices better.

So although the *Second Alcibiades* is a work infused with drama, it is still a philosophic work. Further, it is a drama that shows almost constant interest in the literary heritage of Greece. It can rival the similarly brief *Hippias Minor* or *Ion* for literary interest, but whereas those two engage with interlocutors who claim special expertise regarding Homer, Alcibiades merely has the kind of literary knowledge that one would have expected his aristocratic education to provide. The choice of interlocutor and situation is not sufficient to explain the way in which the work draws its illustrative material from the tragedians and epic poets. Rather we should look to that literary legacy that is so rich with characters who appear to be set upon the paths of good fortune only to seriously stumble in the end. It is not the brilliance of the poets themselves that Socrates needs to appeal to in this work, but rather their part in handing down tales where humans appear to be achieving their goals, only to slip into errors that bring in their wake a reversal of fortune.

If I am right, then, the *Alcibiades II* is something of an experimental work, depicting the Platonic Socrates more as a tragic than as a philosophic hero. Alcibiades has no monopoly on the "fatal flaw," for Socrates is not exempt from it. His philosophic work is relatively easily accomplished, requiring rather less deftness of argument here than in many works of the Corpus Platonicum. Alcibiades can be persuaded rather easily, not through incisive logic but through the able choice of illustrative material that they both understand. Hence it will be one of the shortest works in the Corpus, with a little over four thousand words or about twelve Stephanus pages, as compared with something between eight and ten thousand words or twenty-seven pages for most books of the *Republic* or indeed the *Laws*. Many of the favorite dialogues that seem to be "Socratic" in tone, such as *Apology*, *Charmides*, *Meno*, *Hippias Major*, *Laches*, or *Lysis* are around this length or a little less, while the *Alcibiades I* had been just fractionally more. The present dialogue, however, is not so very different in length from the *Hippias Minor*, *Euthyphro*, *Crito*, and *Ion* among genuine works. It achieves its goals economically, but not with the same haste as some: *Hipparchus*, *Erastae*, *Minos* or *Clitophon*. These last are all often regarded as not the work of Plato himself, and the first two are dialogues that follow directly after the *Alcibiades II* in the Corpus. So can its relative brevity and position in the Corpus tell us something about its authorship?

The Dialogue's Place in the Corpus Platonicum

The *Second Alcibiades* has a special claim to be treated in close relation to the Platonic Corpus itself. That is not because it is *uninteresting* in its own right: as we have seen it has plenty of potential interest, and is only uninteresting if one's interest is narrowly confined to determining the intricacies of Plato's philosophy. Rather, the very doubts about its authenticity that have followed it since antiquity, when some imagined that it might have been written by Xenophon rather than Plato, raise that formidable question of how any dialogue not actually by Plato might have become part of the accepted corpus. Supposing that one work out of thirty-six (counting the disparate collection of thirteen letters as one "work") had been erroneously introduced into the Corpus, what guarantee could there be that other dialogues not explicitly referred to as the work of Plato in fourth century testimony were as "authentic" as we might like to believe? Hence few of the scholars who refuse to accept the authenticity of this work will accept it of all the other thirty-five. The choice would seem to be between accepting all thirty-six works as "genuine Plato" and having to consider the question of the authenticity of a great many other works, getting stuck in issues that often permit no definite answer. Have we got time to embroil ourselves in details rather than study the philosophy of Plato from whatever works seem most plausibly authentic? Is it not a waste of our ingenuity to be forever arguing questions of authenticity?

Issues of authenticity would be easier if we could actually be sure there were no third position in between that of the dialogues of which Plato wrote every word more or less as the best of the manuscripts record it and those which had nothing whatever to do with Plato and his philosophical views. I have come to doubt the wisdom of insisting on such a radical dichotomy, and clearly the ancients also did. Quite clearly those who thought the work to have been written by Xenophon did not believe that there was anything very Platonic about it, but a very different position was taken regarding the *Epinomis*. Here we have a work whose very title suggests that it was a kind of supplement to Plato's *Laws*, and there was a significant tradition that claimed that Philip of Opus, Plato's *anagrapheus* or "recorder" of laws,[13] was responsible for the final organization of the *Laws*, and went on to add the *Epinomis*.[14] But nevertheless we find some authors of the early imperial period such as Theon and Apuleius treating the *Epinomis* as straightforward Plato—indeed it seems that for Apuleius it has the status of a thirteenth

13 Philodemus, *History of the Academy* 3.38–39. The word hints at both the "promulgator" of laws (based on the meaning of the verb in *Laws*) and the "recorder" of in-school discussion, as elsewhere in the *Index*.

14 Evidence in the anonymous *Prolegomena to Plato's Philosophy* 24.13–16 is supported by a quotation from Proclus at 25.6–7; earlier evidence is found in Plutarch, *On Isis and Osiris* 370f.

book of the *Laws*.[15] That need not imply that Plato personally wrote every word, but rather that he intended it to be written and that it was written to reflect his philosophical intentions, much as we today would claim for the *Laws* themselves.

Besides the *Epinomis* and the *Alcibiades II* there were only two other dialogues[16] within the corpus that seem to have had their authorship questioned in antiquity: the *Hipparchus* and less obviously the *Erastae*.[17] In the received corpus, as arranged by Thrasyllus at least, these were the two works that came immediately after the *Alcibiades II*, and this means that our dialogue is from a particularly suspect part of the corpus. The fact that there are two dialogues that bear the same title is also sometimes regarded as problematic, even though there is one other such case in the corpus. Linguistically the *Alcibiades* is interesting for its unusual vocabulary, and it alone employs a Hellenistic grammatical form, so that this too requires explanation from those who wish to regard the work as consistently that of Plato. Yet if it is not by Plato we must look for an explanation of how it had come to be in the Platonic Corpus—no easy task.

Ancient tradition associated the *Alcibiades II* with the subtitle *On Prayer*. By the Roman age several Platonic dialogues had sometimes been known by such topic-related titles instead of by the name of one of their prominent speakers. Hence the *Phaedo* had almost routinely been known as *On Soul*, the *Critias* as *Atlantikos*, the *Menexenus* as *Epitaphios* and so on. Some of Plato's dialogues, in fact, were never known by the name of a speaker even in antiquity, including *Symposium*, *Republic*, *Sophist*, *Statesman*, and *Laws*. Even so, one expected dialogues, especially perhaps dialogues of a type readily known as "Socratic" and of modest length, to be known principally by the names of a speaker, a practice that implicitly acknowledges the dramatic nature of this genre, since many tragedies were named after figures enmeshed in the drama. Since the name "Socrates" was of little use in distinguishing which

15 See Stover 2016, 124–127, and cf. Nicom. *Intr. Arithm.* 1.3.5.

16 Individual epistles are a different matter; in between the twelfth and thirteenth are found the words "It is said against it that it is not Plato's." Precisely which of the two was rejected is less than clear.

17 While Athenaeus 11.506c had discussed the authorship of *Alcibiades II*, Aelian *VH* 8.2 shows the hesitation over the *Hipparchus*, while for *Erastae* note that Thrasyllus in D. L. 9.37 bases his interpretation on the assumption that (εἴπερ) the work was by Plato, implying that some at least had questioned this.

work was meant, it was standard to select the name of one of the other named speakers,[18] not necessarily the most prominent of them.

Two dialogues in the Platonic corpus are known as *Alcibiades*, and they are usually distinguished as "First" and "Second" according to their position in the received corpus. Diogenes Laertius adopted these titles in his list of the corpus at 3.60, just as he spoke of the two *Hippias* dialogues as "First" and "Second" (3.61), even though these are now usually separated rather by their size, as "Greater" and "Lesser." Yet he also spoke of the "greater *Alcibiades*" just afterwards at 3.62. The sixth-century commentator Olympiodorus is unusual in affirming that the *Alcibiades* dialogues were distinguished, like the *Hippias* dialogues, according to their size (*in Alc.* 3.5–8), though his commentary on the *Alcibiades I* was already known by an ancient scholiast on *Phaedrus* 227a as a commentary on the *First Alcibiades*. Other Neoplatonist commentators, such as Proclus (*in Remp.* I 149, 25–26, 186.11, 187.24), and Damascius (*in Phil.* 40.1, 149.6) speak of the *Second Alcibiades* when referring to the dialogue that is the subject of this investigation. Athenaeus (11.114) likewise speaks of the *Second [Alcibiades]* when informing us that some people had supposed that Xenophon was in fact its author.

Several of Socrates' followers wrote dialogues involving Socrates in conversation with others of his time, so it is not surprising that many titles are duplicated; again, the same duplication had existed among the tragedians, so that both Euripides and Sophocles wrote plays with the title *Electra* for instance. Several fragments survive of an *Alcibiades* by Aeschines the Socratic, who in turn is supposed to have made use of a work of this title by Antisthenes (D. L. 2.61). Euclides of Megara is also credited with a work of this title (ibid. 108). On the other hand, it is probably not to be expected that two works of the same title have come from the hand of Plato, or not at least with the intention that both should be published under that name, and the two *Hippias* dialogues are the only other ones in the corpus that share a title. While doubts are occasionally raised about one or the other of these, usually the "Greater," doubts are regularly raised about both *Alcibiades* dialogues. However, we should not be so keen to dismiss

18 The unquestionably genuine Platonic dialogues all employ named speakers; the *Hipparchus*, *Minos*, and *Erastae* as well as some of the acknowledged spuria do not do so, so that the *Erastae* (or *Anterastae* or *Rivals*) simply described participants in the discussion, and the other two are named after famous figures of the past referred to prominently in what seem to be revisionist quasi-historical digressions.

works simply because there is a shared title, given the slight differences in late antiquity about exact titles and considering there is no proof that the titles were Plato's own anyhow. The *Second Alcibiades* is in fact the only one of these duplicated works whose authorship we know to have been suspected in antiquity, thanks to the report of Athenaeus. The Neoplatonists, however, while excluding it from the selection of works that they studied in detail, seem to have accepted that it was written by Plato. In modern times, again, the balance of opinion has tipped against authenticity. Nothing in this study should be taken to imply that I regard the work as authentic, nor that I would deny that any material within it is by Plato. As much of the discussion as possible will be conducted from an agnostic point of view.

One should, however, be prepared to look carefully at what may be learned from the work's position in the corpus as listed in Diogenes. It is the second dialogue of the fourth tetralogy, and no dialogue in this tetralogy has been free from suspicions regarding its authorship in modern times. These four dialogues (with the possible exception of *Erastae*) and the first of the next tetralogy show a few similarities in their working vocabularies,[19] suggesting some similarities in their provenance—though certainly insufficient to prove common authorship. It precedes the *Hipparchus* and *Erastae*, which are the only other dialogues questioned in antiquity apart from the *Epinomis*, and, with the *Minos*, the only ones in which the principal interlocutor remained unnamed.

Furthermore, Diogenes' evidence suggests an *established* order of the two *Alcibiades* dialogues within the corpus. One cannot distinguish two dialogues by their order unless one's readers will all have met them, or be expected to meet them, in precisely the same order. His list appears to be based on the previous work of Thrasyllus early in the first century CE, for Thrasyllus had just been mentioned here (3.56), and is known independently (Albinus, *Prologue* 4) as one who sponsored a similar tetralogical arrangement of the corpus: one postulating nine groups of four dialogues each, and beginning with *Euthyphro*, *Apology*, *Crito*, and *Phaedo*. A certain Dercyllides seems also to have adopted something close to if not identical with Thrasyllus' arrangement, but we cannot settle their relative chronology, although both preceded Theon of Smyrna, another who wrote about the Platonic corpus and seems

19 Tarrant 2013, also 2018.

to have adopted tetralogies of some kind.[20] It appears from Diogenes' text that Thrasyllus had been claiming to have discovered or restored an order that, at least in part, went back to Plato himself, and it could well be that the claim was based on the order in which the dialogues had been preserved in an arrangement that had been passed down in the Academy.[21] Regardless of the exact details it seems that there had long been some reason for regarding the longer *Alcibiades* as "First" and the shorter one as "Second," and perhaps similar reasons for regarding the longer *Hippias* as "First."[22]

The priority of the *Alcibiades I* in the received order agrees with the very dramatic considerations that seem to pervade many groups within the tetralogical arrangement and are a major reason for Albinus' rejection of that arrangement in *Prologue* 4. Something like this applies also to the two *Hippias* dialogues, for at *Hippias Major* 286b–c we meet a forward reference to the display, hosted by Eudicus, that Hippias will give the day after next, along with an invitation to Socrates to come along; it is this display that Socrates seems to have just heard in the *Hippias Minor* in which Eudicus initiates the conversation. Such links are not uncommon in the Platonic corpus, and the last words of the *Theaetetus* appear to imply the immediate priority of the conversation with Theaetetus and Theodorus to the conversation with Euthyphro in *Euthyphro* as well as its happening the day before the conversation involving the Eleatic Stranger in the *Sophist*: thus justifying either the sequence *Theaetetus–Euthyphro–Apology* found in Aristophanes of Byzantium's fourth trilogy *or* that of *Theaetetus–Sophist–Statesman* within the second tetralogy.[23] The forward reference to the *Euthyphro*

20 Tarrant 1993, Ch. 3.

21 An earlier arrangement by Aristophanes of Byzantium (D. L. 3.61), again had once postulated dramatic groups (though this time groups of three like a tragic trilogy rather than a tetralogy). This arrangement dates from around 200 BCE and preserves the relative positions of many dialogues, e.g. *Republic–Timaeus–Critias, Sophist–Statesman, Euthyphro–Apology–Crito–Phaedo*. The arrangement seems to have made no claims to being a complete corpus.

22 While scholars now frequently presume that the *Alcibiades II* did indeed postdate, and to some extent presuppose, the *Alcibiades I*, nobody would argue that such a corpus order reproduced the precise chronological order of works. It had rather been a rival order of dialogues that had claimed to be based on Platonic chronology.

23 That sequence is preceded by *Cratylus* and the rationale behind the tetralogy is explained in a papyrus that may plausibly come from Thrasyllus and was published in Sedley 2009.

is hard to reconcile with the extant prologue of the dialogue,[24] which implies a lengthy process of checking the conversation with Socrates on subsequent visits from Megara to Athens, reminding one that cross-references between works of the same authors may sometimes have been added later, whether by the author or by his followers.

It is not a cross-reference that links the *Alcibiades* works, but the fact that the *Alcibiades I* is supposed to document the first time that Socrates has come forward to initiate a conversation with Alcibiades. Hence, if one regards the two dialogues as interrelated in such a way that they deserve to be placed side by side within a tetralogy, then dramatic considerations demand that the first meeting is given priority, in much the same way as Socrates' pre-trial discussion in the *Euthyphro* must precede his speech in court (*Apology*), his discussion in prison (*Crito*), and his execution (*Phaedo*). Alcibiades also makes an appearance as a character in the *Symposium* and in the *Protagoras*, but there is no philosophical dialogue between them in either. In the former they interact rather as two persons who have *nearly* been lovers but now ceased whatever relationship they had, while in the latter neither of them directly addresses the other since Protagoras' wisdom has temporarily caught Socrates' interest more than Alcibiades' renowned beauty. The order of the dramatic dates of the four works is likely to be as follows: *Protagoras* (relationship not yet started), *Alcibiades I* (relationship begins), *Alcibiades II* (relationship established), *Symposium* (relationship past). Yet Alcibiades is not central to the first and last, and other considerations have resulted in their being placed in different tetralogies. It seems that chronological sequences are not postulated beyond the borders of tetralogies.

Besides dividing the dialogues into tetralogies, Diogenes also offers a classification according to the "character" of the various dialogues. There seems to be little correlation between a dialogue's position in the tetralogical classification and its character, but I doubt that this implies any actual conflict between the two. Rather, it reflects the very different purpose that the two arrangements have. Diogenes tells us nothing of the purpose of the tetralogical order beyond that of its first tetralogy, which was designed to offer a kind of paradigm of the philosophic life (3.57), which would no doubt include the kind of investigation that Socrates pursues in the *Euthyphro* and describes in the *Apology*, some

24 A different prologue had once existed, as seen from anon. *in Tht.* III.

basic tenets mainly concerned with the practice of justice towards other persons and one's city, and running away neither from one's moral principles nor from one's city's decisions. These materials would have been outlined in the *Crito* and *Apology* in particular. Finally, it would involve the description of the philosophic life as a practice of death in the *Phaedo* (64a, 67e), valuing the soul more highly than the body, and avoiding rather than pursuing the pleasures of the body. Hence the philosophic life would, paradoxically, be closely linked with a concept of death, and with the goal of complete disembodiment.

With the assistance of the newly published Oxyrhynchus Papyrus (Sedley 2009) we can get some idea of the purpose of the second tetralogy, where, after a preliminary discussion of names in the *Cratylus*, the *Theaetetus* clears away some false beliefs about knowledge, before the *Sophist* and *Statesman* tackle knowledge from a more positive perspective with an emphasis on definition and division. This tetralogy then is seen as serving an epistemological purpose, offering a Platonic approach to knowledge. The importance of outlining epistemology (4) and logic (5–6) after introducing the Platonic concept of philosophy itself is seen also in the *Didascalicus* of Alcinous, the most important Platonist handbook to have come down to us.[25] Such topics were also afforded pride of place in the Aristotelian curriculum as organized by Andronicus.

No specific evidence tackles the rationale behind individual tetralogies other than the first and second, even though there are features that can be noted, including the late placement of the two tetralogies containing Plato's major political works, the *Republic* (second in tetralogy eight) and *Laws* (second in tetralogy nine). Indeed, the former might be described as having nearly as much to do with other subjects since the same constitutional pattern that can be observed in the Platonic state is likewise present within the human being and in the universe itself;[26] but the latter is more overtly political. The late placement of politics perhaps agrees with the fact that Plato never saw politics as an activity for the young, especially in these works themselves. The *Timaeus* and *Critias* make obvious sequels to the *Republic* given the recapitulation of

25 In point of fact the *Didascalicus* also moves from logic to metaphysics (arguably the topic of tetralogy three), then to physics, psychology, ethics, and politics, all of which are represented in tetralogies eight and nine.

26 The latter is hinted at when one reaches the end of *Republic* IX, but is of course taken up at length in the *Timaeus*.

details of the latter early in the *Timaeus*, and, as mentioned earlier, the *Epinomis* was sometimes regarded as a thirteenth book of the *Laws*.[27] Only the *Epistles* are left after the *Epinomis*, and, while a collection of *Epistles* had already been placed last in Aristophanes' catalogue of Plato's works (D. L. 3.62),[28] there is no shortage of political relevance there either. So, in short, we are not told of the rationale behind any individual tetralogies beyond the first two, but we can be fairly sure that there was one.

While there is much that we cannot say about the purpose of the tetralogies, what we may conclude with reasonable certainty is that the tetralogical arrangement as a whole was intended as a suitable *reading order*, supposedly reflecting any intentions regarding reading order that the mature Plato or his immediate followers might have had. It was not supposed to reflect the order in which Plato had written the dialogues like one ancient arrangement (anon. *Proleg*. 24.13–19), nor that in which he had researched the topics like one employed by al-Farabi.[29] Yet reading orders would ordinarily resemble these in allocating a definite position to each individual dialogue. By contrast, the character classification offered eight different types of dialogue, but the material is not *directly* linked with prescribed reading. Albinus, however, after giving the details of the character classification in Chapter 3,[30] does finally try to link the characters loosely with the five

---

27 See, for instance, Apuleius' summary of the *Laws–Epinomis* in Stover 2016, 124–127; cf. also Nicom. *Intr. Arithm*. 1.3.5.

28 See Mansfeld 1994, 68–69, who appeals to a further rationale for placing the *Epistles* last in the entire sequence, namely its relevance to Plato's life history in an arrangement where the first tetralogy had been illustrating that of Socrates (D. L. 3.58). While this is disputable, it is worth noting that the recently published Apuleian text (13) separates a group of works inspired by Socrates (*Republic–Euthyphro–Menexenus–Apology–Crito–Phaedo*) from another of the Eleatic-Pythagorean works (*Parmenides–Sophist–Statesman–Timaeus–Critias*) preceded by (a) the thirteen books of *Laws–Epinomis* that are thought of as using Plato himself as a character, and (b) the book of [presumably thirteen] *Epistles*, Stover 2016, 110–126. While we do not hear of *Minos* in this text, there seems to be an assumption that all substantial works of the ninth tetralogy concern Plato's views more directly.

29 See Rosenthal and Walzer 1943; Tarrant 1993, Ch. 2; Stover 2016, Appendix, 183–197.

30 Albinus uses the same initial division as Diogenes and the same eight characters (2), but "logical" dialogues are attributed to a different basic genus (6). It seems that the allocation of types to individual dialogues had been similar, though not necessarily the same as those given by Diogenes, but details are obscured by errors of transmission.

stages of his educational theory (6), though it is clear by the presence of three dialogue characters at the third stage and two at the fifth that the character classification was not *designed* to supply the five-part reading order on offer.

Hence, when we look at the fourth tetralogy, in which the two *Alcibiades* dialogues were followed by the *Hipparchus* and the *Erastae*, it is hard to fathom what might have been behind such an arrangement. All these dialogues seem to say something about love, but erotic interest is widespread in the corpus, and the topic of love is confined to the digression on the tyrant Hipparchus in the dialogue named after him. Linguistically, there is a tendency towards a certain type of vocabulary in the first three dialogues, but it is not evident in the fourth and seems to appear rather in the *Theages* that begins the fifth tetralogy. And there are other reasons to suspect that the *Theages* would have been more at home in the fourth tetralogy than the fifth, while the *Erastae* would have sat more comfortably in the fifth. The *Theages* is another rather short, direct (or "dramatic") dialogue, while Socrates narrates the conversation that takes place in the *Erastae* in a manner that resembles the *Charmides* and the *Lysis*, both from the fifth tetralogy. Two rival lovers are the title characters in the *Erastae*, while two friends share the interlocutor's duty in the *Lysis*, a dialogue that may sometimes have been known as *Friends*.[31]

There is a mechanism by which the dialogues could have become confused, for the *Erastae* is plausibly given the descriptive title *On Philosophy* (περὶ φιλοσοφίας) while the *Theages*, according to the manuscripts of Diogenes Laertius, was known either as *On Philosophy* or, no doubt more accurately,[32] as *On Wisdom* (περὶ σοφίας). If the confusion had been present at an early enough date then it could have caused a switch of order to take place in an early listing of the corpus—perhaps encouraged by the desire to place *Theages*, a dialogue well equipped to serve as an introduction and chosen for this purpose by some persons known to Diogenes Laertius,[33] first in some recognizable

31 The problematic evidence is from the Arabic tradition, but it seems that al-Farabi is referring to the *Lysis* when he describes a dialogue that he names as *Philus* (or similar) at the third stage of his supposed research order of the dialogues.

32 The term σοφία and its cognates are indeed prominent in the *Theages*, so that it has been argued that this title is the correct one.

33 See D. L. 3.62. We cannot be sure who these persons were but Tarrant, 1993, 58–72, discusses an arrangement in al-Nadim likely to go back to Theon of Smyrna in which *Theages* was the first dialogue to have been named.

section of the Corpus. If the *Theages* had been part of the same tetralogy as the *Alcibiades* dialogues then that would be at least three works in the tetralogy that highlighted Socrates' interaction with the young men whom he mentored. In theory the *Hipparchus* could have been a fourth, but we really do not know whether or not Socrates' unnamed "companion" in the *Hipparchus* is being mentored or not. What is more certain is that Socrates is not shown mentoring the main interlocutor in the *Erastae* because he introduces the story in such a way as to imply that he does not know the names of either the youths or the lovers involved (132a3–d6). So we are left with little sense of any continuity within the fourth tetralogy beyond the natural coupling of the two *Alcibiades* dialogues.

Perhaps, then, it is more profitable to see a connection between these *Alcibiades* dialogues and what precedes them, rather than to what follows. The immediately preceding works are *Symposium*, which introduces both the character "Alcibiades" and the tale of an unorthodox relationship between him and Socrates, and the *Phaedrus*, which suggests the importance of the main theme of the *Alcibiades I* and the notion that the beloved can somehow see his own reflection in the lover (255d). These connections are obvious, and one does not have to go searching for them in the same way as one must search for connections with what follows. It is easier, therefore, to see them as an appendix to their predecessors than as the start of a new tetralogy. If that were correct, however, then we should probably be looking at a later addition to the corpus rather than something that had constituted a proper part of it. That might have implications for authorship, but not necessarily.[34] One theory that has particularly appealed to me of late is that some of the dialogues of doubtful authenticity result from the

34 I have outlined elsewhere the theory that the Corpus had at an early stage consisted of four groups of twelve books, counting each book of *Republic* and *Laws* separately, so that the *Laws* was complete in itself and the *Republic* merely required the *Timaeus* and *Critias* for completion. The first twelve dialogues of our corpus constituted another group, as did almost all of tetralogies five to seven. I suggest that the *Gorgias* might originally have constituted three books, so that there would be some possibility that two dialogues from these tetralogies were added to the corpus later, possibly *Theages* and *Hippias Minor*. Absent from the list at that time would have been the entire fourth tetralogy, *Clitophon*, *Minos*, *Epinomis*, and *Epistles*. Absence from an early list would (in the case of dialogues at least) invite suspicions of spuriousness but could also be explained in terms of a work's having been temporarily lost or having been considered unsuitable for circulation in its present state.

augmentation and preparation for circulation of sketches left incomplete by Plato, and perhaps originally used for the kind of educated sympotic occasions that he favored.[35]

The Dialogue and the Midwife's Art

According to the "character classification" as presented by Diogenes Laertius (3.49–51), the *Alcibiades* dialogues belong to the major genus described as "zetetic" or "investigative." Whereas the other major genus was "instructional" and its subdivisions were divided according to its subject matter, being either theoretical (involving either physics or logic) or practical (involving either ethics or politics), the zetetic genus was divided rather according to the approach adopted in conversation with a particular interlocutor. Dialogues with younger men and those less confident of their wisdom are described as "gymnastic" or "given to training"; those with sophists and similar intellectuals are described as "competitive," and their subdivisions need not concern us here except to the extent that the more contentious attempts to trip up an opponent, used in conversation with Euthydemus, Gorgias, or Hippias, are not used against Protagoras, who is more interested in fair and proper rules of debate.[36] All this agrees with the fact that *every* zetetic dialogue was routinely named after the interlocutor held to be of most concern, rather than after its subject matter, whereas a majority of titles from the remaining twenty-one works of the corpus were always or often referred to by something related to form or content.[37]

Both of the *Alcibiades* dialogues were characterized as "maieutic" (or "obstetric"), a reference to the intellectual midwifery that Socrates supposedly practices in the *Theaetetus*. The process was understood by the anonymous *Theaetetus* commentator (in the early Roman Imperial period) as involving the reawakening of latent knowledge, such as is postulated by the *Meno* and *Phaedo*, within the interlocutor. The process of giving birth intellectually is therefore identified with Platonic "recollection." No doubt a maieutic dialogue was expected to assist the readers (presumably as Socrates assists the interlocutor) to find

35 The notion is explored in Renaud and Tarrant 2015, 260–269; but see also Tarrant 2018.

36 See *Tht.* 162d–e, 166a–168c; *Prot.* 334d–335a, 350c–351b, 351e10–11, 353a7–8, b6.

37 Always: *Apology of Socrates, Sophist, Statesman, Symposium, Hipparchus, Erastae, Republic, Minos, Laws, Epinomis, Epistles*; often: *Menexenus* (*Epitaphios*), *Critias* (*Atlanticus*).

within themselves truths that they had not previously been aware of. But the distinction seems somewhat opaque, and it is curious that the *Theaetetus* is *not* classified as maieutic, but rather as "peirastic," seemingly implying that Socrates had only made trial of his interlocutor rather than delivering intellectual offspring.[38] One explanation might be that Theaetetus does not manage to bring to light any ideas that withstand Socrates' scrutiny, but that they all in the end prove to have been "wind eggs"—something other than real offspring. The young man has therefore turned out to be less than truly pregnant (210b). And, indeed, the reader has not yet been guided towards seeing where knowledge really lies. All the ideas examined have turned out to be false. It appears from the new "Thrasyllus" papyrus (Sedley 2009) that the *Theaetetus* was seen as removing the obstacles to knowledge, before the *Sophist* and *Statesman* could unveil something of scientific knowledge itself.

If one were to follow this idea through, then the implication for the *Alcibiades* dialogues (as indeed for *Theages*, *Lysis* and *Laches* which are also treated as "maieutic") is that the discussion between Socrates and his interlocutors does succeed in enabling readers to recognize something of importance from within themselves, presumably mirroring a *positive cognitive advance* on the part of the interlocutor. Conversely it would tend to imply that there had not been the same kind of cognitive advance on the part of the interlocutors in the *Charmides*, *Euthyphro*, *Ion*, *Meno*, or *Theaetetus* (the peirastic dialogues). In this connection we should consider the position of the interlocutors who give their name to the titles, Charmides rather than Critias for instance. There seems little doubt that Charmides, who has few ideas of his own, is just as ignorant about the true nature of sound-mindedness (*sôphrosynê*) at the close of his dialogue, where he conspires with Critias to force Socrates into mentoring him (176b–d); much the same could be said for the pedantic Euthyphro, the narrowly focused Ion and the intellectually lazy Meno; and whereas Theaetetus has been improved as a result of his conversation with Socrates, it will take another "pregnancy" for him to have benefitted *intellectually* from his recent examination (210c1–2), and he will otherwise have benefitted only morally through his awareness of his ignorance (c2–4). There is still ignorance of the topics reflected in their second titles: sound-mindedness, holiness, the *Iliad*,[39] virtue

38 I link the term with Theaetetus' own suggestion at 157c that Socrates might be making trial of him.

39 Since Ion must be ignorant about Homer if he is ignorant about other poets (see 532c, 542a–b).

(*aretê*), and knowledge itself respectively. Yet could we not perhaps say that by the end of their dialogues Theages understands a little more about the nature of wisdom (*sophia*),[40] that Laches is much more aware of the cognitive requirements of courage, that Lysis is much closer to appreciating who his "friend" really is,[41] and finally that Alcibiades does in fact make cognitive advances regarding (i) the nature of a human being and (ii) the proper requirements for prayer. The five relevant dialogues were subtitled *On Wisdom*, *On Courage*, *On the Friend*, *On the Nature of Man*, and *On Prayer*.

Hence it seems that the distinction between peirastic and maieutic dialogues was being made according to the absence (in the former) or presence (in the latter) of intellectual progress by the interlocutor named in the titles concerning the topics specified in the subtitles. Could this be a coincidence, or could it rather be that Diogenes' source had been working to coordinate the primary titles (most of them already established), the secondary titles (a few already in use), and the characters, arguably an invention of the early imperial period? It may well be that in the zetetic dialogues at least the dialogue's "character" is to be determined primarily by the way in which Socrates interacts with the interlocutor after whom the dialogue is named, for this would likely explain how the *Protagoras* must be given a different character from those of other anti-sophistic dialogues, in which Socrates adopts

40 It is more accurate to see the *Theages* as having been designated *peri sophias* than as *peri philosophias*, which also has some manuscript authority; for the latter subtitle would double with that of the *Erastae* which precedes it, and it suits the *Erastae* far better. *Theages* begins by wanting to become wise (121d1) and to obtain wisdom (123d2), and by the end of the dialogue he at least understands the implications of this, that Socrates can offer him what he really wants, and some of the problems that studies with Socrates may involve.

41 One might deduce from 222d5–6 that Lysis will now believe that only the good person can be a friend, and from 223b6–8 that Lysis will now understand that Socrates is his genuine friend—more so than Hippothales—and also of Menexenus. Those dialogues that we should see as aporetic could be more positively interpreted in antiquity. At D. L. 2.29 examples are given of Socrates' success in turning the young towards the good and away from the bad, with three examples given from both Plato and Xenophon. For Plato, successful conversations with Euthyphro, Theaetetus, and Lysis are mentioned, all from aporetic dialogues. While the exact outcomes that are claimed for these written conversations cannot usually be documented from within them, it is clear that the conversation with Lysis is supposed to have made him "highly ethical" (if that is the right translation of *êthikôtaton*); while that may not necessarily imply an intellectual advance, it certainly suggests that the dialogue was seen as having a much more positive educational impact on the interlocutor (and reader?) than might be assumed today.

a more polemical stance aiming to entrap and trip up his opponents rather than impartially examining their positions. It is precisely this that Protagoras, as represented in the *Theaetetus*, will not allow, demanding that Socrates' dialectic should avoid playfully tripping (*sphallein*) opponents, and rather concentrate on helping their interlocutors to their feet, and simply pointing out (*anadeiknusthai*) the slips (*sphalmata*) that are of their own making (167e3–168a2).

We have so far spoken as if the "characters" were a rather inflexible set of attributes for characterizing Platonic dialogues. Yet at around 150 CE, Albinus, while preserving the terms for the eight character types, does not arrive at them by dichotomic division, and chooses to regard the "logical" dialogues as belonging to the genus "zetetic" rather than "hyphegetic" (*Prologue* 6). Such a move might imply that dialogues like *Sophist*, *Statesman*, *Cratylus*, and *Parmenides* were not setting out to establish truths by the methods that they unveiled, but were content to communicate the methods themselves.

Three centuries later, Proclus, who was still using much of the terminology as if it remained an acknowledged but flexible tool for the Platonic interpreter,[42] knew of early debates about the "gymnastic" content of the *Parmenides* (*in Parm.* 636.20–23), and whether it merely had dialectical training as its goal, or rather, as in other cases, illustrated that training with genuine problems, finding solutions that could be communicated along with the method. Proclus not only takes it for granted that Socrates practices intellectual midwifery on Alcibiades in the *Alcibiades I* (*in Alc.* 27.14–29.2, 209.11, 283.21, 284.8), he insists that Parmenides is practicing that same midwifery on Socrates in the investigation of his notion of Forms in the early part of the *Parmenides* (*in Parm.* 781.15, 838.19, 873.32, 898.17, 907.8). The "maieutic" method is rarely contrasted with the "peirastic" (a term that he applies to the *Hippias Major* at *in Parm.* 987.15–18); but it is interesting to see him contrasting the "recollective" method, which is virtually another term for "maieutic" (*in Alc.* 28.16–17, 171.8–12), a method that reveals

42 Of the terms that were applied to dialogues like the *Alcibiades II* the following are found in relevant senses: "zetetic" [genus], *in Remp.* 1.15.19–24, *in Alc.* 236.1–14; "gymnastic" [sub-genus], *in Parm.* 636.21, 989.8; *in Eucl.* 70.16; "maieutic" [species], *in Alc.* 27.14–29.2, 209.11, 283.21, 284.8; *in Parm.* 781.15, 838.19, 873.32, 898.17, 907.8, and 987.15 (contrasted with the "peirastic" mode). Some caution needs to be exercised, for though Proclus uses the adjective ἐνδεικτικός, that standardly relates to communication in a riddling fashion, as is evident at *in Parm.* 1027.22–26.

the truth to able young men, with the "cathartic" or "elenctic" one that merely removes problematic falsehoods in those suffering from double ignorance (*in Parm.* 989.11–16; cf. *in Alc.* 171.8). While he cites the *Alcibiades II* only in the commentary on the *Republic* (I 149.25, 186.11, 187.24), it is clear from these references that he takes it seriously as Platonic philosophy, and there is no reason why he should not have regarded that work as continuing Socrates' essentially "maieutic" services to Alcibiades, continuing to help him to see the truth.

One may therefore deduce that Proclus too would have recognized that Socrates' methods in the *Alcibiades II* lead to the acceptance of certain truths by the interlocutor even when those truths were not being directly propounded by Socrates. For Proclus these would include truths recognized following Socrates' suggestions about poetry (*in Remp.* I 186.11–14, *Alc. II* 147b–d) and more especially about the kind of poetry that will offer the most correct account of prayer (*in Remp.* I 187.24–25, *Alc. II* 142e1–143a5). While the modern reader is entitled to question how Socrates can merely be eliciting and investigating Alcibiades' own ideas here, even so the very opening of the dialogue makes it clear that Alcibiades' subconscious is already at work. His agreement with the main points of the argument is established, and, as the dialogue progresses, Alcibiades contributes rather more than one is expecting if one has just read the *Alcibiades I*.[43] There seems to be little inner resistance from false conceits of knowledge preventing him from assenting to all that he needs to assent to. He can draw the necessary conclusions, and redirect his personal aims in accordance with them, postponing his visit to the god until he knows for sure what it would be sensible to ask for. It could be argued that he had shown an innate sense that his present course was dangerous right from the beginning. It is to this beginning that we shall turn, once we have offered a translation of the dialogue.

43 His key contributions come at 143a6–b5, 148a8–b4, and 150b5–7.

Translation

The following translation is included because not all readers will be very familiar with this work, and the chapters that follow are best judged by those who have the dialogue fresh in mind. Brief passages of translations in the later discussions usually match the translation given here, though sometimes I have there preferred to aim at greater precision, while prioritizing fluency here. Nevertheless, the translation was intended to be based on the *results* of the research, and was finalized only after it had been concluded. Words in square brackets have no real equivalent in the Greek, but are easily understood from it, and supplied for the sake of clarity. Greek words in transliteration are sometimes added in parentheses for additional clarification.

[Plato]

The Second Alcibiades

The conversation takes place in an unknown location not far from a temple dedicated to a supposedly powerful male divinity. Alcibiades, presumably accompanied by one or more slaves, is in possession of a garland and a sacrificial victim to be offered to the god, and heading towards the temple. He is preoccupied with his intended approach to the god, and may not have noted the approach of Socrates.

<138a> SOCRATES: Hi Alcibiades. Are you on your way to the god to offer a prayer?

ALCIBIADES: Indeed I am, Socrates.

SOCRATES: You appear to have put on a frown, with your eyes fixed on the ground, as if you were anxious about something.

ALCIBIADES: And what would one have to be anxious about, Socrates?

SOCRATES: The most serious cause for anxiety, Alcibiades, as it seems to me. <b> Please, in heaven's name, regarding the things that we happen to pray for whether publicly or in private, don't you believe that the gods sometimes grant some of them but not others, and to some persons and not others?

ALCIBIADES: Certainly.

SOCRATES: Doesn't it seem to you to require a great deal of forethought so that one doesn't inadvertently pray[44] for bad things when thinking that they are good, and that the gods might happen to be in the frame of mind in which they grant what one happens to pray for? Like Oedipus <c> for example, whom they say prayed that his sons should divide up their father's inheritance with the sword—when he had the chance to pray for some release from his present woes, he uttered a curse, [asking] for others in addition to his present ones. In due course these [prayers] were fulfilled, and in their wake many other terrible woes, which there is surely no need to go through one by one.

ALCIBIADES: But the person you have mentioned was in a fit of madness, Socrates. Who in his right mind, do you think, would pray for that kind of thing?

SOCRATES: Well, does being in a state of madness seem to you to be the opposite of being in one's senses?

ALCIBIADES: Certainly.

<d> SOCRATES: And do there seem to you to be some foolish people, and some wise?[45]

ALCIBIADES: There are indeed.

---

44 Literally "escape one's own notice" (*lêsetai hauton*).

45 I was tempted to translate "senseless" and "sensible" rather than "foolish" and "wise"; this would have preserved the etymological link between the two terms (*aphrôn* and *phronimos*), and made the admission that there can be no third state between them more natural. However, the translation would have been a less familiar one, and obscured the connection with debates about the possible identity of folly and madness.

SOCRATES: Come on then, let us examine who these people are. It is agreed that there are some foolish ones and some wise ones, and others who are mad.

ALCIBIADES: Yes, agreed.

SOCRATES: And some who are healthy?

ALCIBIADES: There are.

SOCRATES: While others too are sick?

<139a>ALCIBIADES: Quite so.

SOCRATES: And they are not the same.

ALCIBIADES: Indeed not.

SOCRATES: Then are there also others who are not subject to either of these states?

ALCIBIADES: There are not.

SOCRATES: That's because it is necessary for a person either to be sick or not to be sick.

ALCIBIADES: It seems so to me at least.

SOCRATES: What about this? Do you have the same opinion about wisdom and folly?

ALCIBIADES: How do you mean?

SOCRATES: [I ask] whether it seems to you that somebody can be either wise or foolish, or whether there exists some third intermediate state, which doesn't involve the person being either <b> wise or foolish?

ALCIBIADES: No, not the latter.

SOCRATES: Then it is necessary to be subject to one or the other of these states?

ALCIBIADES: It seems so to me at least.

SOCRATES: Don't you recall having admitted that madness is the opposite of wisdom?

ALCIBIADES: I do.

SOCRATES: And also that there is no intermediate third state that involves the person being neither wise nor foolish?

ALCIBIADES: Yes, I agreed.

SOCRATES: And yet how could there be *two* opposites to just one thing?

ALCIBIADES: Not at all.

<c>SOCRATES: So folly and madness are probably the same thing?

ALCIBIADES: Apparently.

SOCRATES: So if we made the claim, Alcibiades, that the foolish were mad, our claim would be correct. Take for example people of your age, [consider] whether there happen to be some who are foolish, as indeed there are—just like some who are older still. Well come on, in Zeus' name, don't you think that of those in our city there are few who are wise, while the majority are foolish—the ones you are calling "mad"?

ALCIBIADES: I certainly do.

SOCRATES: Do you think we should get off lightly if we were associating with so <d> many madmen, and that we shouldn't long ago have suffered the consequences by receiving blows and missiles and the other treatment that madmen usually hand out? But look, my fortunate friend, I rather suspect things are not like that.

ALCIBIADES: How could they possibly be, Socrates. Perhaps things are not as I'd thought.

SOCRATES: It doesn't seem right to me either. Rather it should be thought through in the present way.

ALCIBIADES: How do you mean?

SOCRATES: Well I'll tell you at least. We are assuming that there were some people who are sick, is that right?

ALCIBIADES: Certainly

<e> SOCRATES: So does it seem to you to be necessary that the one who is sick should have gout, or a fever, or eye trouble? Or even if he didn't suffer from one of these, doesn't it seem to you that he would

be suffering from a different sickness? For there are many sicknesses surely, and not just these.

ALCIBIADES: To me at least there seem to be.

SOCRATES: So does all eye trouble seem to you to be sickness?

ALCIBIADES: Yes.

SOCRATES: Then does all sickness also seem to be eye trouble?

ALCIBIADES: Not to me at least. But I am uncertain how to put it.

<140a> SOCRATES: Well if you pay attention to me, "When two together go" investigating, with luck we shall discover it.

ALCIBIADES: I am paying attention to the best of my ability, Socrates.

SOCRATES: Haven't we agreed that all eye trouble is sickness, but sickness is not all eye trouble?

ALCIBIADES: We agreed.

SOCRATES: Yes and it seems to me that we were right to agree; for it is also the case that all people with fever are sick, but not that all sick people have fever, or gout, or indeed eye trouble, <b> I suppose. But everything like that is a [case of] sickness, whereas those we call "doctors" say they are different in their symptoms, because they are not all[46] alike nor do they have similar effects, each [affecting us] according to its special nature. Even so, they are all cases of sickness. Similarly we suppose some to be tradesmen, don't we?

ALCIBIADES: Certainly.

SOCRATES: Including cobblers, carpenters, sculptors, and many others by profession, whom there is surely no need to go through one by one?[47] After dividing things up they occupy different professional areas, and <c> all of them are tradesmen, yet all tradesmen together are neither carpenters nor cobblers nor builders.

ALCIBIADES: No indeed.

---

46 Reading πᾶσαι with T rather than πᾶσιν with B.

47 The five words τί δεῖ καθ' ἕκαστα λέγειν (140b8–9) have also appeared after the relative pronoun at 138c5, but searches have revealed no other case in the Greek language.

SOCRATES: So in the same way, then, people have divided up folly, too, and we call those who have the greatest share of it "madmen," while those who have a bit less we call "silly" and "dim-witted." On the other hand, of those who choose to describe them in euphemistic terms, some use "high and mighty" (*megalopsukhoi*), some "naïve," while others use "guileless," or "unrealistic," or "simple"—and if you look for them you'll find many other terms. All these are folly, but they have differences—just as craft appeared to us [to differ] from craft, and sickness from sickness. Is that how it seems to you?

ALCIBIADES: To me it's just like that.

SOCRATES: Let us return again then to the crucial point. It was actually at the beginning of the argument, where the task was to examine who the foolish and the wise actually were. It had been agreed that some such persons existed, had it not?

ALCIBIADES: Yes, it had been agreed.

<e> SOCRATES: Then do you assume that whoever know what they should do or say, those ones are wise?

ALCIBIADES: I do at least.

SOCRATES: And which group are the foolish? Are they the ones who know neither?

ALCIBIADES: That's them.

SOCRATES: Presumably the ones who know neither of these will fail to realize[48] that they are saying and doing what they ought not?

ALCIBIADES: Obviously.

SOCRATES: It was actually among these people, Alcibiades, that I was also including <141a> Oedipus. Furthermore, you will also find many examples among our contemporaries, who don't speak in anger, like he did, and don't believe they are praying for things that are bad for themselves, but for good things. He for his part not only did not pray [for good things], he didn't even think he was doing so; whereas there is another group that have the opposite trouble to this. I think that you'd be the first, you see—if the god to whom you happen to be on your way revealed himself to you, and asked, before you had prayed

48 More literally "they will escape their own notice" (*lêsousin hautous*).

for anything, whether it would be enough for you to become tyrant of the city of Athens; and if you thought this a mean offer and not at all grand, supposing he made the additional offer of [tyranny over] <b> all the Greeks; and if he saw you still under the impression that you had too little without [tyranny over] all Europe, supposing that he promised this too, and not only promised it,[49] but added that on the very day of your wish everybody would perceive that Alcibiades the son of Cleinias was tyrant. I think that you would personally be delighted as you went away, under the impression that you had secured the greatest of good things.

ALCIBIADES: Well I think that anybody else would do so, Socrates, if something like that happened to him.

<c> SOCRATES: All the same, you would not wish to acquire both territory and tyranny of all Greeks and foreigners, assuming that it was in exchange for your own life.

ALCIBIADES: I certainly don't think so. How could I, if I was never going to make any use of them?

SOCRATES: What if you were going to make poor and harmful use of them? You couldn't then, could you?

ALCIBIADES: No indeed.

SOCRATES: So do you see[50] that it is not safe either to accept without a thought things that are offered <by others> or to pray for them oneself—certainly not if one <d> is going to be harmed because of them or to be deprived of one's life altogether. There are lots of people we could mention, including all those who suddenly (*êdê*)[51] conceived a desire for tyranny and worked seriously at getting it on

49 There are a few uncertainties in the text at this point, but the general sense is clear.

50 The singular verb "you see" is characteristic of this work (in the sense of "you realize"), occurring six times at a rate of 0.136 percent of total vocabulary, marginally higher than in *Hipparchus* (0.124), well ahead of *Theages* (0.055), and still further ahead of all other dialogues. This agrees with the overall importance of the theme of sight and blindness. See below, Ch. 3, p. 91–92.

51 Normally "already," *êdê* is used twice in this speech after the aorist participle of *epithumein*, seemingly emphasizing the *immediacy* of the desire (141d3, 142a1); a third case (142b4) follows the aorist participle of *eukhomai*, expressing the desire for the prayer's immediate fulfilment. The only other case of the word in this work (150e2) appears unrelated. For *êdê* in conjunction with *epithumein* see also Ar. *Nub.* 322, Lys. 42.20.8, Pl. *Symp.* 209b2, Xen. *Mem.* 3.11.3, *Anab.* 5.1.2, *Cyrop.* 7.5.37.

the assumption they were achieving something good, but were plotted against as a result of their tyranny and lost their lives. I think you are not unfamiliar with certain things that happened only the other day,[52] when the boyfriend of Archelaus the Macedonian tyrant, conceiving as great a love for tyranny as *he* had done for his boyfriend, killed his lover under the impression that he would then become a tyrant and a happy <142a> man. But after holding onto the tyranny for three or four days, he was himself killed, the target of a conspiracy by certain others.

You can see the case of our own citizens too, and we don't have to rely on hearsay for this, but our knowledge is due to our personal presence—[I mean] all those of them who have conceived a desire this instant for generalship and successfully achieved it and who either are exiles from this city still or have died [as exiles].[53] Those of them who appear to come off best have survived many dangerous and terrifying situations; and it was not only during their actual period of generalship, but, on returning to their own country, they continued being besieged by informers just as viciously as by enemies' armies, so that some of them would pray to have missed being appointed[54] rather than to have served as general. <b> If the dangers and labors had been bringing some benefit, there would have been reason for it, but as things are it is quite to the contrary.

In the same way you will discover much the same situation applying to children as well—that some people have prayed to have them this instant, and as a result of their birth they have got into the greatest personal disasters and discomfort. In some cases, when the children have been unremittingly nasty, people have spent their whole lives in distress; but others, when the children have turned out well <c> and suffered some catastrophe, so leaving them bereaved, have fallen into no less misfortune than the former group, and would have preferred them to be unborn than to have been born. And yet, while these cases and a lot of others similar to these are so painfully obvious, it is very rare to find anybody who would decline these things when offered, or, if they were going to achieve them through prayer, would have desisted from praying. The vast majority would turn down neither a tyranny, if offered, nor a generalship, nor many other things <d> that are more

52 A Homeric phrase, literally "yesterday or the day before," used similarly to bring Macedonian events in the past (and involving Archelaus) to life at *Gorgias* 470d1.

53 I believe that *phugades* ("exiles") must be understood here; otherwise we should be told nothing about the circumstances of their death, and it would not be tragic.

54 Roughly "un-appointed-as-general." On the unusual language see Chapter 3.

likely to bring harm than benefit by their presence—in fact they would actually pray to get them if they didn't happen to belong to one already. Then after a little hesitation (*episkhontes*) they sometimes change their tune, trying to pray away the things they had initially prayed for. For my part I am perplexed and afraid (*aporô mê*) that people might indeed be "blaming the gods" quite pointlessly, when they say that *they* are the origins of their troubles. "Whereas they even of themselves, through their own recklessness," or folly if one should rather call it that,[55] "have sorrows beyond that which is ordained."[56] <e> At any rate, Alcibiades, that [other] poet might perhaps be wise—the one who, it seems to me, had been dealing with foolish friends, and on seeing them both striving and praying for what was less than good, composed a prayer for all of them collectively. He speaks in some such manner as this: <143a> "King Zeus," he says, "give us good things both when we pray for them and when unprayed for," but he tells him to "ward off evils even when we pray for them." It certainly seems to me that the poet is speaking well and safely. But if you have any response in mind to this, don't hesitate to say it.

ALCIBIADES: It's hard, Socrates, to contradict what has been well said. But I do have one thing at least in mind, the number of evils that ignorance is cause of for people, assuming that it is the reason, as it probably is, why we have failed to notice ourselves <b> striving, and in extreme cases praying, for the worst of outcomes for ourselves. That is something that nobody would believe. Rather, everybody would surely think that he has the competence to select for himself the best things to pray for, and not the worst. That would really be like a curse[57] rather than a prayer.

SOCRATES: Though perhaps, my good fellow, some gentleman who happened to be wiser than me or you would claim that we were not right <c> in blaming ignorance in this indiscriminate way,

55 Since it has already been established at 140c that "folly" is the genus under which various kinds of madness and stupidity should be listed.

56 For the quotation of *Od.* 1.32–34 I have used the 1919 Loeb translation by A. T. Murray, which better captures the archaic language of Homer. The words in Homer are given to Zeus. Note that Socrates here does not attribute any special authority to Homer (as at 147c) or to his "Zeus," for *aporô mê* can scarcely indicate a stable commitment to the truth of these words.

57 Alluding to Oedipus' curse at 138c3.

as long as we fail to add that the ignorance of some things and for certain people in a given condition is a good thing, just as it is bad for those ones.

ALCIBIADES: What do you mean? Is it better for anybody in any condition to be ignorant of anything at all rather than to know it?

SOCRATES: It seems so to me at least. Doesn't it to you?

ALCIBIADES: No in heaven, certainly not!

SOCRATES: Well I'm certainly not going to level this accusation against you, that you'd be willing to commit the same act against your own mother that they say Orestes did, and Alcmeon, and anybody else <d> who happens to have committed the same act as them.

ALCIBIADES: Good lord, Socrates, hush [*euphêmei*]![58]

SOCRATES: It's not the one who says that you wouldn't have let yourself do it, Alcibiades, that you should be telling to hush, but far rather anybody who were going to say the opposite, since the deed seems to you so very terrible that one didn't ought to speak so carelessly of it. Do you think that Orestes, if he had happened to have been in his senses (*phronimos*) and known what was best for him to do, would have dared to commit any of these things?

ALCIBIADES: No indeed.

<e> SOCRATES: No, and nor would I think anybody else would.

ALCIBIADES: Certainly not.

SOCRATES: Then apparently ignorance of what's best is an evil, and not to recognize what's best?

ALCIBIADES: It seems so to me at least.

SOCRATES: That surely applies both to him and to everybody else.

ALCIBIADES: I agree.

SOCRATES: So let's go on to examine this additional point. Suppose it came into your head on the spur of the moment,[59] because

58 Used when an utterance seems to involve impiety (*asebeia*), i.e. offences against either the gods or one's parents, etc.

59 The immediacy of the wish to get something done is still a factor, but the language has changed. Here we have a good example of the ability of the author to portray vividly a dramatic sequence of events.

you'd imagined it was better, to [approach] Pericles, your own guardian and friend, with a dagger: <144a> to go up to his door and ask if he was inside, with the intention of killing him and nobody else—and they confirm he is there. And I'm not saying you'd willingly do any of this, but, I'm thinking, *what if* it seemed good to you—surely there's nothing to prevent the thought sometimes coming into the head of anybody ignorant of what's best, so that they actually believe on occasion that the worst course is the best? Or doesn't it seem so to you?

ALCIBIADES: Certainly.

SOCRATES: So *if* you were to go inside and saw the man himself, <b> but failed to recognize him and thought it was somebody else, would you still dare to kill him?

ALCIBIADES: Heavens no, I don't think I would.

SOCRATES: Because you surely wouldn't kill anybody you encountered, but only the person whom you wanted [to kill]. Is that right?

ALCIBIADES: Yes.

SOCRATES: And presumably if you were to undertake the deed many times, but always failed to recognize Pericles whenever you were on the point of succeeding, you would never actually set upon him.

ALCIBIADES: No indeed.

SOCRATES: What about this? Do you think that Orestes would have ever set upon his mother if he had similarly failed to recognize her?

<c> ALCIBIADES: I at least don't think so.

SOCRATES: That's surely because not even he intended to kill any chance woman or the mother of anybody at all, only his own.

ALCIBIADES: That's right.

SOCRATES: Then it is better for people in that condition and with views like that to be ignorant in cases like that.

ALCIBIADES: Evidently.

SOCRATES: So you see that the ignorance of some things is for some people and in some conditions a good thing, not a bad one as it just now seemed to you.

ALCIBIADES: Apparently.

<d> SOCRATES: Then go on to consider this next point, if you like—one that might appear strange to you.

ALCIBIADES: Precisely what, Socrates?

SOCRATES: To put it bluntly, it seems probable that the possession of other kinds of knowledge at least, if one possesses them without knowledge of what's best, is seldom beneficial and for the most part harms the one who has it. Look at it this way: doesn't it seem necessary to you, whenever we make it our intention to do or say something, that we should first either believe that we know, or actually know, about whatever <e> we are more readily intending to say or do?

ALCIBIADES: It seems so to me.

SOCRATES: Take the orators, for instance. On any given occasion it's when they either know or think they know how to advise that they do advise us—some about war and peace, some about the building of walls and the equipping of harbors; and to sum it up, every operation that the <145a> city undertakes regarding another city, or regarding itself internally, all of it happens on the advice of the orators.

ALCIBIADES: True.

SOCRATES: So look at what comes after this.

ALCIBIADES: If I am able.

SOCRATES: You surely call people wise or foolish?

ALCIBIADES: I at least do.

SOCRATES: The majority fools, and the minority wise?

ALCIBIADES: Correct.

SOCRATES: Don't you have something in view in both cases?

ALCIBIADES: Yes.

<b> SOCRATES: Do you call this kind of person wise, who knows how to give advice, without knowing which course is better and when it is better?

ALCIBIADES: No indeed.

SOCRATES: Nor, I believe, the one who knows just how to wage war, without knowing when it is better and for how long? Right?

ALCIBIADES: Yes.

SOCRATES: Nor indeed anybody who knows how to have people executed, fined, or exiled from their country, irrespective of when it is better, and who it is better to do it to?

ALCIBIADES: Certainly not.

<c> SOCRATES: Then whoever has knowledge of such things, if it is accompanied by knowledge of what's best[60]—this being the same surely as [knowledge of] what's beneficial, is that right?

ALCIBIADES: Yes.—

SOCRATES: That is the person we shall claim to be wise and to be a competent advisor for the city and for himself. For the other sort we'll claim the opposite. Or how does it seem to you?

ALCIBIADES: Just like that to me.

SOCRATES: What if somebody knows how to ride horses and shoot arrows, or to box, wrestle, or compete in some other way, or any other <d> of the kind of things that we know through some skill? What do you call the person who knows what is better from the point of view of that skill? Don't you call the one who knows from the equestrian art a "horseman"?

ALCIBIADES: I do at least.

SOCRATES: And again, the one who knows from boxing's art a "boxer," from the *aulos* playing art an *aulos* "musician," and so on, with other skills on the same principle? Or is it different somehow?

ALCIBIADES: No, just like that.

SOCRATES: So does it seem to you to be necessary that the one who is knowledgeable about one of these should therefore be a wise man, or <e> shall we say he falls far short of it?

ALCIBIADES: A long way, heavens yes.

60 The sentence continues into Socrates' next speech, after the parenthetic exchange.

SOCRATES: What kind of society (*politeia*) do you think it would be if we had good archers and *aulos* players, plus athletes and craftsman of other kinds; and intermingling with them those about whom we have just now spoken who know about war-making narrowly conceived or about securing executions narrowly conceived; and in addition rhetoricians, bellowing forth their public bluster—all of these, but without the knowledge of what's best, or the person who knew when it was better to employ each of these, <146a> and upon whom?

ALCIBIADES: A rotten one in my view, Socrates.

SOCRATES: You would certainly say so, I believe, when you see each one of them taking sides, and "attributing the greatest role" in that community (*polis*) "to this [role] in which he happens to be at his most excellent"[61]—I mean the one in which he is best by the standards of his actual craft, but for the most part mistaken about what's best for the city, his own self included, presumably because he has put his trust in opinion without intelligence.[62] <b> This being the case, shouldn't we be right to claim that such a community was rife with confusion and lawlessness in abundance?

ALCIBIADES: We'd be right indeed, by heavens.

SOCRATES: Didn't it seem to us necessary that we must first of all think we know, or actually know, about whatever we were readily going to undertake or say?

ALCIBIADES: It seemed so.

SOCRATES: And also that if a person was doing what he knew about or thought he knew about, and it turned out that he was doing so beneficially, we should have a profitable situation, <c> not only for the community but in his case for himself as well.

ALCIBIADES: Of course.

---

61 The author has adapted Euripides' *Antiope* (fr. 184), presumably imitating *Gorgias* 484a6–7, and rejecting the kind of society to which Callicles' ideas would lead. For discussion and an alternative translation and comment see Chapter 4, pp. 109–110.

62 A phrase that will be repeated at 146c12–13, and recalls the themes of the *Gorgias*, especially 454c–e, 467a, and 466e (quoted in Chapter 4, p. 111), as well as *Meno* 99e.

SOCRATES: Then again, I presume, if he acted in the opposite fashion to this, [we should have profit] neither for the community nor for the man himself.

ALCIBIADES: No indeed.

SOCRATES: Well then, does it still seem the same to you now, or somewhat different?

ALCIBIADES: No, just like that.

SOCRATES: Then didn't you say that you called the majority foolish and the minority wise?

ALCIBIADES: I certainly did.

SOCRATES: And we are reaffirming that the majority are mistaken about what's best, because for the most part at least they have put their trust in opinion without intelligence.

<d> ALCIBIADES: Yes, we do affirm it.

SOCRATES: Then it is profitable for the majority neither to know nor to think they know anything, presuming that they are more eager to undertake whatever things they know about or think they know about, in doing so to be harmed for the most part rather than to be benefited.

ALCIBIADES: You speak with a lot of truth.

SOCRATES: So you see, when I was making the claim that, just perhaps, possession of the other kinds of <e> knowledge, if one has obtained it without knowledge of what's best, seldom benefits and for the most part harms its possessor, didn't I in fact turn out to be speaking the truth?

ALCIBIADES: Even if it didn't seem so then, it does seem so to me now, Socrates.

SOCRATES: Then it is necessary both for the community (*polis*) and for the person (*psukhê*)[63] that is going to live correctly to grasp hold of this knowledge, just as a sick man must hold onto a doctor or the

---

63 As at 141c1 the word does not easily translate as "soul," as it would normally mean in a Platonic text. However, the word may well be intended to recall the *Republic*'s analogy between *polis* and *psukhê*, and there "soul" would be the normal translation.

man who is going to travel safely by sea must hold onto a helmsman. <147a> So to the extent that one more readily (*pro<kheiro>teron*)[64] gives a tail wind to the object of one's prayer[65]—for without this [knowledge] it will involve either the acquisition of property or the strength of the body or some such thing—to that extent, as is likely, are greater upsets inevitably going to arise as a result. As for the man who has made himself into a so-called polymath or jack of all trades, but is left without the protection (*orphanos*) of this particular knowledge and driven on by each of the others singly, will he not actually deserve to experience "a perfect storm"—because it is with no helmsman, I think, <b> that he continues on his ocean course—throughout his brief life. And so it seems to me that here too the line of the poet comes to fulfillment, which he presumably utters in condemnation of somebody, saying that "many were the deeds he knew, but badly did he know them all."

ALCIBIADES: How on earth is the poet's line fulfilled, Socrates? To me it does not seem to have been composed to any purpose at all.

SOCRATES: It's very much to the point. In fact, my good fellow, this poet speaks in riddles like almost all of the other ones as well. The entire poetic art, you see, is by nature enigmatic, and <c> not for the man in the street to discern. And further, in addition to being such by nature, whenever it takes hold of a grudging man, who does not want to unveil his wisdom for us but rather to keep it hidden as far as possible, it becomes terribly hard to work out the matter of what each of them means. You would surely not imagine that Homer at least, the most godlike and wise of the poets, was ignorant of the fact that it wasn't possible to know something *badly*. After all, he is the one who states that Margites knew many things <d> but knew all of them badly.[66] Rather, I think, he is speaking in riddles by introducing the adverb "badly" for the adjective "bad," and [the second] "he knew" for

64 The received text of this passage is very difficult, and caution should be exercised. This emendation is discussed on pp. 114–115. The meaning here is close to "hurriedly," but I translate it as I do at 144d9 and 146b6. I also consider a similar alternative *pro<thumo>teron*, "more enthusiastically."

65 On this sentence see Chapter 4, pp. 114–116, where the proposed text (much closer to the manuscripts than anything usually printed) is first translated more literally.

66 This claim is now controversial, but was probably accepted at the time of writing, when Aristotle and others seem to have accepted Homeric authorship. The character Margites came to the fore in public discourse in the third quarter of the fourth century, and was compared to Alexander.

the infinitive "to know." So with this addition it turns out—no longer in meter certainly, though it's what he meant at least—that he knew many deeds but that it was bad for him to know all of them. So it is clear, given that knowing many things was bad for him, that he was actually a worthless fellow—at least if one should trust the claims that were argued before.

<e> ALCIBIADES: Well it seems to me that we must, Socrates. I'd surely be hard pressed to trust any other arguments, if I didn't even trust these.

SOCRATES: Yes, and you are right to take this view.

ALCIBIADES: Once again it seems so to me!

SOCRATES: Well come along then, in heaven's name. I mean, you surely see now the magnitude and nature of the problem, and you too seem to me to be one of those involved in it. You just don't stop veering this way and that even for a moment. Instead, whatever it is that seems most obvious to you, it has soon sunk out of sight <148a> and no longer seems the same. So if the god to whom you happen to be going even now were to stand revealed to you, and asked before you had uttered any prayer whether one of those things of which we were first speaking would suffice for you, or whether he should actually entrust you with making a prayer, what do you think would have the timeliest outcome, accepting one of his offers or offering your own prayer?

ALCIBIADES: Goodness gracious, I'd have nothing to say to you, Socrates, straight out. It[67] seems to me to be rather buffoonish,[68] <b> and really a matter for[69] considerable caution so that a person does not inadvertently pray for bad things when thinking that they are good,[70]

67 What precisely, is buffoonish here? Carlini 1963, 187, proposed a lacuna, to be filled with something like "to accept offers without thinking." But perhaps it is the hypothetical situation with which Socrates has confronted him.

68 The word used echoes the name of Margites, and hence I have used a word that captures the quality of the comic "hero." While it is possible that the word means something closer to "crazy," it has no obvious link with the dialogue's theme of madness.

69 Again, it may be that the verb *deisthai* or *prosdeisthai* ("to require") has fallen out, picking up 138b6 (cf. also 149c6). It seems to me, however, that the received text will suffice.

70 There are clear echoes of 138b6–8 early in the dialogue.

then, "after a little hesitation," as you too were saying, "change his tune, trying to pray away the things he had initially prayed for."[71]

SOCRATES: Then was it not with some knowledge greater than ours that the poet whom I mentioned at the start of the discussion asked [Zeus] to "ward off evils even when we pray for them"?[72]

ALCIBIADES: It seems so to me at least.

SOCRATES: Well then, Alcibiades, it is in emulation of this poet, <c> or else by a similar examination [of the issues], that the Spartans regularly employ a very similar prayer both in private and in public, once again asking the gods to bestow upon themselves what is noble as well as what's good. Nobody could hear those people praying for any more than this. Accordingly, right up to the present time they have been no less successful than any other people. Even though the result for them was not invariably successful, at least this [lack of success] didn't happen because of <d> their own prayer, and it is in the power of the gods, I presume, both to give whatever somebody happens to pray for and [to give] quite its exact opposite. I now want to tell you another story, too, which I once heard from some of my elders.[73]

It told how, when conflict broke out between the Athenians and Spartans, the result for our city was always misfortune, both by land and by sea whenever a battle took place, and that it was never able to secure victory. So the Athenians, grumbling about this business, and wondering by what <e> means they should find release from their present woes, decided on deliberation that it was best to send people to Ammon and ask him.[74] And further, in addition to this, to ask *in return for what* the gods gave victory to the Spartans rather than to themselves: "Us, who, of all the Greeks," they claimed, "conduct the greatest number and most splendid sacrifices, have adorned their

71 Apart from singulars for plurals and the subjunctive for the indicative, this reproduces Socrates' words at 142d2–4.

72 See 143a1–2, where the verses make it plain that it was Zeus who was being addressed.

73 I see no reason to delete the words "of my elders" as Burnet did; the telling of stories in ancient Greece routinely involved older persons communicating with younger ones, as is particularly evident at *Protagoras* 320c2–4, *Gorgias* 527a5, *Republic* 377a, and *Timaeus* 20e–21d. Reference to the provenance of the story tends to confirm its mythical status, and there is no historical time that the details could fit.

74 The idea of a state mission to the Libyan desert to consult the Egyptian god Ammon would appear to be anachronistic, though Alcibiades would consult it privately. See Chapter 5.

sanctuaries with dedication like no other peoples, annually offered to the gods the most sumptuous and solemn processions, and <149a> spent more money on it than all the other Greeks combined. Whereas the Spartans," they claimed, "were never ever concerned for any of these things, but had such a contemptuous attitude towards the gods that they regularly sacrifice physically impaired beasts and show far less regard for all the other matters than us, even though they had just as much money as our own city." When they had said this, and asked what they must do to find release from their present ills, no other answer was given by the <b> prophet—obviously because the god would not allow it—but he called and said "Ammon says this to the Athenians: he affirms that he would prefer for himself the respectful language (*euphêmia*) of the Spartans rather than all the offerings of the Greeks put together." That's all he said, nothing more.

As for this phrase "respectful language" at any rate, it seems to me that the god means nothing else by it other than their prayer, for it is in fact far <c> superior to the rest. For the other Greeks, some when assembling golden-horned cattle and others when offering other dedications to the gods, make prayers for whatever it may be, whether good or bad. So, on hearing their ill-conceived words, the gods refuse these sumptuous processions and sacrifices. Rather, it seems to me that there is a need for considerable caution and investigation over what must be said and what must not.

You will find that other things similar to this have been said in Homer. <d> For he says that the Trojans, on making their camp:

Offered up to the gods perfect hecatombs,[75]

And the "winds bore" the "aroma from" the "plain into heaven,"[76]

Delicious; but of it the blessed gods did not partake,

And refused it; for greatly were they hated by them,[77] holy Troy,

<e>And Priam and the host of Priam with the ashen spear.

And so it was pointless for them to sacrifice and to offer up gifts in vain, when they were hateful to the gods. For the way of the gods

75 *Iliad* 2.306, grammatically adjusted.

76 Close paraphrase of *Iliad* 8.549.

77 There is no known parallel in Homer for the two lines up to this point. What follows is formulaic, and found three times, at *Iliad* 4.46–47, 4.164–165 and 6.448–449.

isn't such as to be diverted by gifts like some bad moneylender. Rather, we [Athenians] too are making a naïve claim if we demand that we should get the better of the Spartans in this way. For it would actually be a dreadful thing for the gods to be looking at our gifts and sacrifices rather than at whether somebody's inner self (*psukhê*)[78] happens to be holy and just. <150a1> Yes, [they look at this] far more, I believe, than at these expensive processions and sacrifices, which could just as easily have been provided for each year, either on an individual basis or as a community, by those who had committed many crimes against the gods and men alike. But they [the gods], as they are not susceptible to bribes, despise all these things alike, as the god [Ammon] and his prophet affirm. It is surely to be expected that justice and wisdom have been exceptionally prized both among the gods and among men of good sense. <b> And the wise and just are precisely those who know what one should do and say both towards the gods and towards humans. I would be pleased to hear from you, too, what you are minded to respond to this.

ALCIBIADES: Well, as for me, Socrates, it seems no different than it did to you and to the god, since it would scarcely be reasonable for me to be casting my vote against the god.

SOCRATES: Don't you remember saying that you were in great perplexity <c> about how you could avoid inadvertently praying for bad things when thinking that they are good?[79]

ALCIBIADES: I do indeed.

SOCRATES: You see then that it is not safe for you to go and pray to the god, in case when this happens the god hears your disrespectful words and accepts none of this sacrificial ceremony, and you perhaps get something quite different into the bargain. So it seems better to me to keep quiet, because, given your high and mighty nature—to give it the finest of all names suggestive of madness, I don't suppose you'd be willing to employ the Spartans' prayer. <d> Accordingly, it is necessary to wait until one learns what attitude one should adopt both towards gods and towards humans.

---

78 To translate "soul" might well be sufficient, but since the first meaning of the word in this dialogue has been "life" (141c1), and the second little more than "person" (as contrasted with "city," 146e4), I prefer a translation that resonates less with the details of Platonic psychology.

79 Cf. 143a–b and 148a–b.

ALCIBIADES: So when will that time arrive, Socrates, and who will be my educator?

SOCRATES: This person here who is concerned for you. But it seems to me that he should act just as Homer says Athena did for Diomedes, taking away the mist from his eyes,

So that he might reliably recognize both god and man.

<e> He must act in this way for you, taking away from your mind (*psukhê*) the mist that now happens to be there, and only at that point applying [the cures][80] by which you will recognize both good and bad. Right now it doesn't seem to me that you would be able to do so.

ALCIBIADES: Let him take it away, whether mist or anything else that he wishes! I have braced myself so as not to flinch from any of his prescriptions, whoever that person may be, just assuming that I'm going to be better.

<151a> SOCRATES: Well then, he too is indeed showing an amazing keenness in your case.

ALCIBIADES: In that case it seems best to me to postpone the sacrifice, too, until that moment.

SOCRATES: Yes, and you are right to think so. It is safer than to subject oneself to a danger of such magnitude.

ALCIBIADES: How could I, Socrates? Very well, I am going to crown you with this garland here, seeing that you seem to me to have given great advice. <b> As for the gods I'll give them garlands and all the other customary honors just as soon as I see that the day we have spoken of has arrived. It will come without too much delay if they are willing.

SOCRATES: Well not only will I accept this, but I'd also be glad to see myself accepting another of the gifts that come from you. Think how Euripides depicted Kreon, on seeing Teiresias crowned with

80 The verb for "applying" is frequently used of medical remedies, something that Alcibiades will pick up in his response.

garlands and on hearing that he has received them as first fruits from [Athens'] enemy plunder in return for his skill, as declaring:

> I take your crowns of glorious victory as a [victory] portent,
> For we lie in the path of a storm, as you know yourself.[81]

In the same way I too regard this token of esteem from you as a portent. It seems to me that I am in the path of no less a storm than Kreon was, and I'd like to have "glorious victory" over your lovers.[82]

81 Euripides' *Phoenissae* 858–859, spoken by Kreon to Teiresias.

82 The sinister complexities of the ending can only be fully appreciated with a knowledge of Euripides' *Phoenissae* in which the vocabulary of glorious victory is consistently ironic. Interestingly, Socrates may be thought to compare himself with Kreon *qua* viewer of the garland, and with Teiresias *qua* wearer of it, the former being a tragic character about to learn of impending horror, the latter the prophetic instruments of the gods.

Chapter One
The Opening

The Occasion of the Conversation

If the *Alcibiades II* had employed the voice of a narrator, most likely that of Socrates retelling the story to his friends, then some early lack of clarity could have been avoided. A narrative voice added considerably to our appreciation of the setting and of the dynamics of the situation in dialogues like the *Charmides* and *Lysis*, and Plato's skills in this regard emerged most clearly in *Protagoras*, *Euthydemus*, *Symposium* and the first book of *Republic*. It seems to have been mainly later in his creative career that Plato also managed to build up a picture of the setting and the interactions of the characters through the skilled use of direct speech, where speakers drew attention to features of their surroundings, as is at its most obvious in the *Phaedrus*—though the *Laches* is also interesting in this regard. But many dialogues give us comparatively little scope for imagining how and where the conversation got started, as for instance in *Meno* and *Cratylus*, or even in the late *Philebus*. The shortest dialogues, with the exception of the *Erastae*, do not employ a narrator, and afford the reader little scope for picturing the scene or for understanding how the conversation originated. Since it is probable that authors of dialogues originally expected to be reading their work themselves, or having their slaves read it in their presence, they had the opportunity to supply whatever background information they thought was necessary prior to the actual reading.[83] Only if it was anticipated

83 Note that Zeno is reading from his own work at the start of the *Parmenides* (127c), while Euclides has already introduced his work before having his slave read it in the *Theaetetus* (142d–143c); Socrates offers some words of introduction before reciting his memorized conversation with Diotima (*Symp.* 201d1–e7). Not only the preface of the *Theaetetus* (which, as anon. *in Theaetetum* III shows, was one of two prefaces to this dialogue known in antiquity) but also that of *Protagoras* (a narrated dialogue)

that the work would circulate widely would any written preface be needed.

In the *Alcibiades II* Socrates opens the conversation by simply asking Alcibiades whether he is on his way to pray "to the god." A lack of further background details leads Nails (2002: 311) to declare:

> There is no particular indication of dramatic date, but the two men do not seem to be on campaign during the conversation, so the dialogue is probably conceived to take place just after *Alcibiades* (i.e. before Potidaea), though it could also be after their return more than two and a half years later (after May of 429). Since Pericles I is still alive (143e), a date after August–September 429 is ruled out.

Standard historical methods might indeed lead to such a conclusion, but some rather basic aspects of the setting are missing, so that the absence of indications that the two are on campaign can scarcely be a conclusive indicator that they are not. Further, the dialogue is known for one of the most flagrant chronological inconsistencies in the corpus: the assassination of Archelaus of Macedon, which according to 141d had taken place "yesterday or the day before,"[84] actually happened in 399 BCE, five years after Alcibiades had been assassinated himself, and thirty years after the death of Pericles. In the *Gorgias*, too, there are chronological inconsistencies involving the recent death of Pericles (429: 503c) and the accession and injustices of Archelaus of Macedon (413: 470d–471d), with the latter certainly in conflict with the likely date of the conversation (427).[85] So such inconsistencies may have

---

is not integrated with the main discussion, and both would surely reflect the author's practice of giving his own introduction, tailored to the particular audience, prior to performance. Note that separable prefaces, usually dedicatory, may also be used by later writers of dialogues, including such figures as Cicero (e.g. *Timaeus*) and Lucian (*Nigrinus*).

84 Translated literally in this way by Johnson 2003, 64, the words χθιζά τε καὶ πρωϊζά preserve the epic diction of their Homeric original at *Iliad* 2.303, where they actually refer to events that are *comparatively* recent, but remembered vividly. The diction contrasts with Plato's use of contemporary forms of the words (ἐχθὲς καὶ πρώην) when talking again of Archelaus at *Gorgias* 470d1.

85 I have argued (Tarrant 2008) that there may well be no great inconsistency with the date of Euripides' *Antiope*, since stylistic evidence marks it as a much earlier play than the one given by the scholiast.

seemed acceptable or even especially Platonic to the author of the *Alcibiades II*, and not too much should be built on the fact that the dialogue assumes that Pericles is still alive.

But what is the point of these connections with the inconsistent chronology of the *Gorgias*, involving Pericles' last days, the story of Archelaus, and coupling of the phrase "yesterday or the day before" with that story? Surely Plato was unlikely to feel the need for this kind of inter-textual link, and even less likely to indulge in such flagrant violations of chronology. A later author, at the end of the fourth or in the early third century, might have raised fewer eyebrows with his references to Macedonian events that occurred decades later than the supposed conversation between Athenians. The details of the chronology had receded further into the past, and there may have been nobody left to remember them. The point, I presume, is that readers, as long as they are not too distracted by historical reflection on the cautionary story of Archelaus, will be able to use the *Gorgias* as well as the *Alcibiades I* to plot where in the relationship the *Alcibiades II* fits. The *Protagoras* and the *Gorgias* also involve Alcibiades, albeit in minor ways.[86] He is a secondary character of the narrated conversation in the former, where Socrates takes the young man's support of his own position in the debate with Protagoras (336b–d, 347b) as a hopeful sign of his interest (309b). And, while he does not appear in the *Gorgias*, Socrates announced there that philosophy and Alcibiades are his two loves (481d), with philosophy ever saying the same thing but Alcibiades expressing different views at different times (482a)—and therefore, it seems, philosophy now has the greater influence.

Considered in this way, the fact that Pericles is still alive means that the dramatic date of the *Alcibiades II* precedes that of the *Gorgias*, and suggests that the relationship is still flourishing, while it is already waning in the *Gorgias*. The dramatic date *relative to the progress of the relationship* is the one that matters to its ultimate author, not the absolute date. Let us presume then that this author would identify Athens as its setting, the location where Socrates spent nearly all his time when not on campaign;[87] and let us suppose that it is not far from the center, perhaps

86 For discussion of Alcibiades in these two works see Ramsey 2012.

87 If no effort has been made to smooth over the chronology then there remains a chance that Alcibiades and Socrates are somewhere on campaign together, presumably either at Delium (*Symp.* 220e) or, less likely, at Potidaea (*Symp.* 219e), but was Alcibiades then at liberty to stroll off to visit temples on personal business? The chronology would be problematic in either case, though chronological consistency is violated elsewhere in

near Socrates' usual haunts in the agora, for no picture of the location ever emerges as it does in some dialogues. The fact that Socrates says "the god," using the masculine of the article,[88] seems to imply that he had some particular Greek divinity in mind, but this god's identity is never revealed. One might naturally assume that we are dealing with one of the more powerful gods of the Greek world, such as Zeus, Apollo, or Poseidon, but it is hard to think of a site sacred to any of these individually at Athens that Alcibiades could be approaching. In any case, one might genuinely wonder why he was not instead approaching Athena, the divinity most closely associated with Athens and by no means indifferent to power and conquest. Philosophically there is little at issue, since Platonism did not accept that the various gods quarreled about the fortunes of humans, and the issues concerning prayer that will be raised might apply to prayers offered to any of the gods. But historically the choice of which god one should pray to was so important that this very question was often asked of the Delphic Oracle.[89] Hence the name of the god was no irrelevance, even though there is no obvious candidate for him to be identified with assuming that the action is within Athens. The absence of the god's name detracts from the dialogue's realism.

However, let us consider for a moment the possibility that the dialogue was reconstructed from a sketch that went back to Plato himself. Would Plato have been so willing to sacrifice realism here at the outset, or would he perhaps have always intended to supply the kind of background in an unwritten preface about how and where the conversation took place. What god's name might he have supplied? That of Zeus? But the dialogue repeatedly uses the expressions *pros Dios* ("by Zeus") and *nê Dia* ("Yes by Zeus") without a hint that Zeus might

---

the dialogue. The attraction of postulating a setting at Delium is the presence there of a temple of Apollo, seemingly a suitable god for Alcibiades to be addressing and a divinity of background relevance. But in that case it seems hard to show why the setting should have been omitted, unless a scene-setting prologue has been lost or deliberately dropped.

88 One cannot simply emend to the feminine, as the same god is again masculine in two almost identical passages at 141a6–8 (εἴ σοι ἐμφανὴς γενόμενος ὁ θεὸς πρὸς ὃν τυγχάνεις πορευόμενος, ἐρωτήσειεν, πρὶν ὁτιοῦν εὔξασθαί σε, εἰ ἐξαρκέσει σοι . . .) and 148a2 (εἰ οὖν σοί γ' ἔτι καὶ νῦν ἐμφανὴς γενόμενος ὁ θεὸς πρὸς ὃν τυγχάνεις πορευόμενος ἐρωτήσειε, πρὶν ὁτιοῦν εὔξασθαί σε, εἰ ἐξαρκέσει σοι . . .).

89 Verseln 2015, 451–452; see Xen. *Anab.* 3.1.5–6.

be the relevant god.[90] That of Apollo? Where would Alcibiades go for this purpose, and what is his connection with the god? As for Poseidon, one might again wonder where within the walls of Athens his temple would be found, but there is no doubt that as god of horses Poseidon could have been seen as being of special relevance by Alcibiades, whose horse-racing exploits outshone those of all the other Greeks (Plut. *Alc.* 11–12).[91] Early in Aristophanes' *Clouds* the young man Pheidippides, who then thought only of horse-riding (1401) and appeared to model himself on Alcibiades in many ways,[92] swears by "Poseidon, god of horses," much to his father's dismay (83–84). But where within the walls of Athens did one go to pray to this god? Socrates and Alcibiades would have encountered such a temple rather in Potidaea, just outside of the central area of the city,[93] for Poseidon was the primary god associated with that city and appears on many coins, mounted but with trident. An introductory prologue could once have explained that the conversation took place when Socrates and Alcibiades were on campaign in the Chalkidike, and that the latter had been approaching the temple of Poseidon just outside the citadel of Potidaea.

That much is what I should postulate if the dialogue is based partly on material that went back to Plato himself. However, it seems to me that the author primarily responsible for the preservation of this text did not in fact need any such information. As far as he is concerned, what we are intended to notice about Alcibiades is simply what Socrates notices about him.

90 πρὸς Διός at 138b1, 139c6, 143d2, and 147e5; νὴ Δία at 145e2 and 146b4. The former is three times preceded by φέρε, the latter on both occasions by μέντοι. Now the combination μέντοι νὴ Δία only occurs thirteen times in the whole Platonic corpus (*Euthphr.* 1, *Ap.* 1, *Phd.* 3, *Alc. I* 1 [133d4], *Chrm.* 1, *La.* 1, *Hp. Ma.* 1, *Ion* 1, and *Rep.* IX 1); the combination φέρε πρὸς Διός is unique to this dialogue. Even the simple expression πρὸς Διός is only found thirty-nine times in the rest of the corpus.

91 Matters concerning horses enter the discussion at *Alc. I* 111d, 121e, 122d, and 124e; and at *Alc. II* 145c–d.

92 On his mother's side he too appears linked to the Alcmaeonids (63–70); he is fond of special game-birds (108–109) like Alcibiades (Plut. *Alc.* 10, cf. *Mor.* 799d; *Alc. I* 120a9), modeling his behavior on that of the cockerel (1427–1431), and he has a speech-impediment (870–873).

93 See Herodotus 8.129.3, Thucydides 4.129.3.

Knowing Alcibiades

The most obvious sign that might lead one to deduce Alcibiades' intentions would be close proximity to a temple or shrine, but what he or his servant carries may also betray his intentions, for the end of the dialogue (151a) will show that he has an animal intended for sacrifice and a garland to be given to the god. However, no attention is paid to their presence at this stage, and it is possible that we are deliberately being invited to ask ourselves, "How does Socrates deduce that?" His failure to mention any of the expected signs is not due to his being unobservant, for he notices that Alcibiades is off to pray, he observes his worried appearance, and he correctly guesses not only that the youth has something on his mind but also what this worry is. So the focus of his observations is Alcibiades himself, suggesting that some powerful erotic attraction is still present for him. In the *Alcibiades I*, too, both its opening (103b–105c) and elsewhere, he shows himself to be an astute observer of the young man and a confident and accurate interpreter of his secret thoughts. This theme will continue in the *Alcibiades II* at 141a–c, and that is no accident. It is a continuing indication that Socrates is the one through whom Alcibiades must get to know himself. Socrates can give Alcibiades a better account of his actions and his thoughts than he could himself.

So Socrates does not so much notice temples or garlands or sacrificial animals, but looks above all into the face of Alcibiades. He is still a lover, demonstrating a determined interest in the young man, and hence it is Alcibiades' worried appearance upon which he remarks. The unusual[94] verb *skuthrôpazô* (σκυθρωπάζω) is employed to describe a big frown that has come over his face, particularly unusual for Plato;[95]

94 Searching for forms of the verb using the search string σκυθρωπα one encounters five matches involving this verb or one of its compounds in fifth and fourth century comedy: 2 in Aristophanes, 1 in Amphis, and 1 in Antiphanes; in fourth century oratory: 2 in Demosthenes and 2 in Aeschines; in fourth century history: 3 in Xenophon; in tragedy: 1 in Euripides; and in fourth century philosophy other than here: 1 in Theophrastus, that being *Characters* 14.7. At an early stage the word seems to have been more characteristic of comedy than anything, but it is used more widely among later authors: 8 matches in Lxx, 7 in Plutarch, 6 in Diogenes Laertius, 6 in Athenaeus, 5 in Philo, and so on. Besides this dialogue, the perfect active form is found in Demosthenes (2) and Alciphron, Diogenes Laertius (2), Plutarch (2), Arrian, Cassius Dio, Appian, Epictetus, Themistius (2), and various later authors or scholia.

95 Note the perfect infinitive ἐσκυθρωπακέναι. The word is surprising, being the only case of the verb in the Platonic corpus, while the adjective σκυθρωπός is found

Alcibiades looks down at the ground as if he had some concern on his mind, highlighted by another rare verb, the participle of *sunnoeisthai* (συννοούμενος).[96] Apart from an isolated occurrence at *Symposium* 220c3,[97] this verb is only found in relatively late Plato (according to traditional chronology), having next appeared in *Republic* VII. But in the middle voice it does not occur outside the *Alcibiades II*, all other cases being in the active. Alcibiades now repeats this middle voice of the verb as he asks for further explanation from Socrates. Socrates uses the associated noun *sunnoia* (σύννοια: "anxious thought," again rare)[98] in his reply. Alcibiades shows himself less than willing to share his private thoughts, and it appears he is aware that he is about to undertake something that may have important consequences for himself. Certainly his mind is troubled. But does he fully understand the internal conflict that he experiences? Those who have read the *Alcibiades I* in a particular way may feel that here too in the opening pages of the *Alcibiades II* it is only through the mirror of Socrates' words[99] that Alcibiades is coming to appreciate the precise nature of his present condition.[100]

On closer inspection, then, some of the quirkier features of this opening may have been deliberately designed to suggest Socrates' continued infatuation with Alcibiades himself, and the accuracy with which he could read the other's mind. So it is not so much spuriousness that this unusual and unexpected language signifies, but rather the precise intentions of the author. One might argue for the spuriousness

---

only at *Symp.* 206d6 of something "pregnant" but frustrated because it cannot find something beautiful in which to beget. Second, a search of TLG reveals that infinitives in -κέναι are found 90 times altogether in the first twelve dialogues of the corpus, never in *Alc. I* or *Hipparchus* (twice in *Amat.*), but 9 times in *Alc. II* alone (also at 139d, 142b, 146c, 147b, 147e [twice], 149a, 151a) suggesting a strong liking for such perfect forms. Other forms range from the common εἰρηκέναι (twice) and δεδωκέναι, to the longer and rarer ἐστρατηγηκέναι, διημαρτηκέναι, κεκοινωνηκέναι, ἐκδεδυκέναι, συμβεβουλευκέναι. Note also εἰληφέναι at 151b8 (19 in -φέναι elsewhere in corpus) and πεπονθέναι at 139b3.

96 Kenny 1999, 597, has "you seem preoccupied," while Johnson 2003, 59, has "as if you were concerned," cf. Brisson 2014, 24; Carlini 1964, 257, had "come se riflettessi a qualcosa" and Aronadio 2008, 209, has "come se stessi meditando a qualcosa." The exact sense is difficult to determine.

97 Interestingly Alcibiades is the speaker, and it is Socrates who is there lost in meditation.

98 Found in *Republic* IX and *Laws* VII. The translation given is one offered by LSJ, but the general sense seems clear given the frown.

99 For a *logos* as something with mirror-like properties see *Tht.* 206d1–5.

100 As at *Alc. I* 109d, 116e, 118b, 124a–b, 127d.

of almost any work on the basis of the unusual features of its vocabulary, but individual linguistic quirks might equally derive from the particular needs of the individual dialogue. Here the author is not concerned with background scenery or with Alcibiades' choice of divinity, but rather with what the man himself was feeling. Hence if there is more linguistic overlap with comic drama than with other philosophy then it may be due to the fact that comedy does not look at idealized individuals in a particular circumstance, but at particular individuals' responses to situations that reveal their quirks and imperfections. Again, if this work is striving for dramatic effect, then it is natural that our focus should be directed, with some precision of language, towards the current feelings of the person at the center of the drama. Perhaps the author is creating a kind of tragicomic mask for Alcibiades through what Socrates can see rather than through what a spectator in the theatre can see. Socrates now proceeds to further develop our picture by the suggestion, readily assented to, that Alcibiades' worries have something to do with the gods' perceived habit of granting some wishes and denying others, and granting them to some and denying them to others. The question in Alcibiades' mind must be all about whether he is going to find the god sympathetic to his prayers. What, he is thinking, if the god does not grant his wish? But it is the wrong question.

Escaping one's Own Notice

The question in Socrates' mind is quite different, with its focus on whether Alcibiades will actually be asking for something that is advantageous to him at all. The fear in this case is that the god *might* grant the wish, and prove the young man's undoing. He asks whether Alcibiades does not think that one needs to give a great deal of forethought to this act of supplication "so as not to escape one's own notice praying for great evils that merely appear good" (138b7–8). Already we are introduced to what will become a refrain in this dialogue, that of not realizing what one is doing. It typically involves the verb *lanthanein* ("to escape notice") with a reflexive. It occurs here at 138b7, at 140e7, and at 150c1 in Socrates' words, and at 143a8 and 148b1 in those of Alcibiades. In a sense this is a variation on the Delphic theme of the *Alcibiades I*, but while that dialogue took self-cognition to be a positive foundation upon which ethical qualities could be built, the emphasis in the *Alcibiades II* is all upon what happens in its absence—or, more precisely, what happens in its absence at times when there is a particular need for it.

The *Phaedrus* (229e4–230a6) had implied that self-knowledge (seen as knowing about one's *inner* self—what kind of beast one really was) was somehow basic, and preliminary to the pursuit of other knowledge. Yet the hiatus avoiding dialogues that we are accustomed to think of as late Plato are mainly concerned with the need to avoid a second level of ignorance here: thinking that we know certain things about ourselves when we do not. The chief material is in the *Philebus* and *Laws*.[101] The ignorance of concern in the latter was the supposition that one had knowledge in cases where one did not, somewhat reminiscent of Socrates' concerns in the *Apology*. So neither dialogue was concerning itself either about one's not knowing oneself qua human being, nor even about not knowing oneself qua *this* human being.

In the *Philebus* (48c7–e11) mention of the Delphic inscription is followed by a threefold division of self-*ignorance*: ignorance about one's external goods, ignorance about one's body, and ignorance about one's state of soul. One can be mistaken about one's wealth, about the quality of one's physique, or about the quality of one's inner person—thinking oneself wealthier, of superior physique, or superior in virtue to what one really is. And, according to *Philebus* 49a, it is the ones who have an inflated view of their own wisdom that are the worst, and special dislike is reserved for the kind of self-delusion about one's own expertise that is found in people of power (49b1–c5),[102] as opposed to the comic self-delusion of those who lack the strength to harm the fabric of society. Here the matter about which one is ignorant is not what kind of beast one is (as in *Phaedrus*) nor what one's own self really is (as in the *Alcibiades I*); it is more about what qualities one has *in comparison with* those of others. Rather earlier (19c), the interlocutor Protarchus, having asserted that it would be wonderful for the sensible man (σώφρων) to be able to recognize everything, says that a "second sailing" would be to avoid escaping one's own notice. Again Plato stresses the need to avoid this kind of cognitive error, which is presumably a failure of self-recognition. Protarchus, a relatively astute interlocutor, seems almost to be accusing Socrates here of some kind of lack of self-knowledge.[103]

---

101 I discuss this material in Tarrant 2019.

102 It is hard not to think of people like Alcibiades, Charmides, and Critias at this point.

103 He accuses Socrates of failing to honor his promise to assist them in their search for the greatest good, not because he intends to disappoint them, but because he fails to see that his present tactics are ill-suited to his audience.

But again, it is not a complete failure to recognize what species he belonged to or what the basic characteristics of that species were, but simply about the kind of individual he was.

In the *Laws* (IX 863c–d) the Athenian Guest suggests that whereas "Socratic ignorance" is merely a single ignorance, the kind of ignorance against which Socrates contended was somehow a double ignorance. It involved the supposition that one knew those things of which one was in fact ignorant. One knew neither *p* nor if one knew *p*. This was especially culpable, and more so in the powerful (c6–d1). The emphasis here is less on freeing the individual from the ignorance that affects him (as it had been for the Socrates of the *Apology* for instance), and more on cleansing the community from such self-deception in the hands of those who govern. Indeed, it would appear from XI 923a that individual members of the state are being given no encouragement to get to know themselves or what's theirs in the Delphic manner because it will be too difficult; the lawgiver will tell them!

Assuming a continued association between self-knowledge and the virtue of being sensible (i.e. *sôphrosynê*) in the *Sophist*, then there too self-knowledge would turn out to imply very little more than avoiding the false conceit of knowledge. For at 230d5–6 "Theaetetus" declares that the best and most sensible (*sôphronestatê*) of states is the one in which people have had the obstacle to learning removed by the elimination of false conceits of knowledge, and the Stranger makes no attempt to disagree with him. So being sensible is an awareness of one's ignorance rather than the knowledgeable assent to actual propositions regarding the identity and nature of one's "self." In this dialogue Plato does not use the term "self-knowledge" nor does he employ any Delphic theme, but the passage agrees well with those in other late Platonic discussions that put their primary emphasis on the awareness of one's own deficiencies *in wisdom*.

One cannot claim that the avoidance of this kind of self-deception was absent from the *Alcibiades I*, for at 117a–118b Socrates can be quite scathing about Alcibiades' supposition that he knows important matters relating to politics when he does not. It is rather that it is not explicitly suggested that this has anything to do with Delphic self-knowledge. And when Delphic self-knowledge is first mentioned at 124a–b it involves something more positive: the knowledge that our real adversaries are in foreign lands where educational preparation is thought vital, and also that they can only be overcome by careful practice (*epimeleia*) and by skill (124b). We have to correctly evaluate our own situation relative to that of others. The next occurrence of the Delphic theme is associated with the demand that we should identify the "self" in order to know how to take care of ourselves (129a–b), and this appears to involve identifying what we really mean when we say that "we" do something. When the oracle is finally mentioned at 132c it seems that it is interpreted as meaning that we should work out what our real self *is like* by looking into something else that *resembles* our own real self. One might in other circumstances discuss the passage at 132c–133c at great length, but it seems clear that Delphic self-knowledge in the *Alcibiades I* involves establishing what we really are, what we are really like, and what, in the case of adversaries (124b) and much else (133c21–e3), is "ours" and what belongs to what is "ours."

If we recognize that there is something of a gulf here between the Delphic self-knowledge of the *Alcibiades I*, which involves both serious positive content and reflection upon the nature of the self, and such self-knowledge as features in the late Platonic dialogues that involves little more than an awareness of our own ignorance, then we can perhaps allow that the theme of avoiding deceiving ourselves in the *Alcibiades II* is in closer agreement with the late dialogues. It will emerge later that the kind of self-deception that this dialogue is most concerned with is the incorrect evaluation of what will be *good or bad for us*, not so much mistaking either our own selves or their qualities, but mistaking what a course of action will be like *for us.*[104] This will also be in agreement with the general tendency of this work to examine things as they are relative to ourselves rather than in absolute terms.

The theme of self-deception, then, is introduced by Socrates as follows (138b):

> Do you think that it requires a great deal of forethought to avoid escaping one's own notice by praying for great evils that only seem to be good, in a situation where the gods *happen to be* in the frame of mind in which they personally grant what one *happens to be* praying for?

There is no immediate indication that escaping our own notice is to be something of a theme within the dialogue, and no indication

---

104 Note here the emphatic ἡμῖν αὐτοῖς at 143b2, which may also be assumed to apply when the material is repeated at 148b1–2.

yet of epistemological relevance. But if one considers the practice of prayer within such a society, where prayers are recited aloud and often accompanied either by a meaningful gift to the god or the promise of such a gift, then one soon realizes that things are not asked for that aren't expected to be to one's benefit: either directly or by benefitting one's family or community. So in every case of voluntary prayer the assumption is that what is prayed for is beneficial, and often the belief that one *knows* it to be good. Mistakes are usually either cases of double ignorance, or something similar. Who would take extreme action to gain something that merely *might* be beneficial? One is far likelier not even to question the desirability of whatever one is praying for.

It also seems from this quotation that praying is a chance business. The verb for "happen" is *tunkhanein*, and therefore related to the concept of chance or luck (*tukhê*). It is not only people's prayers that are subject to the vagaries of fortune, for it seems that the moods of the gods are rather unpredictable too. We are dealing here with the gods as conventionally portrayed by Homer and others, not the predictably good gods of Plato who would never disagree among themselves and never change their minds. There is no problem here for anybody insisting on Platonic authorship, for Socrates needs to talk to Alcibiades in terms of the gods *as he understands them*, and as he would suppose the god being addressed to be. More particularly, we are dealing with mythical or poetic gods rather than Platonic ones because the dialogue regularly introduces material from poetic myth. Enter Oedipus.

Oedipus' Blindness

Blindness, literal and metaphorical, is a significant theme in the dialogue.[105] The impairment of vision itself features early in the repeated use of the example of eye disease (139e–140a), and late where there is talk of the lifting of mist from our eyes (150d). The latter talk parallels Alcibiades' need to have the "mist" lifted from his mind (150e), a more constant concern throughout the dialogue. The first mythic figure introduced is Oedipus, whose failure to see in the metaphorical

105 See for instance Sharpe 2012, 136–142.

sense earlier in life had resulted in him ending his days blinded by his own hand.

Oedipus was notorious for having his requests to the gods rebound against him. The best known example is in Sophocles' *Oedipus the King*, where he utters a series of prayers, underlined by the words *kateukhomai*, *epeukhomai*, and *eukhomai* (246, 249, 269), subjecting the murderer of Laius and any accomplices to his curse. He is not only unwittingly cursing himself, but also praying further to be subject to the same curse should he himself knowingly share his hearth with this man. He follows this up by prayers for those who assist in bringing the man to justice and others condemning those who fail to assist. By the end of the play, having exchanged his earlier mental ignorance for physical blindness, he realizes that his prayers and solemn orders given to his fellow citizens have backfired upon himself (1378–1383). But myth spoke of similar curses called down on the brothers Eteocles and Polynices, who were not only Oedipus' sons but also his half-brothers, leading upon fulfillment to their deaths at each other's hand. The story seems to have been told in the lost *Thebaid*, but allusions or variations occur in the tragedians Aeschylus (*Sep.* 785–789), Sophocles (*OC* 1383–1392), and, most importantly, Euripides (*Ph.* 66–68).[106] Given the sacred nature of the household for the Greeks, and the importance of one's children in the Greek concept of happiness, a curse on one's sons is tantamount to a curse upon oneself, and something that no sane person is likely to utter.

Accordingly, Socrates selects Oedipus as a key *example*[107] of one who unwittingly utters prayers that result in his own detriment. Curses for the present purpose are simply a subset of prayers,[108] as the text makes clear:

> When he had the chance to pray (*eukhesthai*) for some release from his present woes, he uttered a curse (*katarasthai*) [asking] for others in addition to the

106 See above, note 7.

107 The mistranslation of αὐτίκα (here "for example," LSJ II), as in Johnson 2003, 59, as "suddenly" obscures this, but it is quite clear in Carlini 1964, 258, Aronadio 2008, 209, "per esempio," and Brisson 2014, 25, "par exemple"; Kenny 1997, 597, seems to hedge his bets.

108 Compare Versnel 2015, 454–456.

> present ones.[109] In due course not only these [prayers] were fulfilled, but in their wake many other terrible [woes] that there is no need to enumerate.

Cursing can be viewed as a kind of prayer that requests that an evil be brought down upon somebody. A curse, in this sense, asks for something from the gods as much as a prayer.

The example of Oedipus is clearly being used to illustrate the kind of trap that Alcibiades might unwittingly fall into if he does not give forethought to what he intends to pray for. It is an extreme example, but not necessarily inappropriate, and it is apparent that the author wants to suggest that the example of Oedipus might be pertinent. He too had been raised under the guardianship of another man, and he too was is search of his true destiny and seeking to involve a god in his own success story. It might even have been the same god that was implicated in Oedipus' fate, Apollo.[110] Already the *Alcibiades I*, with its Delphic theme, had laid something of an Apollinine foundation for the relationship between Socrates and Alcibiades,[111] though the oracular site relevant to the *Alcibiades II* is rather that of Ammon in the Libyan desert. One might also be intrigued that Socrates invites Alcibiades later (143e–144b) to imagine that he had quasi-patricidal intentions, directed against his guardian Pericles—his nearest living equivalent to a father.[112] Is Socrates picturing an Alcibiades who could develop into some kind of Oedipal character himself, with the direst of consequences?[113]

Alcibiades' reaction to this comparison is to imagine that it could not happen to him. He protests that Oedipus was crazy, whereas anybody

109 The text of Euripides too had brought out that Oedipus was already under pressure from other evils when he made this dreadful mistake.

110 It certainly would have been if the action had been set in Delium, since Thucydides (4.90–101) tells us that much of the action centered upon the sanctuary of Apollo, which the Athenians fortified.

111 It had even touched on Alcibiades' refusal to play the aulos (106e), his reasons for which according to Plutarch (*Alc.* 2.5) included Athena's dislike and Apollo's utter contempt for it.

112 Pericles' death is usually placed in the second half of 429 BCE, following Th. 2.65.6.

113 Should readers question the relevance of patricide to the idea that Alcibiades might murder his guardian, they might bear in mind the next example used of somebody who would be better off not recognizing their intended victim is the tragic matricide of Orestes, who would have been better off not recognizing Clytemnestra as his mother.

in a healthy condition (including himself of course) would never pray for such things. Yet Alcibiades, though not sharing the reputation of his brother Cleinias for madness,[114] is known for some of the traits one might associate with craziness: impetuosity and unpredictability, for instance, and a tendency to indulge in such illegal activity as he thinks he can get away with.[115] The first dialectical section must now argue that Oedipus' so-called "madness," even though it involved anger (141a2), is not generically dissimilar to the kind of condition that Alcibiades might fall prey to. Socrates is taking him rather to be an example of one who does not know what things they must say and what things they must carry out (140e1–141a1). All such persons will escape their own notice (*lêsousin hautous*, 140e7) saying and carrying out things that they should not. Surely Alcibiades is not exempt from that kind of limited self-ignorance: the ignorance of the role proper to oneself.

---

114 This is "Clinias IV" in Nails 2002, 101; for Alcibiades' description of him as "crazy" see *Alc. I* 118e4, and compare *Prot.* 320a–b.

115 This comes over reasonably well in Plutarch's *Life*, where the charge of unpredictability occurs already at 2.1, and there is regular mention of his violent and hybristic behavior (e.g. 4.6: τῶν οὖν ξένων δυσχεραινόντων καὶ λεγόντων, ὡς ὑβριστικῶς καὶ ὑπερηφάνως εἴη τῷ Ἀνύτῳ κεχρημένος ὁ Ἀλκιβιάδης; 8.2: περιβοήτου δὲ τῆς ἀσελγείας ἐν τῇ πόλει γενομένης; 16.1: πολλὴν αὖ πάλιν τὴν τρυφὴν τῆς διαίτης καὶ περὶ πότους καὶ ἔρωτας ὑβρίσματα) and it was precisely these traits that made him vulnerable to charges over the religious crises of 415 BCE, whether or not he was really involved in them.

Chapter Two
Going Wrong

The Investigation of Madness

Since Alcibiades is not prepared to accept that there is any danger he might utter the kind of prayer that Oedipus' curse would constitute—in his view the kind that only a madman would utter since the granting of his wish would bring an acknowledged evil on his whole household—Socrates must either show that Oedipus' situation is not very different from Alcibiades', or be prepared to convince Alcibiades of his vulnerability by some other means. He will do both. First, he will argue that wisdom (or the sort that ensures a sensible approach to practical affairs: *phronêsis*) is opposed to craziness as well as to folly (*aphrosynê*: a term that *sounds* like its opposite), but since one thing can only have a single opposite, craziness and folly must be identical.

The argument has something in common with the argument used in the *Protagoras* (332a) to suggest to those present that sensibleness (*sôphrosynê*) is the same as wisdom (here *sophia*) because both can be seen as opposite to folly (again *aphrosynê*). The premise that each thing has only one opposite (139b11; *Prot.* 332c8–9) seems to be common to both arguments, though the author of the *Alcibiades II* consistently employs a slightly different term (*hypenantion* rather than *enantion*), one that may perhaps specify a particular type of opposite: one by privation or something similar.[116] In any case, he also feels the need to exclude specifically there being any third intermediate condition involving

116 After the challenge to the premise that each thing can have only one opposite, one can still plausibly argue that any given quality can have only one opposite by privation. On the rare term *hypenantion* see below where we tackle language (p. 78).

neither opposite, first between physical health and its privation, sickness (139a4–9,) and then between their mental equivalents (139a13–b4). If:

1. Madness is the opposite of wisdom;
2. Wisdom and foolishness are opposed in such a way that there is no third state in between them (*dia mesou*);

Then, to conclude, madness and folly are one and the same thing. The most obvious explanation of the need for excluding a third intermediate condition, a need that had not occurred to the Socrates of the *Protagoras*, is that the Aristotelian doctrine that moral virtues are a mean (or some similar doctrine)[117] had already been introduced and broadly accepted. Aristotle requires that the mean is opposed to the extremes as well as their being opposed to one another.[118] So if the premise that any given thing has only one opposite is challenged on the grounds that the mean is also opposed to opposite extremes, then that objection can be found not to apply to the case in question.

It does not take long for Socrates to cast doubt on the conclusion. Lots of people are foolish, indeed a majority of their fellow citizens are foolish. Yet one could scarcely expect to lead much of a life if most of one's fellow citizens were madmen. Just as there are many kinds of disease of which eye disease (*ophthalmia*) is merely one, or many crafts of which cobbling is just one, so too there can be many kinds of folly, and it is merely those with the greatest share in it who are called "crazy," with others being called "simpletons" or "dullards" and so on, with many euphemisms possible too. So craziness will merely be a certain type of folly.

One might expect after this retraction for Socrates to say what was wrong with the preceding argument, involving the principle of there being only one opposite for each thing, but that argument seems to have had little purpose other than to make Alcibiades unsettled. What Socrates wants to examine is just folly, something that Oedipus had suffered from (as long as madness is viewed as a species of folly), and

117 More on this will follow in Chapter 7. Speusippus is also reported to have insisted that the "more" is opposed to the "less" as well as to the "equal," and tried thereby to show that pleasure's being good did not necessarily follow from pain's being, by general agreement, bad. He no doubt thought that both pain and pleasure, besides being opposed to each other, were opposed to the neutral state. See Arist. *EN* 7.13 1153b1–7 = Speusippus F80 Tarán. Speusippus may in turn be influenced by *Statesman* 286c6–d2, where long and short are not just opposed to one another, but to the fitting length.

118 See particularly Arist. *EN* 1108b13–15; *EE* 1220b30–32, 1222a19–21, 1227a37–38.

that Alcibiades is equally susceptible to. It seems that folly had been the real opposite, but madness had been one of the various types of this opposite. The foolish are simply all those who do not know how to behave or to speak, and, without realizing it, end up behaving or speaking in the wrong way; the crazy are among them (140e–141a). But, Socrates will argue, so might Alcibiades.

Socrates had virtually admitted that the example of Oedipus might not have been the most appropriate. He only wanted to use Oedipus as an example of somebody who was foolish, and so did not realize the full implications of what he was saying (and what, by saying this, he could in fact be bringing about). So why would an author have chosen the example of Oedipus in the first place? The first point to be made is that he can thus hint that Alcibiades is suffering from a certain type of craziness without actually having to have Socrates argue with Alcibiades' presumption that he is not at all like Oedipus. He never says that Alcibiades is suffering from a type of folly quite distinct from that of Oedipus, only that he might be vulnerable to some kind of folly. Certainly, Socrates could not be plausibly depicted as choosing the example of Oedipus purely to introduce the reader to the distinction between a genus and its species. So perhaps we are meant to think that "there is no smoke without fire"—the suggestion would not have arisen at all if Alcibiades had not been just a little mad. It was not such a strange suggestion after all, given that Alcibiades acknowledged the craziness of his own brother (*Alc. I* 118e4) and had a reputation for rash and unpredictable behavior.[119]

But can anybody be "just a little mad"? It may well be that Alcibiades became a principal example in discussions of this very question, a question that we have come to associate with the Stoics in particular.[120] In book 11 of Athenaeus' *Deipnosophistai* we are told of Chrysippus' discussion of the Stoic notion that madness is not far from being universal (SVF 3.667; cf. 3.480). He claimed that madness was widely

119 See above, p. 65.

120 If the *Alcibiades II* had been written late enough it is easy to suppose that the author, in ultimately rejecting the thesis that all who are not wise are mad, implies criticism of Stoic theory. Even so, to put the argument that all folly is madness into the mouth of Socrates might also be seen as an acknowledgment of the Socraticity of this kind of extreme Stoic theory. Furthermore, it seems rash to suppose that the passage cannot be explained without reference to any polemical attack on the Stoics or on similar proto-Stoic beliefs.

associated with a great many people, when their critics used terms like "woman-mad," "quail-mad,"[121] or "glory-mad" (*doxomanês*). Plutarch's *Life of Alcibiades* testifies adequately to the near manic preoccupation with women (8), his affection for the quail that he carried beneath his cloak (9), and his burning ambition for glory (e.g. 6) even when he was a young man. Alcibiades is not, so far as we are aware, named in discussions of degrees of madness, but it would surely not be surprising if he had been so named—especially in view of his relevance to this discussion in the *Alcibiades II*.

Madness and the Introduction of *Megalopsukhia*

Here we should consider the possibility that the whole discussion of folly, to which the key example of madness contributes, arises from inter-school polemic. That might be a little easier to believe if only it were clear what view of madness is being promoted here. What theory of madness does this seem to be? It can certainly be said that madness is discussed from a wholly negative point of view, and one that stands in sharp contradiction to the opening of the palinode of the *Phaedrus* (244a–245a; cf. 265b), in which four more welcome kinds of madness are outlined: the state of "madness" in which prophetic utterances are given; another involved in various rituals, mostly involved with religious purification; a third the "rapture" that overtakes the inspired poet; and the fourth the madness that afflicts the lover. All involve benefits, and all are the gifts of divinities. These were opposed to those caused by human illnesses (265a9–11). In the *Alcibiades II* the superior kinds of madness are never mentioned, first because one does not normally expect divinely bestowed ecstatic states to be the cause of rash and foolish prayers, and second because they seem irrelevant to Oedipus' prayer for the destruction of his household. So the concept of madness as an unfortunate and dangerous sickness comes to prevail.

Rather than an organized division of madness such as is presented in the *Phaedrus*, this dialogue offers a division of folly, of which

121 The term *ortygomania* is used (though no independent use of the term is attested), shortly followed by *ornithomanês* ("bird-manic"); the latter term for "bird-crazy" is used in a rather different sense in Ar. *Birds* 1284 and 1344, but in Chrysippus it would probably have covered those crazy about cock-fighting as well as those who loved quail-striking; perhaps also those who prized other gallinaceous birds, such as the pheasants which Pheidippides esteems so highly in Ar. *Clouds* 108–109.

madness (seen as a mental illness) can be viewed a species. A theory of madness would be expected not simply to say *that* it is a species of a given genus, but also to explain *what* species it is. This is all the more true, because according to Xenophon Socrates "often used to investigate *what* difference there was between madness and ignorance" (*Mem.* 1.2.50), noting that madness required physical restraint while ignorance just required teaching. Xenophon also affirmed that Socrates saw madness as an opposite of wisdom (here *sophia*); he resisted the idea that it was the same as a lack of knowledge, but saw self-ignorance, in the form of thinking one knows what one does not know, as "very close" to madness (*Mem.* 3.9.6). Only if it involved knowledge of the kind that normal people were not mistaken about would this be called madness. While Xenophon is trying briefly to capture the essence of a Socratic theory of madness, the *Alcibiades II* tells us rather less in a much longer discussion, without actually making any points that are in obvious disagreement with Xenophon's account. Even though some in antiquity had considered the possibility that Xenophon had written the *Alcibiades II*, we are not entitled to postulate an especially close relationship between the two. Xenophon is merely trying to give the reader a clear idea of the flavor of Socrates' conversations on such topics, and much of his material is likely to have parallels elsewhere in Socratic literature. Is the *Alcibiades II* really trying to do much more than exploit some unsettling possibilities of a traditional Socratic *topos*?

Our answer may be influenced by the date we would postulate for the dialogue. It might make a significant difference if the Stoic concept of madness had already been developed. A key piece of evidence occurs at D. L. 7.124, where, because of the Stoic strategy of characterizing all error and vice as intellectual mistakes, and all sins as equal, madness and folly are simply identified. Those who commit a foolish error through seemingly minor ignorance are just as mentally deficient as those who can be described as wholly crazy.[122] The Stoics, then, held the kind of position that the author of the *Alcibiades II* had first outlined, only to reject it on the grounds that life would not be livable if that were the case. This probably happened as part of Zeno's own adoption of a

---

122 SVF 3.664: πάντας τε τοὺς ἄφρονας μαίνεσθαι· οὐ γὰρ φρονίμους εἶναι, ἀλλὰ κατὰ τὴν ἴσην τῇ ἀφροσύνῃ μανίαν πάντα πράττειν. The doctrine is attested by other authors (SVF 3.662, 665–667, and especially 3.663 = Long and Sedley 41 I). Examples of those whose madness any of us non-sages can equal are Orestes, Alcmaeon, and Heracles (SVF 3.668).

radical version of Socratic ethics, perhaps as mediated by Antisthenes and Diogenes.[123] Hence, if we do not believe the dialogue postdates the arrival of Zeno at Athens as Neuhausen does,[124] then we might be tempted to look rather to the Cynics for an opponent. Though they were certainly not averse to introducing madness, as in Antisthenes' alleged retort that he would rather go mad than feel pleasure,[125] or in Diogenes' assertion that the majority were but a finger away from madness,[126] they are still not credited with any relevant *theory* as radical as Zeno's. Hence anti-Stoic motivation for this passage does seem somewhat more probable, assuming that it was written at a date that allows this. Even so, if it is being claimed that Zeno is taken seriously as an opponent, then the fact that the initial (Stoic?) position on madness and folly is soon painlessly dismissed counts against taking the passage as straight polemic. The dialogue certainly does not answer Stoic theory adequately, and the character of its dialectical exchanges would seem to be "protreptic-elenctic" (to use Neuhausen's concept) rather than agonistic.

Some scholars, however, have detected such polemic particularly at the point where the description "high and mighty" (*megalopsukhos*) is offered as a euphemism for a certain type of foolishness (140c9). In effect *megalopsukhia* in this dialogue has become something akin to what we call "megalomania," implying that there is something "mad" about somebody's inflated sense of their own worth. Even so it is not affirmed here that it is a type of madness, only that it is a type of *folly*. Even calling it "folly" stands in sharp contrast with Aristotle's *Nicomachean* and *Eudemian Ethics* (where this virtue-related terminology occurs

---

123 Cf. Neuhausen 2010, 30: "die stillschweigende Radikalisierung einer sokratisch-antisthenischen Thesen."

124 Neuhausen 2010, 242. Zeno's arrival is placed in 312/11, but Zeno would have to make his mark on the Athenian intellectual scene if he were to attract a polemical response. If it is true that he studied with Polemo for a time, then he could have made his mark within the Academy, already perhaps undergoing a Socratic revival, well before his school was founded at the turn of the century.

125 D. L. 6.3: ἔλεγέ τε συνεχές, "μανείην μᾶλλον ἢ ἡσθείην." The retort was presumably uttered in specific situations, where Antisthenes believed that one should avoid taking any pleasure. Madness in such cases would be a lesser evil than pleasure, an attitude that is at odds with the *Alcibiades II*.

126 D. L. 6.35: τοὺς πλείστους ἔλεγε παρὰ δάκτυλον μαίνεσθαι· ἐὰν οὖν τις τὸν μέσον προτείνας πορεύηται, δόξει μαίνεσθαι, ἐὰν δὲ τὸν λιχανόν, οὐκέτι. But the fact remains that a distinction is still being made between everyday behavior and madness.

21 and 34 times respectively),[127] and allegedly also with Cynic ethics, where qualities reminiscent of *megalopsukhia* are reckoned to be cases of virtue—hardly surprising when it is the semantic equivalent of the term "magnanimity." Here, however, I shall resist any suggestion that even this much is to be understood *simply* against the background of inter-school polemics.

While it is often possible to find meaningful comparisons with Antisthenes in the *Alcibiades II*,[128] I am not happy that the case for anti-Cynic motivation regarding *megalopsukhia* is here as strong as is made out.[129] In Diogenes Laertius the quality is attributed to the Eretrian Menedemus (2.132); it is mentioned in the Platonic-Aristotelian divisions (3.89); it is acknowledged as one of the secondary Stoic virtues (7.92–93, cf. 128); and works are devoted to it by Demetrius (5.81) and by the Epicurean Metrodorus (10.24). But it does not figure in the sixth book devoted to Cynics. While *something like* this quality is certainly associated with Cynic heroes, I find little evidence that the term *megalopsukhia* was a key one in any early Cynic's ethics.

By contrast, the term's importance to Aristotle's ethics can hardly be questioned. Yet even here Aristotle is not doing anything that runs counter to prevailing opinion, for the term is reasonably widespread and often occurs in orators such as Isocrates and Demosthenes.[130] In fact, such a wide range of fourth-century authors is happy to use this term, and ordinarily as one of approval, that it is odd (though explicable)[131]

127 I have used figures based on the number of matches to the pattern μεγαλοψυχ in the TLG. Besides these two major ethical works several others from the Aristotelian Corpus have multiple matches, including the *Rhetoric* (10), *Politics* (3), and (Peripatetic if not "Aristotelian") *Magna Moralia* (6) and *On Virtues and Vices* (5). Another with Peripatetic connections who seems to have used the concept is Heraclides Ponticus (fr. 55).

128 While Diogenes of Sinope does not rate a mention in the index of Neuhausen 2010, Antisthenes features several times, with two and a half columns of citations in the *Index Locorum*, and he would have had relevant things to say about matters of madness, of self-deceptive pride, of the traditional heroic virtues that led one to praise figures such as Ajax, Achilles, or Heracles, and indeed of prayer itself (ibid. 182–185); but this is usually a matter of Antisthenes' influence rather than of critical reaction against him.

129 E.g. Hutchinson 1997, 596–597; Sharpe 2012, 137 and 139–140, repeats many of Hutchinson's claims, but is actually quite cautious and turns the argument in a different direction.

130 There are 5 matches to the pattern μεγαλοψυχ– in Isocrates, 9 in Demosthenes, 3 in Aeschines, and 1 each in Hyperides and Lycurgus.

131 The term is such that it would naturally be associated with the timocratic society of book VIII of the *Republic* rather than the ideal society.

that it is absent from undisputed Plato. It features again at 150c8, where it is described as the most attractive of the names applied to folly, and one that can be applied to Alcibiades himself.

Commenting on Socrates' assessment of Alcibiades' self-esteem at *Alc. I* 105c4–6, Sharp observes that "There could hardly be a better example of somebody who deemed himself a *megalopsuchos* in the exact sense Aristotle describes in the *Nicomachean Ethics*: namely, "the man who, deeming himself worthy of great things, really is worthy of them" (*NE* 1121b1–2). One may quibble about Alcibiades' *real* worth for sure, particularly in a dialogue that plays with ideas of self-deception, but it is nevertheless quite interesting to find that Alcibiades' rather outrageous level of self-esteem is taken as a case of this quality that almost everybody except this dialogue's "Socrates" regard as praiseworthy. In this connection we should surely mention a passage of Aristotle's *Posterior Analytics* (98a15–20):[132]

> For instance, if we were inquiring what *megalopsukhia* was, we should inquire in the case of several *megalopsukhoi* what one thing they all have in respect of this attribute. For instance, if Alcibiades were a *megalopsukhos*, or Achilles, or Ajax, what one thing do they all share? The refusal to put up with being insulted—for one went to war, the next went into a rage, and the next committed suicide [to avoid it].

So Aristotle had clearly been aware that Alcibiades was somebody liable to be regarded as a *megalopsukhos*, and, commenting on this passage, Eustratius (*in Anal. Po.* 214.13–14) affirms that Alcibiades, Achilles, and Ajax were chosen since *they were agreed to have this quality* "because they did not put up with being insulted."

There is, then, a substantial question of how far the revaluation of *megalopsukhia* here arises out of the desire to criticize other schools of philosophy, and how far it is due to the need to challenge a quality that

132 οἷον λέγω, εἰ τί (15) ἐστι μεγαλοψυχία ζητοῖμεν, σκεπτέον ἐπί τινων μεγαλοψύχων, οὓς ἴσμεν, τί ἔχουσιν ἓν πάντες ᾗ τοιοῦτοι. οἷον εἰ Ἀλκιβιάδης μεγαλόψυχος ἢ ὁ Ἀχιλλεὺς καὶ ὁ Αἴας, τί ἓν ἅπαντες; τὸ μὴ ἀνέχεσθαι ὑβριζόμενοι· ὁ μὲν γὰρ ἐπολέμησεν, ὁ δ' ἐμήνισεν, ὁ δ' ἀπέκτεινεν ἑαυτόν.

many had found attractive in highly ambitious persons. Among such persons Alcibiades could naturally be included, but there may have been other characters closer to the time of writing who were just as much in the forefront of the author's mind. Two such possibilities, dependent on the work's date, are Alexander the Great, for whom Aristotle had acted as intellectual mentor, and Demetrius of Phaleron, the Peripatetic overlord of Athens who had himself written of *megalopsukhia* (fr. 74 = D. L. 5.80). It is interesting to note that in his *Lives* Plutarch applies the notion of the *megalopsukhos* to Pericles (*Per.* 36.9), and more often to Alexander (*Alex.* 4.8, 30.11, 42.10; cf. *de Alex. Fort.* 327e) or Dio (*Dio* 7.1, 32.1, 52.1), but not to Alcibiades. Athenaeus (1.3d) likewise mentions the *megalopsukhia* of Alexander in a context that mentions Alcibiades too, but does not credit him with this quality. It seems that Alcibiades was a *plausible* example, but that Alexander was the *paradigmatic* case. With Socrates, the reader is subjecting Alcibiades, and any others like him, to scrutiny. After the death of Alexander he too would be one of those being re-evaluated as part of the same process. But when was this episode actually written?

Unexpected Vocabulary, 138a–140e

We have now met some of the distinctive language that characterizes the *Alcibiades II*, and it seems appropriate to discuss it more generally at this stage. The term *megalopsukhia* does not occur elsewhere in the Platonic corpus. We have likewise discussed some surprising language at the opening of the dialogue, such as the middle *sunnoeisthai* and the verb *skuthrôpazein*. These, too, are not found elsewhere in the corpus, and yet they are not included in the extensive list of words and expressions that serve as linguistic hints for the dating of the dialogue by Neuhausen (2010: 243)—for something unique within the corpus is not necessarily something that belongs to a date beyond the bounds of Plato's creative life. Even so, *any* words or phrases that do not seem to be Platonic would increase the chances of Plato not having been responsible for the vocabulary of a particular part of the dialogue, and most of those who argue against Platonic authorship would argue for a later date. If there are good reasons for the choice of certain vocabulary in this work of the corpus only, then that weakens the argument against Platonic authorship insofar as it may depend on the vocabulary concerned. In general, however, it is the cumulative picture built up that can most convincingly call Platonic authorship into question.

My examination now involves more Greek than some readers might appreciate. I beg their indulgence and suggest they may like to proceed directly to the final paragraph of this section. Meanwhile, I invite those with greater facility for dealing with the technicalities to take a look at Neuhausen's list for 138a–140e, which includes the following words or phrases:

138b1/139c8: ἐπεὶ φέρε πρὸς Διός
138b9: ἐν ταύτῃ ὄντες τῇ ἕξει
139a14: τι διὰ μέσου τρίτον πάθος
139b8: μηδὲν . . . διὰ μέσου τρίτον πάθος
140a1: τυχόν
140b2: τὴν ἀπεργασίαν
140c8–9: ἐν εὐφημοτάτοις ὀνόμασι . . . κατονομάζειν
140c9: μεγαλοψύχους
140d1: ἐνέους
140d6–7: ἦν γὰρ δήπου καὶ ἐν ἀρχῇ τοῦ λόγου

The following observations can be made about these cases:

138b1 and 139c8: There are only three cases of φέρε πρὸς Διός in the entire corpus, the third also being in this dialogue at 147e5, while these are the only two of ἐπεὶ φέρε πρὸς Διός. It is hard not to believe this to be the distinctive language of an author other than Plato. The lone πρὸς Διός occurs one other time in this dialogue, and a further 39 times in the corpus. Dialogues with regular uses of the phrase include *Euthyphro* (3: 0.55 cases per thousand words), *Lysis* (3: 0.41 per thousand words), and *Euthydemus* (5: 0.38 per thousand), as compared with this dialogue (4: 0.90 per thousand). Usually it is used when the protagonist is expressing some surprise at the responses or attitudes of the interlocutor, or at a sudden thought of his own as at *Alc. I* 129b5, but neither applies to examples in this dialogue. There is no corresponding attraction to νὴ (τὸν) Δία, found 55 times in the corpus, and twice in this dialogue.

138b9: At *Protagoras* 344c1 we meet ἐν ταύτῃ τῇ ἕξει, which may be a sufficient parallel, though ἕξις is a term that increases in philosophical importance with Aristotle.

139a14 and b8: Not only can I not match the phrase διὰ μέσου τρίτον πάθος, I cannot even find a comparable example of τρίτον πάθος in TLG.

140a1: The lone τυχόν is found twice in this dialogue as little more than "perhaps," occurring also at 150c5. Of five other occurrences of the word within the corpus, those in the *Republic* and *Timaeus* involve the article, while two in *Laws* and one in *Epinomis* have dependent genitives.

140b2: While τὴν ἀπεργασίαν is a rare case of this noun with the article (cf. *Prot.* 312d3, *Rep.* 504d7), the noun is found only nine times in the corpus outside our dialogue, most commonly in the *Euthyphro* (4 times, 13d–14a), a passage that may well have inspired its use here. But this may be a very rare medical sense, and is translated as "treatment" by Johnson (2003: 62). Cf. LSJ IV, "les effets" in Brisson (2014: 30), and "i loro effetti" by Carlini (1964: 266), but "symptom" by Kenny (1997: 599), with greater sensitivity as to its context.

140c8–9: Regarding the expression ἐν εὐφημοτάτοις ὀνόμασι . . . κατονομάζειν, one may first note that the dialogue will shortly (149b) present two occurrences of the corresponding noun, of which there is only one example in the *Phaedo* (117e1) and six in the *Laws* elsewhere, and one instance of the verb (143d2), which is marginally commoner. The adjective is otherwise found only three times in the corpus. But note that this is ordinarily *religious* language, and may be appropriate to our dialogue.

140c9: I have treated μεγαλοψύχους (*megalopsukhous*) above.

140d1: With ἐνεούς one may compare *Crat.* 422e4 and *Tht.* 206d9. This cannot contribute to a case against Platonic authorship.

140d6–7: The words ἦν γὰρ δήπου καὶ ἐν ἀρχῇ τοῦ λόγου could conceivably be a gloss in any case, but they contain the combination γὰρ δήπου, which is found at six other points of the dialogue (139e3 [with added γε], 144b4, 144c2, 145a6, 147c6, 147e5), twice in the *Alcibiades I* (110c6, 118d6), possibly once in the *Hipparchus* (226d2), and a maximum of 33 times in the rest of the corpus. It seems difficult to escape the conclusion that somebody other than Plato is responsible for the gross overuse of this combination.[133]

While we should not be content to discuss Neuhausen's list, it already contains enough to lead us to doubt whether Plato could be the author, and those who might still accept his authorship should be prepared to explain why this unusual language is appropriate to this context in particular. One might also ponder the words τί δεῖ καθ' ἕκαστα λέγειν (138c5 and 140b8–9), which in both cases occur after a relative pronoun, a use for which I can find no parallel elsewhere.[134] However, there is quite a lot of vocabulary that is not un-platonic, but seems to occur at rates that would not be expected of a genuine Platonic dialogue.[135] In the not unlikely scenario of the author being a Platonic imitator, this gives insights into those features of Plato's style that were being noticed at that time, with some potentially interesting consequences.

Tentative Judgments and Limited Perspective

One of the first things a Greek reader would have noticed is the frequency of the limiting form of the first person singular, in both nominative ("I at least," *egôge*, found already at 139b7, c9, and 140e3) and dative ("to me at least," *emoige*: 139a9, b4, e5, e9, and 140a1). Was this an exceptional rate for a Platonic text? I calculated the rates per thousand words of both forms (whether the final epsilon was elided

133 Of δήπου itself there are ten examples in each of the two *Alcibiades* dialogues, with another 309 examples across the corpus. Given their size both have rather more than would be expected, and the *Alcibiades II* considerably more. *Hipparchus* has five, *Erastae* and *Minos* two each, *Theages* one only.

134 Elsewhere, the *earliest* occurrence of τί δεῖ in close conjunction with καθ' ἕκαστα is from the first century BCE (Dionysius of Halicarnassus, *De Isocrate* 14). This suggests that the expression found here is a mannerism of the author.

135 Here I should mention the word for "opposite" (*hypenantios*), occurring at 138c9, 139b5 and b11, and only three other times in the whole corpus (four other times if one counts the *spuria*). Whether the sense differs at all from that of *enantios* here is unclear, but the compound form was used throughout the argument based on the premise that each thing has only one opposite, while the latter is found elsewhere in the dialogue at 141a5, 142b2, 143d5, 145c7, 146c3, and 148d2. In that argument the term *hypenantios* is always used for the opposite of the *positive* condition (madness or folly), never of wisdom. That would agree with the word's use at *Tht.* 176a, where it is used of opposition of the bad to the good. Cf. *Statesman* 306e3 referring to inactivity as the contrary of quickness, and *Laws* 810d6 referring to little as the contrary of much.

or not). The results (table 1) must certainly be considered with care, as many dialogues would simply offer few opportunities for such forms, chiefly those with little personal content or a great deal of monologue. Very low rates may not be significant. However, the overall results do appear interesting:

Dialogue	Words	*egôg-*	*emoig-*	Nom. %	Dat. %	Total %
Euthyphro	5,464	15	6	0.275	0.110	0.384
Apology	8,854	10	1	0.113	0.011	0.124
Crito	4,329	3	3	0.069	0.069	0.139
Phaedo	22,633	25	14	0.110	0.062	0.172
Cratylus	19,201	27	28	0.141	0.146	0.286
Theaetetus	23,803	38	13	0.160	0.055	0.214
Sophist	17,414	7	3	0.040	0.017	0.057
Statesman	18,592	2	4	0.011	0.022	0.032
Parmenides	16,434	6	5	0.037	0.030	0.067
Philebus	19,054	11	8	0.058	0.042	0.100
Symposium	17,530	10	3	0.057	0.017	0.074
Phaedrus	17,221	7	7	0.041	0.041	0.081
Alcibiades I	11,317	26	15	0.230	0.133	0.362
Alcibiades II	4,422	10	9	0.226	0.204	0.430
Hipparchus	2,426	11	6	0.453	0.247	0.701
Erastae	2,424	2	0	0.083	0.000	0.083
Theages	3,650	12	5	0.329	0.137	0.466
Charmides	8,410	22	8	0.262	0.095	0.357
Laches	8,021	19	9	0.237	0.112	0.349
Lysis	7,319	11	9	0.150	0.123	0.273
Euthydemus	13,030	28	9	0.215	0.069	0.284
Protagoras	18,077	21	7	0.116	0.039	0.155
Gorgias	27,824	69	29	0.248	0.104	0.352
Meno	10,396	34	24	0.327	0.231	0.558
Hippias Ma.	8,911	14	12	0.157	0.135	0.292
Hippias Mi.	4,505	6	3	0.133	0.067	0.200
Ion	4,091	5	3	0.122	0.073	0.196
Menexenus	4,908	1	0	0.020	0.000	0.020
Clitophon	1,575	1	0	0.063	0.000	0.063
Republic I	9,451	19	12	0.201	0.127	0.328
Rep. II–X	79,907	61	25	0.076	0.031	0.108

Tim.-Criti.	29,144	0	0	0.000	0.000	0.000
Minos	3,078	3	5	0.097	0.162	0.260
Laws	106,298	28	12	0.026	0.011	0.038
Epinomis	6,389	0	0	0.000	0.000	0.000
Epistles	17,213	2	1	0.012	0.006	0.017

Table 1: Comparison of rates of *egôg-* and *emoig-*

The six highest overall rates are *Hipparchus* (about 7 cases per thousand words), *Meno* (5.6), *Theages* (4.7), *Alcibiades II* (4.3), *Euthyphro* (3.8), and *Alcibiades I* (3.6).[136] This is another case where the language of the *Alcibiades II* comes close to that of *Alcibiades I*, *Hipparchus*, and *Theages*—as if the dialogues in this part of the corpus, except *Erastae*, had some similar background of which we are not aware. Yet it would be hard to claim that Plato could not have been responsible for such rates when the *Meno* is the second highest.[137]

We should next ask *why* this dialogue should offer a high rate of such forms as this. A possible answer is that the author is acutely conscious that assent to the steps in the argument is constantly being offered from a personal and limited perspective. If the author was putting more stress than usual on the limited perspective that each individual can bring to philosophic problems then another way it might show up is in higher rates of the expression "it seems to me," either *moi dokei* or *dokei moi*. Here are some figures for this:

Dialogue	Words	*dokei moi*	Rate %	*moi dokei*	Rate %	Combined	Comb. Rate %
Hipparchus	2,426	0	0.000	0	0.000	0	0.000
Clitophon	1,575	0	0.000	0	0.000	0	0.000
Tim.-Criti.	29,144	0	0.000	0	0.000	0	0.000
Epinomis	6,389	0	0.000	0	0.000	0	0.000
Laws	106,298	7	0.007	4	0.004	11	0.010
Sophist	17,414	0	0.000	2	0.011	2	0.011

136 I have examined the corresponding second person singulars σύ γε and σοί γε, and, while results are far less striking *Alcibiades II* has the third highest rate.

137 Interestingly, the first third of the dialogue, Stephanus pages 71–80, is responsible for precisely half of the relevant cases. Nearly half the cases in the *Alcibiades II* are found in the first quarter (138–140).

Parmenides	16,434	0	0.000	2	0.012	2	0.012
Epistles	17,213	1	0.006	1	0.006	2	0.012
Statesman	18,592	1	0.005	2	0.011	3	0.016
Crito	4,329	0	0.000	1	0.023	1	0.023
Minos	3,078	0	0.000	1	0.032	1	0.032
Phaedrus	17,221	4	0.023	2	0.012	6	0.035
Euthyphro	5,464	1	0.018	1	0.018	2	0.037
Philebus	19,054	3	0.016	4	0.021	7	0.037
Symposium	17,530	2	0.011	5	0.029	7	0.040
Erastae	2,424	1	0.041	0	0.000	1	0.041
Alcibiades I	11,317	0	0.000	5	0.044	5	0.044
Hippias Ma.	8,911	0	0.000	4	0.045	4	0.045
Euthydemus	13,030	0	0.000	6	0.046	6	0.046
Rep. II–X	79,907	15	0.019	23	0.029	38	0.048
Theaetetus	23,803	2	0.008	10	0.042	12	0.050
Gorgias	27,824	0	0.000	15	0.054	15	0.054
Theages	3,650	0	0.000	2	0.055	2	0.055
Charmides	8,410	2	0.024	4	0.048	6	0.071
Protagoras	18,077	2	0.011	12	0.066	14	0.077
Apology	8,854	0	0.000	7	0.079	7	0.079
Phaedo	22,633	3	0.013	16	0.071	19	0.084
Republic I	9,451	1	0.011	7	0.074	8	0.085
Hippias Mi.	4,505	1	0.022	3	0.067	4	0.089
Menexenus	4,908	2	0.041	3	0.061	5	0.102
Lysis	7,319	5	0.068	3	0.041	8	0.109
Ion	4,091	0	0.000	5	0.122	5	0.122
Laches	8,021	2	0.025	8	0.100	10	0.125
Cratylus	19,201	8	0.042	20	0.104	28	0.146
Meno	10,396	6	0.058	13	0.125	19	0.183
Alcibiades II	4,422	3	0.068	7	0.158	10	0.226

Table 2: Rates for *dokei moi* and *moi dokei*

Since these figures are difficult to digest when considered independently, it may help to list the seven highest for each of the three rates:

Dialogue	*dokei moi* %	Dialogue	*moi dokei* %	Dialogue	Combined %
Laches	0.025	*Republic* I	0.074	*Menexenus*	0.102
Menexenus	0.041	*Apology*	0.079	*Lysis*	0.109
Erastae	0.041	*Laches*	0.100	*Ion*	0.122
Cratylus	0.042	*Cratylus*	0.104	*Laches*	0.125
Meno	0.058	*Ion*	0.122	*Cratylus*	0.146
Alcibiades II	0.0678	*Menexenus*	0.125	*Meno*	0.183
Lysis	0.0683	*Alcibiades II*	0.158	*Alcibiades II*	0.226

Table 3: Highest rates in ascending order

Clearly the *Alcibiades II* has the highest density of such forms, more than double that of all but its five nearest rivals, though it is just edged out of top place when the verb precedes the dative, the preferred order in the *Lysis*. It is noticeable that none of the hiatus avoiding dialogues make this list, and overall they tend to have very low rates (less than one case per book of the *Laws*). This picture alters little when one considers the phrase *emoi dokei*, using the stronger form of the personal pronoun which only occurs in this combination *before* the verb.

Dialogue	Words	No.	Rate %
Laws	106,298	1	0.001
Gorgias	27,824	2	0.007
Theaetetus	23,803	2	0.008
Alcibiades I	11,317	1	0.009
Republic II–X	79,907	8	0.010
Protagoras	18,077	2	0.011
Hippias Ma.	8,911	1	0.011
Apology	8,854	1	0.011
Symposium	17,530	2	0.011
Charmides	8,410	1	0.012
Laches	8,021	1	0.012
Phaedo	22,633	3	0.013
Lysis	7,319	1	0.014
Euthyphro	5,464	1	0.018
Meno	10,396	2	0.019
Euthydemus	13,030	3	0.023

Epistles	17,213	4	0.023
Cratylus	19,201	7	0.036
Erastae	2,424	1	0.041
Alcibiades II	4,422	2	0.045

Table 4: Rates for *emoi dokei* in dialogues containing the phrase

So once again the *Alcibiades II* has the highest rate, with *Erastae* also high, and *Cratylus* quite high. And, again, the hiatus avoiding dialogues have very low rates—all except *Laws* have zero rates.

The figures for the combination of *moi* and *dokei* are similar to those of the combination of *soi* and *dokei*,[138] for which the figures greater than zero appear below:

Dialogue	Words	*soi dokei* %	*dokai soi* %	Total	Comb. Rate %
Laws	106,298	0.003	0.001	4	0.004
Statesman	18,592	0.005	0.000	1	0.005
Sophist	17,414	0.006	0.000	1	0.006
Epistles	17,213	0.000	0.006	1	0.006
Alcibiades I	11,317	0.000	0.009	1	0.009
Symposium	17,530	0.006	0.006	2	0.011
Philebus	19,054	0.010	0.010	4	0.021
Apology	8,854	0.000	0.023	2	0.023
Parmenides	16,434	0.018	0.006	4	0.024
Republic II–X	79,907	0.016	0.010	21	0.026
Theaetetus	23,803	0.017	0.013	7	0.029
Republic I	9,451	0.021	0.011	3	0.032
Lysis	7,319	0.014	0.027	3	0.041
Hippias Mi.	4,505	0.000	0.044	2	0.044
Crito	4,329	0.046	0.000	2	0.046
Theages	3,650	0.027	0.027	2	0.055
Charmides	8,410	0.000	0.059	5	0.059
Phaedo	22,633	0.040	0.022	14	0.062

138 Absent from both *Phaedrus* and *Laches*, as also from *Hipparchus*, *Clitophon*, *Timaeus-Critias*, and *Epinomis* from which δοκεῖ μοι and μοι δοκεῖ were also absent.

Euthydemus	13,030	0.069	0.000	9	0.069
Protagoras	18,077	0.017	0.055	13	0.072
Ion	4,091	0.049	0.024	3	0.073
Hippias Ma.	8,911	0.045	0.045	8	0.090
Euthyphro	5,464	0.018	0.073	5	0.092
Minos	3,078	0.000	0.097	3	0.097
Cratylus	19,201	0.057	0.042	19	0.099
Gorgias	27,824	0.054	0.065	33	0.119
Meno	10,396	0.077	0.048	13	0.125
Erastae	2,424	0.165	0.041	5	0.206
Alcibiades II	4,422	0.136	0.181	14	0.317

Table 5: Rates for *soi* and *dokei* together—late dialogues in **bold**

Evidently the *Alcibiades II* and to a lesser extent the *Erastae* have exceptional rates, while *Meno* again has the highest rate among undisputed dialogues. *Gorgias, Cratylus, Euthyphro, Hippias Major,* and the suspect *Minos* all show high rates. On this criterion the *Alcibiades II* would differ considerably from its neighbors in the fourth tetralogy, *Hipparchus* and *Alcibiades I.* The *Erastae*, however, did not show any comparable frequency for *egôge* ("I at least," etc.), while the *Theages*, with a very similar rate to the *Alcibiades II* for *egôge*, looked closer to average on the other tests—so that none of these neighboring dialogues share all the same traits. This should act as something of a warning for any who are tempted to postulate a common origin for all these dialogues. To judge from the *Memorabilia*, those ancients who suspected the author of the *Alcibiades II* was Xenophon were also wrong, for that work is no more than mid-range in the tests applied.

These tests for which the *Alcibiades II* gave such high results were for language that tended to limit any statement, or the invited answer in the case of a question, to be a personal perspective of one of the participants in the conversation. So in this dialogue there is additional emphasis on the fact that the views stated are only those of Alcibiades himself or those of Socrates. But surely there are other words through which one could make this apparent. For instance, the term *phainetai* ("it appears," "it is apparent") can be used in close proximity to *moi* or *soi* to indicate what appears to be so to one of the participants in the conversation. High rates of *phainetai* (>2 cases per thousand words) can be found in *Hippias Minor* (3.55), *Cratylus* (3.07), *Parmenides* (3.03),

Hipparchus (2.47), *Alcibiades I* (2.12), and *Theaetetus* (2.06), but in the *Alcibiades II* the rate is only 0.90. However, if one then calculates how often the verb is construed with the personal pronouns *moi*, *soi*, or *emoi*, the highest rates are *Cratylus* (0.99 per thousand), *Phaedo* (0.71), *Crito* (0.69) and *Charmides* (0.59). This verb, which generally implies that one has a much *more distinct* view of the matter, is not so common in limiting that view to the individual, and is not found in that role in the *Alcibiades II*, nor indeed in the *Hipparchus* and *Theages.* Overall, it is a less suitable term for an author wishing to emphasize the dangers of relying on one's own limited perspective. It was tentative judgments based on a limited perspective to which the author wished to give prominence.

These tests suggest we should conduct a rather wider examination of the vocabulary and style of the *Alcibiades II* before our examination of the dialogue is complete. But at this stage we have discovered that the dialogue places an unusual emphasis on the personal perspectives of its participants. Does that mean it is pervaded by an almost Protagorean view of the world? Does it mean it was written at a time when certainty was receding from Academic discussion? And does it mean that it marks already a step on the road to the new Academy and to "skeptical" methodologies? All such questions are complicated, and all are worth trying to answer. However, it would be more appropriate at this stage to continue further with our examination of the dialogue in order that we may have the whole in view before finalizing our assessment.

Conclusion

Both the work of Neuhausen and my own observations about the language of limited perspective have pointed to numerous ways in which the language of the *Alcibiades II* is unusual, to the extent that if it is to be regarded as genuine a great many words and phrases need to be better explained as appropriate to the content, along with the high frequencies of other words and phrases to which I have pointed. But it is more probable that the work is not ultimately by Plato himself, or not in its entirety, so that there is no objection to placing its final version significantly later than the death of Alexander. As our task progresses it will become still more difficult to ignore the effects of Alexander's brief reign upon many of the details.

Chapter Three

Power and Violence: Nothing to do with Alcibiades?

A Mistaken Attraction to Tyranny

For all the initial emphasis on Oedipus and his madness, Socrates makes it plain at 141a that it is not really this kind of outburst that he fears from Alcibiades. Plenty of people in their own time do pray for things that are bad for them, but whereas Oedipus, in a fit of anger, was knowingly praying for something harmful, these people are praying for things that they presume to be good (141a1–3). In view of this contrast between ignorance and anger as two distinct causes of error, it seems that the kind of "Socrates" envisaged here is not the one who believed "nobody does wrong willingly" and denied the existence of incontinence (*akrasia*) as he had apparently done in early dialogues—most dogmatically at *Protagoras* 345d–e. This is more like the Socrates of the *Republic* (IV), who acknowledges that passionate feelings including anger can take control of the individual even when their reason tries to object that there is some better course.

Alcibiades, however, is not accused of being swayed by the passions and so acting against his better judgment. He is rather accused of acting according to an erroneous assessment of what is best for him. The accusations and examples that follow pay curiously little attention to the kind of intentions the young Alcibiades might conceivably have had some time between 432 and 429 BCE, and seem to suggest that his understandably high ambitions and his hubristic tendencies might in certain circumstances have reached Macedonian heights. Socrates readily admits that there are limits to Alcibiades' quest for glory and to his ruthlessness, but that does not stop him from using these extreme examples of conduct that he might contemplate.

In a passage reminiscent of *Alcibiades I* 105a3–c6, Socrates first imagines circumstances in which the god on whom Alcibiades is relying to fulfill his prayers forestalls his request by asking him, successively, whether he would be content to be the tyrant of Athens or, failing that, of all Greece, or even of Europe as a whole. While in *Alcibiades I* the god making the offer was entirely unspecified, here it is the particular god to whom Alcibiades intends to appeal (141a6–7). The other major difference is that, while the Alcibiades of their first encounter was ready to die rather than to accept limitations to his glorious achievements, the Alcibiades of the present encounter will not sacrifice his life in return even for world domination—he observes in fact that by dying he would be losing his chance to make use of the enormous acquisitions he had made (141c4–5). He does not deny that in normal circumstances he would accept the offer of tyranny across the European world, and believes that anybody would do so in the expectation that such an achievement would be the greatest of goods. Following Alcibiades' admission that he would not want to acquire tyranny if he had no chance to enjoy it, Socrates also succeeds in getting him to admit that he would not want to acquire it if he were going to use it badly and harmfully (141c6–8).[139]

It seems questionable whether the young Alcibiades could have thought of his political ambitions as a desire for *tyranny*. For him more than for most Athenians the obvious model for political power must have been his guardian, Pericles, whose power was firmly rooted in the support of the citizens. In the well-known statement of Thucydides (2.65.9) the city was "nominally a democracy, but for practical purposes under the rule of one man." In the first instance it was for this kind of power that subsequent leaders unsuccessfully contended, and one notes that in another doubtful dialogue the young Theages thinks that Socrates is mocking him in deducing that his desire for rule at Athens aims at tyranny.[140] It is hardly surprising,

139 The conjunction of these terms (κακῶς τε καὶ βλαβερῶς) seems to be a case where the latter term further specifies the sense in which the former is to be taken.

140 See 125e3. At 124e1–10 Theages has been forced to admit that the kind of rule that a number of potentates had over the whole population of their cities is called "tyrannical," and that in seeking rule of this kind he would be seeking tyranny. Socrates' reaction implies that this is a disgraceful ambition, and Theages now insists that what he said he desired was the kind of rule over his fellow citizens that comes through their consent rather than force, like that exercised by those who have become renowned at Athens: Themistocles, Pericles, or Cimon. While Theages does admit that he, like most people, would pray to be the tyrant of all people, or as many as possible, he views this as on a par with praying to be a god (125e8–126a4), not as a realistic ambition; and he never says that he would pray to be a tyrant of Athens.

then, that Helfer is able to describe the evidence for Alcibiades' quest for tyranny as "vanishingly thin."[141]

The comparable passage of the *Alcibiades I* starts from the premise that Alcibiades will want to show the city that he deserves to be honored (*axios . . . timasthai*) *even more than Pericles* (105b2–3), and the expected outcome is that the city will put the greatest of power in his hands. We are talking of leadership that is freely granted by the governed, and granted because he deserves that much honor (*timê*). That is the kind of leadership Pericles had according to Plutarch (*Pericles* 33.2), who tells us that it was because Socrates wanted to maximize Alcibiades' "love of honor" (or "ambition," *philotimia*) in things fine (or "glorious," *en kalois*) that he ceded the prize for valor to Alcibiades (*Alc.* 7.5), probably because his would-be corruptors had already been making use of his "love of honor" and "love of ambition" (*philodoxia*), which had so far been poorly directed. Allegedly these corruptors tried to persuade him that he could outdo Pericles (*Alc.* 6.4). The language of *philotimia* abounds in Plutarch's *Alcibiades*, and the potential relevance of *timê* is confirmed by the passage on the young man's ambitions in the *Alcibiades I* (105b2: *timasthai*), so that one naturally questions why neither concept is at any stage applied to Socrates' young friend in the *Alcibiades II*.[142]

Such leadership of Athens, freely given in response to Alcibiades' genuine worth, would in the *Alcibiades I* mean that he is without rival among all the Greeks or even foreigners in Europe (105b4–7). Admittedly Socrates thinks that Alcibiades would not be keen to have his power limited to Europe, and he would like to have the opportunity to demonstrate his superiority to Cyrus and Xerxes, which looks as if it would have to come about by invasion and conquest, but the strongest term that is ever used in this passage is *dunasteuein* (105b8), which implies being in a position to exercise power, but does not describe the manner in which the power is acquired or maintained. This is not

141 Helfer 2017, 176. Later in Alcibiades' career it is reported that his extravagant ways caused some Athenians to worry he might have tyrannical ambitions (Th. 6.15.4), but there is no suggestion that Thucydides would have considered their views helpful to Athens' cause.

142 Note that there is one use of the verb φιλοτιμεῖσθαι (146a4 of craftsmen in the dystopia, and apparently unrelated to the *Antiope* as quoted in *Gorgias* 484e), and two of the verb τιμᾶν in Socrates' second monologue (149a5 and 150b1, neither having relevance for Alcibiades). No other vocabulary from the root *tim-* is present.

unexpected, because Alcibiades is aiming above all at being honored, and the exercise of tyrannical power does not enhance how one is regarded by others. The vocabulary of tyranny occurs only twice in the *Alcibiades I*, both at its close (135a1, b3), where it is used to illustrate the *unchecked* power that Socrates must demonstrate to be dangerous.

In the *Alcibiades II*, however, the vocabulary of tyranny occurs ten times between 141a and 142c,[143] so that one might justly call it thematic here. The author has no hesitation in imagining the god offering to make Alcibiades "tyrant of the city of Athens." The term is implicit when the god is imagined to increase his offer and make him "[tyrant] of all the Greeks." The concept is then extended to cover tyranny over all Europe, with everybody aware that very day that he is "tyrant" (141b2–5).[144] This is an unusual sense of the word *turannos* since it would ordinarily apply to a single Greek city state, other words being employed for those who rule larger regions. But then Socrates, in reminding Alcibiades of what he would *not* sacrifice in return for an empire of *any* magnitude, refers to "the territory of, and tyranny over, all Greeks and foreigners." It seems that even *universal* domination can be referred to as "tyranny" in this context.

In the course of this brief section on Alcibiades' ambitions (141a–c) there occur no particular words or phrases that are noted by Neuhausen (2010: 243) as indications of a late date or as extreme rarities, though he rightly draws attention to the unusual Hellenistic spelling of the word for "nothing" at 141c4 (μηθέν). One might also note the term for "this very day" (*authêmeron*) has only two parallels in Plato (*Republic* 374d2, *Laws* 936a1). Since this term twice occurred in Thucydides in relation to regime change (6.55.3, 8.89.3), it does not seem inappropriate here.

The Switch to Monologue

After getting Alcibiades to admit that he would not accept any such mega-tyranny in exchange for his life, nor even if he couldn't make good use of it, Socrates gives a rather long speech (141c9–143a5) that appears designed to reinforce powerfully the message of their preceding conversation. Alternatively, one might prefer to see the preceding

143 The noun for "tyranny" occurs six times, and the noun for "tyrant" four.

144 The text here is not totally certain, as, unlike Burnet, Carlini does not accept Sauppe's proposal to repeat the words καὶ τοῦτο, but the sense is clear, and the word "tyrant" not in doubt.

exchange on Alcibiades' lust for unrivalled political power as a suitable introduction for the monologue on the dangers of prayer. It had taken a theme from the opening pages of the *Alcibiades I*, and then handled it in a fashion somewhat unsuited to the actual ambitions of the historical Alcibiades, but well suited to providing an occasion for the theme to be explored in the monologue: the gulf between people's most earnest desires and what will actually be in their interests.

That Socrates launches into a longer speech should cause no surprise, since even in dialogues where he makes a virtue out of brevity (or *brachylogy*) he does not always adhere to his preferences.[145] It should now be well known, first, that Plato often employed a substantial discursive central section in his works[146] and, second, that several of the doubtful dialogues have Socrates launching into an extended monologue somewhere near the center, though in the *Theages* that monologue comes almost at the end. In a study of such passages I have ascertained that the doubtful dialogues typically show greater linguistic variation between the dialogic and monologic sections than dialogues of unquestioned authenticity.[147] This is particularly clear in the *Alcibiades* dialogues, the *Hipparchus*, and the *Theages*.

The *Alcibiades II* differs somewhat in splitting the monologue into two parts. I do not mean simply that there are two such monologues, but rather that what appears to be the same theme, the theme of what kind of prayer it would be prudent to utter, is broken off at the end of one monologue and then resumed after a repetitive reminder later on. In the first and last lines of these monologues there are signs of a token effort to link this theme, which would have been of relevance to a great number of individuals and indeed to whole cities, with the issues facing Alcibiades himself,[148] and such verbs as

145 For the term see particularly *Protagoras* 335a–b and also (within a longer speech at 341d–347a) 343b; also *Gorgias* 449c, comparing also 465e (within a longer speech at 464b–466a).

146 See most recently Thesleff 2017.

147 See Tarrant 2018.

148 For instance, while it is clear from second person singulars throughout the earlier monologue that there is a single intended addressee, a vocative at 142e1 reinforces the impression that it is specifically tailored to Alcibiades, and at 143a5 the addressee is openly invited to express his opinion. A vocative occurs in the first line of the second speech, and the final sentence (150b3–4) again inquires what the interlocutor has to say about the claims just made.

"you see" (*horais*, 141c9, e3)[149] and "you will find" (*heurêseis*, 142b3, 149c8),[150] both typical of this dialogue, remind the reader of the presence of an interlocutor. But the material might have been addressed to anybody who was intending to pray, and the advice on suitable formulae for prayers will ultimately go unheeded by Alcibiades, because the wider discussion will lead him to avoid praying at all. The twin monologues encourage us to modify our prayers—the dialogue as a whole encourages us to abandon them. At this point what is required is that we note the different nature of the monologic sections, and bear in mind that it may possibly have been adapted from elsewhere. But even if this should prove to have been so, the monologues have become an integral part of the work, and must be considered as part of the overall design.

The first part of the monologue, then, commences with the claim that it is not safe either to accept randomly what is on offer or pray to acquire things, assuming one is going to be harmed or even lose one's life because of them. It is argued that there are many examples of men who set their hearts and minds on tyrannical power on the assumption that they would be doing very nicely, only to find that once the prize was theirs they become the object of a conspiracy and lose their lives. But if there are so many examples, as Socrates claims, it is odd that the sole one given involves a considerable anachronism. With an Homeric phrase for "only the other day," he introduces the same lawless Macedonian tyrant introduced with an Atticized[151] version of that same phrase by Polus at *Gorgias* 470d1. Both passages involve the violent death of a Macedonian ruler and his unlawful replacement by an assassin, the *Gorgias* with the replacement of Perdiccas by Archelaus in 413 BCE (despite indications of a dramatic date of about 427 BCE),[152]

149 This second person singular indicative form is found six times in the *Alcibiades II*, three times in the *Hipparchus*, twice in the *Theages*, and just once in the *Alcibiades I*. As it is only found in just over seventy cases in undisputed Plato (some technical, as at *Theaetetus* 165c x 4) the rate for the *Alcibiades II* is very high. Corresponding optative and imperative forms are found at 139d3, 145a4, and 146a3.

150 The four cases in the *Alcibiades II* overall (one in *Alc. I*, one in *Minos*) seem excessive compared with just fourteen cases in undisputed Plato.

151 As opposed to the Homeric text (χθιζά τε καὶ πρωιζά), the correct text in the *Gorgias* is probably that offered by Dodds (see 1959, 242) that accords with *Laws* 677d6 (χθὲς καὶ πρῴην). The reversion to the Homeric form is perhaps due to the tendency of the *Alcibiades II* to pay close attention to literary matters.

152 Dodds 1959, 17–18, finds passages that suggest a whole variety of dramatic dates.

and the *Alcibiades II* with the short-lived replacement of Archelaus by one of his young male sexual partners in 399 BCE.[153] This is the final year of Socrates' life, by which time Alcibiades is already dead, and given that Pericles is supposed to be still alive at the time of the conversation (143e) this involves an anachronism of at least thirty years. Interestingly, the *Theages* has also been suspected of introducing Archelaus, as an example of a tyrant, anachronistically,[154] thus also following the example of the *Gorgias*.

So what is the author of the *Alcibiades II* trying to achieve here by this flagrant anachronism? Perhaps he was keen to use this particular example because it involved a ruler so temporary that he could never have received any benefit from his rule prior to his death, and perhaps he was imitating the *Gorgias* both in glossing over a blatant anachronism with a Homeric phrase and in choosing an example from the lawless history of Macedon. The text emphasizes this lawlessness by designating Archelaus himself as a "tyrant" rather than a "king" (a term that Aelian 8.9 would have thought more appropriate) or simply as a "ruler" (as preferred by Plato at *Gorgias* 470d6).[155] Here too, it seems, the word

---

Tarrant 2008 argues that the scholiast whose evidence would make Euripides' *Antiope* a late play, contrary to the dating suggested by the number of resolved feet, should be ignored, leaving the reference to Archelaus as the only real anomaly.

153 The *Alcibiades II* mentions no name, referring to one man only and offering the information that he was Archelaus' παιδικά. Aelian (8.9), who quotes the whole of 141d7 (Ἀρχέλαον) to e3 (ἐτελεύτησεν), adds parenthetically that "tyrant" rather than "king" was what Plato called Archelaus, and also includes the name Crateuas, with a subsequent change of the participle (ἐρασθέντα) from n.pl. to masc.s. In Aristotle's version (*Pol.* 5.10 1311b6–20) the leading assassin receives the name Crataeas or Crataeus, and Hellanocrates of Larissa is made an accomplice. Later (1311b30–34) we learn that Decamnichus had spurred them on. Both Crateuas and Hellanocrates were here supposed to have been motivated by the way that Archelaus used them for physical gratification, though the former also resented the failure of Archelaus to give him the hand of one of his daughters as promised. Some other sources disagree regarding the motivation, and for most of the 390s, before the ultimate emergence of Amyntas III, instability prevailed. A version in Diodorus Siculus (14.37.6) makes the name Craterus, and his killing of Archelaus, an accident.

154 See Nails 2002, 329. But I am not entirely sure that the phrase τὸν νεωστὶ τοῦτον ἄρχοντα ἐν Μακεδονίᾳ (124d2–3) implies that Archelaus is already dead. Joyal 2000, 156n78, thinks that it implies that Archelaus had only recently *come to power* (hence that it is consistent with a dramatic date of 409 BCE), but if so, why would the author not have written νῦν rather than the vague νεωστὶ?

155 Aelian uses βασιλεύς, Plato ἄρχων (cf. 471b2: τὴν ἀρχήν). However, the Platonic conversation does rapidly move on to consider those who seize tyrannical power, but without retaining the Macedonian context.

"tyrant" has been deliberately chosen, and one may ask whether it underscores a certain anti-Macedonian attitude.

While the allusion to the *Gorgias* is obvious, the desire to allude to certain other prominent works of the Platonic corpus also seems clear from the suggestion that Alcibiades is "not unfamiliar with" recent events in Macedon, employing a term that is prominent in the *Phaedrus* (243e5, 259b3, b6, 261b8) for "not having heard" something (*anêkoos*), but with a different construction.[156] The contexts are also a little different, for in the *Phaedrus* it usually signifies something poetic or mythic that Phaedrus should have heard, and even at 243e5 it foreshadows the poetic and mythic voice that Socrates is about to adopt. So the term sounds a little pretentious there, suiting a literary conversation with Phaedrus perhaps. In this Macedonian story, however, there is nothing poetic and little that is mythic—at least when seen from the perspective of 399 BCE. By the date when the dialogue was written, however, we may already be dealing with an established cautionary tale.

As if to acknowledge that Alcibiades might make a serious mistake without his having ambitions of either tyrannical or Macedonian proportions, Socrates now switches to the kind of thing that could more readily happen in classical Athens: the acquisition of the rank of *stratêgos* (141e3–142b3). This is the position that had enabled Athenians to achieve political leadership in the polis, and the position best seen as underpinning Pericles' continuous power. And we are no longer talking of what people pray for or receive with divine approval: most prominent Athenians simply desired high office, as is apparent at 142a1 (*epithumêsantes*),[157] and it is the Athenians themselves who bestow it. Even those who have successfully handled the challenges that it brings can live to regret not just the military horrors involved in leadership but also the siege tactics of the informers who work for their downfall. So some of them would now pray to have been without the office at all rather than to have served in it. So too with children, suggests Socrates

156 The difference is that the *Phaedrus* uses the genitive for what one has not heard, and the *Alcibiades II* substitutes the accusative.

157 In the tripartite psychology of the *Republic* the part of the soul motivated by *timê* would ordinarily be the spirited part (*thumoeides*), not the appetitive part characterized by desire (*epithumia*). Socrates speaks as if either the motivation for generalship was not the pursuit of *timê*, or the pursuit of *timê* was no more noble than any other self-interested desire. It is indeed regarded as illogical that people should pursue such office when no personal benefit ensues (142b1–3).

(142b3–c7): there are plenty who have prayed to acquire the children who have been the source of disaster for them—whether because they grew up constantly displaying bad character, or because they grew up virtuous and were then tragically lost.

There is an interesting parallel here between those who would prefer to have been "unappointed [as general]" (*astratêgêtos*) than to have served [as general], and those who would prefer their children to have been "unborn" (*agenêtos*) rather than to have been born:[158] the constructions are parallel,[159] and after the unusual adjective "unfamiliar" (*anêkoos*) at 141d6 we now meet two other interesting adjectives formed with the alpha privative (analogous to the English "un-"). What we are encountering here is the general idea of perceived benefits that most people would pray (or at least prefer) to receive, which are liable to turn out so badly for the recipient that they often, with hindsight, wish they had never had them. And even so, it is difficult to find people who would neither accept nor pray for what are popularly perceived as advantages (142c4–d2). But many will change their minds, and just as the original desire can be represented as a prayer, so too (in a strange sort of way) can the change of mind be represented as a reversal of an initial prayer. Here (142e3) the author devises another strange word, *aneukhesthai* (something like "unpray"), though there seems little point in praying that something had never actually happened. The general cannot in ordinary language "pray" that he had never been a general, nor the father that he had never had a child. But what the Greek seems to mean is that the language of prayer is used to express this forlorn wish for the reversal of the past. Another word employed here is *palinôidousin* (παλινῳδοῦσιν: "they change their tune"), which indicates a public

---

158 "Born" is something of an over-translation, but no good alternative presents itself. The text is not entirely reliable here, owing to the ease of confusing the rather colorless ἀγένητα (normally found in Plato in the sense of things being "ungenerated," e.g. *Phdr.* 245d1, d3, 246a1; the adjective is found also at *Prot.* 324b3 and *Laws* 934a7, both in the sense of "undone" or "unaccomplished") and the more personal term ἀγέννητα (cf. *Tim.* 41b7; but 52a1 uses this adjective in the same sense as the *Phaedrus* had used the other term). Both readings are found in the manuscripts, with the latter having the authority of B, C, and D, as against T. But ἀγένητα does contrast nicely with the aorist infinitive γενέσθαι.

159 As follows:

142a8:	[pray] unappointed, to be, rather, than, to have served.
142c3:	[wish] unborn, rather, to be, than, to have arisen.

and often poetic change of one's original stance, and is a term well known from Plato's *Phaedrus*.[160] Alcibiades at 148b3–4 will repeat the whole phrase, including both of the colorful verbs, in the singular but otherwise virtually word for word.

Socrates' cautionary speech continues with the traditional (and also Platonic)[161] idea that people are far too ready to blame the gods rather than their own stupidity when their hastily conceived prayers are answered, and Homer (*Od.* 1.32–34) is brought in as a confirmation of this view. Then Socrates continues his respectful nod towards the tribe of poets by partly quoting and (on the face of it) partly paraphrasing two hexameters from an unnamed source that otherwise appears only in ancient anthologies and sources quoting Plato.[162] Yet, while the partial re-quotation at 148b6–7 suggests that the poet's name was unknown to Socrates,[163] he is prepared to speculate here about matters that one could hardly be sure of without knowing the author. The lines, he thinks, were written for friends who were inclined to act and to pray according to their own inaccurate assessment of what was best. The actual lines offer a prayer to Zeus that he will grant them[164] what is best whether they pray for it or not, and ward off evils even when we pray for them.

At the conclusion of the initial monologue Socrates invites Alcibiades to agree that the lines present splendid and prudent policy,

160 See *Phdr.* 243b2, b5, 257a4.

161 Compare for example *Rep.* X 619b7–c6.

162 *Anth. Pal.* 10.108, and Orion, *Anthologion* fr. 17 (headed "from the Pythagoreans"); cf. Julian fr. 170b. The manuscript text of our dialogue concludes with the infinitive ἀπαλέξειν (with κελεύει), while other texts have ἀπερύκοις and even Proclus (who discusses the *Platonic* text) has this alternative verb (in the form ἀπέρυκε), and also the correct λυγρὰ rather than δεινὰ. Orion does not have βασιλεῦ, but rather Κρονίδη. While it is possible that our MSS have the correct text of this dialogue, and that the author has modified two lines of pre-existing verse, one should also consider the possibility that the author has invented the lines, which have subsequently suffered in transmission. The principal reason for suspecting that the lines were invented is the adjective ἀνεύκτοις, which must involve the root "pray" in conjunction with either the alpha privative ἀν- or the elided prepositional prefix ἀνὰ; and so it would *either* be formed similarly to the adjectives for "not having heard," "not having been general," and "not having been born," *or* be directly related to the curious verb for "unpray." Either way, the most distinctive language of the preceding part of the monologue is matched by something directly comparable in the epic lines.

163 Note the periphrasis "the poet whom I mentioned at the beginning of the discussion."

164 The first person plural ἄμμι ("to us") presumably refers to the poet and his friends.

even though there had actually not been much in this speech to mark it as an address *to* Alcibiades. Rather it is the first part of the core *theoretical* contribution on prayer, containing some of life's overall tragicomedy that Plato had spoken of in the *Philebus* (52b3). People's prayers go on making the same mistakes even though the dangers are there for all to see, and when things turn out badly they blame it on supernatural forces rather than on themselves. We go from praying for a thing to wishing that it had never come about. We change our tune and reverse-pray, blaming the very beings we pray to. We really ought to learn to pray more prudently. These themes are echoed at 148b as if to reinforce them, and in very much the same language. So this speech is central to the philosophy of prayer rather than to the dramatic confrontation between Socrates and Alcibiades, and its significance is actually for all of us. Tyrannical desires, ambition for high office, and the longing for children are no more than typical reasons for earnest acts of prayer, which may all result in disaster if the prayers are successful. They are not the special desires of Alcibiades: the siring of legitimate children is unlikely to have been of concern to him at this youthful stage, and his political ambitions would have taken a more typically Athenian form.

Various issues arise about the exact reasons for the choice of some of the language in this speech. While some of it is unusual, all of it serves a purpose, and could be regarded as clever enough to encourage the belief that, here at least, Plato was the author. Neuhausen draws our attention to two cases of unusual spelling at 141d8 and 141e4,[165] so that the author has indeed adopted an unusual orthography. On the other hand, Neuhausen only includes three terms from the initial monologue (141c9–143a5) in his lists of words and phrases that are rare or indicative of lateness, and these are three of the terms with an alpha privative that we drew attention to above.[166] Such words have been shown to be *thematic* in this discussion, and appear to be present for special effect. If this is Plato, he has indeed been choosing some unusual vocabulary, but this has successfully served to emphasize the way people often wish for the non-fulfillment of a wish already fulfilled.

I have given reasons elsewhere for believing that some of the long speeches in works of doubtful authenticity do in fact preserve a Platonic

165 Neuhausen 2010, 243: the spellings are οὐθέν for οὐδέν and οἴδαμεν for ἴσμεν, respectively.

166 Neuhausen 2010, 243: 142a8: ἀστρατηγήτους; 142d3 [& 148b3]: ἀνευχομένοις; 143a2: ἀνεύκτοις.

kernel of material around which a less Platonic dialogue (linguistically speaking) has been constructed.[167] We shall deal with that possibility at greater length after we have examined the second installment of Socrates' monologue. For now it is enough to note that so far the linguistic oddities in Socrates' speech do not justify suspicions of non-Platonic authorship. The *Alcibiades II* follows the pattern of many doubtful dialogues, where the language of the monologic passages is such as to attract rather less suspicion of spuriousness than that of the regular dialogue. And we should also bear in mind that what looks at first to be a complete monologue is such as to lead *directly* into the other main monologue on prayer starting at 148b9. That is precisely why the content, and especially the closing statement, of the earlier speech must be so mechanically recalled at 148b1–8. It looks almost as if one continuous monologue, on the type of prayer that human beings ought to settle for, has been broken up artificially by the psychological and epistemological material more typical of the dialogue.

The Virtues of Ignorance

The last few words of the monologue re-engage with Alcibiades, and ask him how he feels about the kind of prayer proposed by the unnamed poet. Alcibiades seems to think the lines well said, but rapidly changes the subject. What he has noticed are not just the consequences of human ignorance for the way we should engage with the divine, but the potentially devastating nature of ignorance more generally. There had been some terminology broadly connected with stupidity and foolishness, beginning with the Homeric quotation, where *atasthaliaisin* is glossed with the more prosaic and relevant term *aphrosunais* ("instances of folly"). It is then suggested that the poet whose lines will follow is a *phronimos tis* ("a sensible person") writing for *philois anoêtois* ("foolish friends"). Such terminology can be seen as having as much to do with ethics as epistemology (supposing Plato and his followers would acknowledge that the two can easily be separated), but what follows is more directly concerned with the theory of knowledge. In a word, Alcibiades thinks that *agnoia* ("ignorance," "failure to recognize" something) is to blame for all the human woes that result from tyranny, high office, or children. People do not realize they are working for, and ultimately praying for, the very worst of things for themselves.

167 See Tarrant 2018.

They find it impossible to comprehend that they cannot be trusted to choose what is best for themselves rather than what is worst. Their prayer turns out to be a curse no better than Oedipus' at 138c! They are unaware that they are ignorant in this regard, so that they are in fact doubly ignorant.

One does not expect the Socrates of the *Apology* or even of the *Alcibiades I* to disagree violently with Alcibiades' rejection of this "double ignorance": the mistaken belief that one knows something that one does not in fact know. This dialogue, however, wants readers to be looking more carefully at the intersection of epistemology and ethics. Socrates does not, in fact, raise the objection as his own, but as something that another, wiser than them, might raise against them. The objection turns out to be a relativist one: fairness demands that, if one is to blame ignorance, then one should specify ignorance *of something in particular*, and *for which persons and in which conditions* it might be good, just as for the persons under consideration it is bad. Alcibiades' perplexity provides the occasion for the reiteration of these details: "What do you mean? Is there anything at all, for anybody in any condition, that it is better to be ignorant of than to know?" Socrates now demonstrates to Alcibiades that he, too, in certain circumstances that do not currently apply, would be better off not knowing certain things. These circumstances may apply when he does not know what it is best for him to undertake.

There follows a strange passage that employs themes of matricide and patricide. Socrates begins as follows:

> Well I am certainly not going to bring this accusation against you, that you'd like to have committed against your own mother what they say Orestes did and Alcmaeon and any others who have committed the same act as them.

The act was matricide. Alcibiades is horrified that Socrates has even raised such a possibility, and calls for him to keep quiet in the religious sense of avoiding unholy utterances. Orestes and Alcmaeon were the most famous matricides of Greek mythology, in both cases having done the deed in order to repay a perceived obligation to their fathers, the former after encouragement (in some versions of the myth) from the Delphic Apollo and with revenge of his father's murder in mind, and the latter at the behest of his doomed father Amphiaraus, who required revenge upon his wife who had wanted him to go with the force that attacked Thebes. Alcibiades, whose father Cleinias had long ago died in battle free from suspicious circumstances, could have no similar excuses, and must have felt especially close to his surviving parent Deinomache.

Socrates tells Alcibiades that it is whoever says that he *would* do this that he should be silencing, but he does in fact want Alcibiades to react to it as a horrific act and one that nobody, not even Orestes, would have done had they been able to distinguish properly between good and bad. This leads to the conclusion that it is ignorance *of what is best* that is bad *for everybody* (143e). The relativism that applies to all other cases of ignorance does not, apparently, apply to ignorance of what is best. But at this stage we have not yet met a case of ignorance that is good. Therefore, Socrates invites Alcibiades to imagine a case where he would commit a murder if he were able to recognize the target of his attack, and where non-recognition would save him from a particularly despicable crime.

In order to make the situation more vivid, Socrates describes what might happen in more detail than would ever be required to make the philosophical point. We are to imagine that the young man had suddenly determined, on the assumption that this was *best* for him, to take action against Pericles, his guardian (and thus the nearest thing he had to a living father) and friend. He would take a dagger, go up to his door, and ask if he was at home, with the murder of this single individual in mind: the closest thing to parricide that Alcibiades could commit—given the legal parental rights that Pericles had acquired over him. Socrates is careful to reduce the indignation with which the young man might again be expected to react by making it plain that he is not claiming that Alcibiades would willingly do such a thing, but rather that there would be nothing to prevent anybody unable to distinguish the best from the worst deeds from arriving at such a decision. With Alcibiades' consent the story advances. If after coming inside he had seen his intended victim and failed to recognize him, thinking the person seen to be somebody else, would he still kill him? Not if it was this single individual's murder that he was bent on. Unless Alcibiades were at some stage able to recognize Pericles, he would never accomplish his murder. Nor indeed would Orestes have ever accomplished the murder of his mother if he had failed to recognize her. In all such cases non-recognition would be better for the individuals concerned.

There is no doubt that Alcibiades is now aware of cases in which ignorance, in the form of non-recognition, could be a good thing. But is that the kind of "ignorance" that he was describing as an origin of human evils at 143b8? That was the kind of ignorance that could underlie both our actions *and our prayers*, and it involved *self-ignorance* too. He was therefore talking about some type of moral ignorance that was not the immediate result of sense perception. Alcibiades had been blaming one kind of ignorance, while Socrates has been defending another. Hellenistic philosophy had a name for this latter kind of ignorance: *akatalêpsia*, the failure to grasp a piece of sense-based evidence—the kind of ignorance supposedly embraced by the New Academy from Arcesilaus on. The foundations of moral knowledge, and particularly the knowledge of good and evil, have not at all been found wanting, nor indeed is there any intention of criticizing such knowledge as that. If there is anything "New Academic" about this dialogue it is not at all at the expense of the moral indifference sometimes linked with its so-called "skepticism."

So in this passage Socrates has, firstly, not been concerned with the way that Alcibiades himself might have represented his ambitions. Secondly, he has taken advantage of his criticism of ignorance to defend non-recognition in certain circumstances. Thirdly, he has chosen to illustrate his argument by selecting the most extreme cases of intended action that could be envisaged, and asking the young man to envisage himself embarking upon the crime of matricide and something very close to parricide. Aside from the discussion of generalship it seems that an argument is being made with scarcely a concern for anything that Alcibiades might reasonably be contemplating. And the discussion of generalship has now receded into the background for one very good reason—matricide and parricide are the type of crimes that are intentionally committed in the course of struggles within ruling families. There can be no such troubles within Alcibiades' family, because, if anything, the power of Pericles has been a huge advantage for Alcibiades himself, as the *Alcibiades I* makes clear (104b), and there is no machinery at Athens that allows for transfer of power within the family as would be the case within an inherited monarchy. Examples of matricide are drawn from the royal families of Greek myth, while none was offered for parricide—the most famous case having been committed by the mythical figure that featured at the beginning of our dialogue at 138b–c: Oedipus himself. But far from having planned the deed and having failed to recognize his opportunity, Oedipus had tried his utmost to avoid it and committed it only because of non-recognition! For Alcibiades the world into which Socrates has invited him to step is sheer fantasy. Tyranny and murders within the ruling family were not part of the world he grew up in.

Throughout the fourth century, however, these things were a distinct possibility in Macedonia. Even since the death of Archelaus in 399 BCE, violent deaths had continued among Macedonian rulers, including those of Pausanias (394), Alexander II (369), Ptolemy of Alorus (365), and Philip II himself (336). Archelaus II may or may not have been killed accidentally. Close family involvement was sometimes suspected, as in the latter case and that of Philip II, when the assassination was curiously convenient for Alexander the Great's mother Olympias—and thus for Alexander himself (Justin 9.7, Plut. *Alex.* 10.6–7). Rival claimants to the throne had continued to be disposed of since the notorious deeds of Archelaus I, with Philip II being responsible for the deaths of sons of Amyntas III by another marriage, and Alexander being responsible for that of Amyntas IV who had been dethroned but not eliminated by Philip II in 359 BCE. Many of the details relevant to the deaths of Macedonian monarchs were shrouded in mystery, but what is important is the way in which Macedonians were *suspected* of behaving in order to secure personal power. It is no wonder that an appropriate Macedonian example of a brief and disastrous tyranny was offered, even at the expense of believable chronology.

Chapter Four
Good and Sometimes Bad Knowledge

Ignorance and Knowledge of the Best

The demonstration that there can exist such knowledge that individuals might be better off without it has been effected with a somewhat foreign emphasis on tyrannical ambitions and intra-familial murders, making us wonder whether the author really wanted to have his "Socrates" address the young Alcibiades, or whether, had the conventions of dialogue allowed it, he might rather have chosen the young Alexander III of Macedon. Alcibiades now realizes that all sorts of horrific possibilities might seem good to any individual operating in ignorance of what is best (*beltiston*). This theme word occurs regularly from 143d to 146e[168] and, intriguingly, the relevant passage is framed by two references to Alcibiades himself as *beltiste* ("best one").[169] It is an unexpected address given that it is usually used between mature adults in the course of a disagreement,[170] though this seems not to be the case in the doubtful

168 The neuter plural is first introduced at 143b4, but thereafter it is the neuter singular that is found (143d8, e3, e4, 144a4, a5, d5, 145c2, e8, 146a7, a8, c12, and e1 [also, with a variant, 150c6: a key point]). The thematic significance is clear from the fact that there are only about sixty cases of the neuter singular in undisputed works. The highest rates of *beltiston* per thousand words in the corpus are as follows: *Alcibiades II*, 0.294; *Clitophon*, 0.063; *Republic* I, 0.063; *Gorgias*, 0.047; *Phaedo*, 0.031; *Theages*, 0.027. The extent to which *Alcibiades II* leads the field is quite surprising.

169 For another obvious theme word that is chosen for a vocative see the address of Hippias as a *kalos* at *Hippias Major* 281a1.

170 There are just over thirty cases of the vocative in undisputed Plato. Socrates addresses Alcibiades himself as *beltiste* (vocative masculine singular) at 143b6 and 147b7. Others in Plato whom Socrates addresses more than once in this way are usually his opponents: Callicles (*Gorg.* 482b7, 491b5, 494c4, 511c4, 515a1, d9), Euthyphro (*Euthph.* 4a7, 15e2), Ion (532b2, 541c7), and Hippias (*Hp. Ma.* 301d5; *Hp. Mi.* 373b6), though one should not see "Young Socrates" as the Stranger's opponent (*Plt.* 263a5, 295b7). Other opponents so addressed are Meletus (*Ap.* 24e1), Critias (*Chrm.* 162d7), Prodicus (*Prot.*

dialogues, as there are also examples, with Socrates as the speaker, in the *Alcibiades I* (113c6, 118b6), *Hipparchus* (226e3), *Erastae* (139a4), *Theages* (126d8), and above all *Minos* (315d6, 318d11, and 320e2). Could it be that an address that was typically used with great irony in Plato himself lacks it in the work of imitators, so that it is no longer reserved for any special kind of situation?[171]

But the vocative is a peripheral issue. The key question is why it is the knowledge of what is best rather than of the good (or of good and evil) that has been chosen here as the key to human success. The concept of some supreme knowledge that will in effect be the source of the goodness of any other knowledge is by no means foreign to the Platonic corpus. The *Euthydemus* fails to come up with a name for it but explores the concept (291a–293a), whereas the doubtful *Erastae* find embarrassingly many names (138c). The *Charmides* gives prominence to the "knowledge of good and bad" in that role (174b10–c3, d6–7), and this is also known there simply as "knowledge about the good" (174e2). Nicias' conception of courage in the *Laches* is likewise turned into a knowledge of all things good and bad (199c7, cf. d5–7). Again, the supreme wisdom of the "more ingenious" people in the *Republic* is "wisdom of the good" (505b9–10), and the aim of the guardians' higher education will of course be to prepare their vision of "the Good." While there is another term for "best," *ariston*, I see little sign that this has in any work of the corpus become more prominent than *beltiston* as an object of knowledge. So in tackling this passage of the *Alcibiades II* it is imperative that we try to explain why the author has deliberately chosen to use the superlative.

Here we need to go back to 143b, where Alcibiades complains that we humans fail to realize that we are aiming, or even praying, for what is "worst for ourselves," when everybody would trust themselves "to pray for what is best for himself, and not for what is worst." Essentially we are dealing with human choices: in any given situation we human

---

358b1), Polus (*Gorg.* 461e1), Thrasymachus (*Rep.* 337e4), Euthydemus (*Euthd.* 300c5), and Dionysodorus (*Euthd.* 297e6). In a few cases opponents address Socrates (Critias at *Chrm.* 163e5, Thrasymachus at *Rep.* 338e6) in this way, and Nicias so addresses a disgruntled Laches (*La.* 195e8).

171 Such situations are so scarce in the *Republic* that they are never found in books II–X. The address occurs just once in *Laws*, which is the only "late" instance outside the *Statesman*. The highest rates of *beltiste* per 1,000 words are as follows: *Minos*, 0.97; *Ion*, 0.49; *Alcibiades II*, 0.45; *Erastae*, 0.41; *Hipparchus*, 0.41; *Euthyphro*, 0.37; *Theages*, 0.27; *Gorgias*, 0.25.

beings claim to be able to make the best choice available for ourselves *out of those available to us*. It is not a matter of what is absolutely good or absolutely best, but rather of what is best out of the options available. Since the *Republic* an expression like "knowledge of the Good" would tend to suggest some overriding vision that can explain why any particular instance of something's being good is good. No such vision can be referred to here by Alcibiades, for we are not dealing with remote theory but with what can be observed in everyday human practice. Again, suppose that one prays for a lighter sentence after a conviction rather than a heavier one. There are, realistically, no good options to be prayed for in such situations, only less bad ones: a modest fine rather than exile or a cup of hemlock, for instance. So throughout this passage, *beltiston* will imply a comparison with all other options, not something that would be the best thing of all for any human being.

This is why Socrates here repeatedly invites Alcibiades to examine scenarios, including Orestes' act of matricide and his own hypothetical attempt on Pericles' life. The singular *beltiston* first occurs in relation to the matricide, and it is jointly concluded that Orestes would not have killed his mother if he had known "what was best for him to be achieving" (143d8). We are looking at a given individual in a given situation, and concluding that he had a better option for himself in that situation. It is argued from this example that ignorance of what is best is the type of ignorance that is simply bad, so that the particular example leads to a universal conclusion (143e6), but this universal conclusion need mean no more than that, for any given person in any given situation, ignorance of the best course of action for that individual in those circumstances is a bad thing. And we had already been warned that ignorance ought only to be blamed if we specify ignorance *of what* and ignorance *for what persons* and in *what situations* (143b6–c5). At 144c9–10 it is then claimed that they have discovered cases of ignorance *of specific things* that is actually good *for specific persons in specific circumstances*. And that is because such ignorance can only be a good thing *for individuals who are unaware of what is best for them in the relevant situation*.

The fact that *beltiston* is not being used in any absolute sense but in comparison with other options that are available becomes clear at 143e9 when Alcibiades is imagined to have decided that it is "better" (*beltion*) to kill Pericles. The comparative had already occurred at 142e4, and will again occur at 144c6, six times at 145b2–10, and again at 145d2, and e9: mostly in relation to when a given action is better, for how long, and in what other circumstances. This means that the comparative is nearly as thematic as the superlative, and far more frequent than in any other dialogue, except possibly the *Alcibiades I*.[172] Another clue that we are dealing with the best *of the options available* comes at 144a5–7: such near-parricidal activity is possible in cases where one is ignorant of what is best "so as to believe at times even that the worst is the best." The *Theaetetus* (190b–c) rules out the possibility, even in a moment of insanity, of thinking that beautiful is ugly, unfair fair, or odd even. It does not of course rule out the possibility of thinking that a beautiful jug is an ugly thing, that an unfair contract is fair, or that a given odd number is even. Hence the passage that refers to believing that the worst is best cannot be postulating a person who thinks the one *concept* to be the other, and in fact the very opposite concept. However, it is entirely possible for one to mistakenly believe that what would in fact be the worst *outcome* is actually the best outcome available. It will be concluded at 144c6–7 that for those who are bent on a course of action that has been so wrongly evaluated it will be better (*beltion*) for them to experience some ignorance or non-recognition that prevents them from carrying it out: better, that is, than for them to be fully aware of how to achieve their goals. There can be little doubt that the author, throughout this passage, applies the terms *beltiston* and *beltion* to the best of a finite number of possible courses of action and to the better of just two.

So, in a dialogue in which the language of one's personal perspective is surprisingly prominent, affording a suspicion that the author may be some kind of Neo-Protagorean, the terms *beltiston* and *beltion* refer consistently not to any kind of absolute "best," but to the best or better of the options available. And these options will in each case be those that are, or seem to be, available to a given individual in a certain situation. The conclusion offered at 144c9–10 will run as follows:

> You see then that ignorance of *some* things, and for *some* people in *some* particular condition, is a good

172 There are a total of 11 cases of the neuter singular in the *Alcibiades II*, 2.49 per 1,000 words, as opposed to the *Alcibiades I* (1.50), *Crito* (0.46), *Minos* (0.36), and *Gorgias* (0.29). There are fewer cases in all other dialogues. If all cases and genders, singular and plural, were included, the *Alcibiades II* would have only a marginally higher rate.

thing and not a bad one as you were inclined to believe just now.

At this point the argument switches to matters of clear relevance to Alcibiades and to the consequences of ignorance of what's best for the city as he knew it.

Ignorance: Individual and City

It may be occurring to readers that we have heard little about prayer, the nominal subject of the dialogue, for a while. The last references to prayer and praying was at 143b, immediately before Socrates launched an investigation into ignorance, and into whether it was a good or a bad thing. Prayer will be forgotten for some considerable time while that investigation continues, now with a greater emphasis on the extent to which a whole community might benefit from less knowledge among some of its citizens.

At 144d1 Socrates moves on to making the next point (*to meta touto*), though he will introduce the overall notion with a fair degree of caution, qualifying his statement with both "so to speak" (*hôs epos eipein*) and "there is a risk that" (*kinduneuei*: little more than "perhaps"). The claim itself is also far from being a universal one: the acquisition of branches of knowledge (other than that of the best), when acquired "without (that of) the best" (*tou beltistou*),[173] is seldom beneficial, and *for the most part*[174] harmful for the possessor. The mechanism by which harm results is allegedly as follows: Whenever we are about to do or say something, we must first either imagine we know or actually know about that thing that we are more readily[175] inclined to say or do. Knowledge or the illusion of it will give one the confidence to act or speak. The combination of prayer and ritual in approaches to the god has made the conjunction of acting and speaking here natural, but

173 This exact phrase recurs at *Gorgias* 465a2.

174 Such a qualification, using τὰ πλείω or τὰ πολλὰ occurs five times in similar contexts in the *Alcibiades II*, the former at 144d6, 146d5, and 146e2 (but not otherwise in the Platonic corpus except for *Clitophon* 409e1) and the latter, which is moderately common in Plato, at 146a8 and c12.

175 The MSS have "more readily," and unlike Sauppe I am inclined to accept their reading simply because of the importance of the comparison between available options in this passage. However, the comparative can easily sound awkward in translation, and is often omitted. Carlini translates "senza esitazione," for instance, and Johnson "so ready."

the spotlight now (144e) falls on a different kind of speaking: public oratory. Everything that the city tries to achieve, either in its dealings with another city or for itself internally, happens on orators' advice. Applied to them, the principle introduced at 144d will mean that they must either know how to advise, or imagine they know, every time they offer public advice, be it on war and peace, or walls and harbors, or whatever.

The examples given are quite important. War and peace are what Alcibiades thought he would soon be advising on at *Alcibiades I* 107d3–4, and it is in fact what he did historically advise the Athenians on. Walls and harbors, however, are typical of what is pointed to by Gorgias in a memorable passage of the *Gorgias* (455d8–e3; cf. 455b6–7, 514a7, 519a2–3) as examples of the achievements of fifth-century public orators rather than craftsmen.[176] It was important to the *Gorgias* that orators are normally thought of as able to persuade by means of their experience of human interactions (cf. 463a8), but unconcerned about "the best" (*to beltiston*, 464d1, 465a2, 501d5, 502e3) unlike the craftsmen who they imitate (464c4, 501b4, 503a9, d7, 513d4, e2, 521d9).[177] At 145b it is further agreed that an orator of the kind to give advice without knowing whether it is better or when it would be better is not wise (*phronimos*), nor the person who knows about war without knowing when it is better and for how long, nor the person who knows about killing an opponent, confiscating his property, or procuring his exile without knowing when to do this and to whom. The questions about war are directly reminiscent of *Alcibiades I* 107d8–e3, and Alcibiades' inability to offer an answer there at 108e–109c showed him to have been an intending orator without that important extra knowledge of who one should make war on and when and for how long. The other example, however, is reminiscent of another passage of the *Gorgias*, beginning with Polus' glorification of the orator's ability to exact whatever penalties he likes at 466b11–c2, repeated by Socrates

176 The word for dockyards (*neôria*) is also present in all these passages, while harbors (*limenes*) is omitted at 514a. But I think it is plain that the *Alcibiades II* intentionally alludes to this theme in the *Gorgias*.

177 Note that our calculations above indicate that the *Gorgias* had the fourth highest rate of *beltiston* in the corpus, behind only the *Alcibiades II*, the doubtful *Clitophon*, and *Republic* I (when taken separately).

at c9–d3, 468b4–6, c1–2 and d1–2. The penalties mentioned at these five points are again death, confiscation of property, and exile.[178]

The result of offering such examples is that Socrates is now (145c1–7) able to draw the conclusion that somebody who knows how to do such things and is also in possession of the knowledge of what is best, now identified with what is beneficial, should be called "wise" (*phronimon*) and an adequate advisor both for the city's and for his own purposes. If such additional knowledge is not also present then he is quite the opposite. The same applies to a whole range of skills, from the combative activities of archery and horse riding, and the competitive sports of boxing and wrestling, to the recreational art of flute playing. One can know what is *best according to each of these crafts*, but this does not make one wise without the knowledge of when it is best that they should be applied. Socrates is thus able to envisage a strange dystopia in which the city is full of people with knowledge of particular skills of those types, plus people with a knowledge of warfare and homicide and finally orators blasting forth their political word storms,[179] all without knowledge of what's best and without anybody who knows when it is better to apply such arts and against whom.

At this point there is yet another reminiscence of the *Gorgias*, this time from Callicles' utilization of Zethus' words at Euripides' *Antiope* at 484a6–7.[180] It is more likely that the quotation is derived from here than from the original. The *Gorgias*, in Zeyl's translation (1987), runs as follows:

> where he says that "each man shines" in this and
> "presses on to this,
> allotting the greatest part of the day to this,
> where he finds himself at his best."

178 Polus makes the change to death, confiscation, and imprisonment at 468e8–9. The passage concerned directly compares the orator with the tyrant when discussing these powers (466b10, d1, d7).

179 The phrase πολιτικὸν φύσημα φυσώντων reminds me somewhat of Aristophanes' decision to call Cleon "the Paphlagonian" (because of his huffing and puffing) in *Knights*, and at least the last two words may have a comic origin, but if so they are not extant.

180 Fr. 183 Nauck^2; *Antiope* fr. 184 in Collard, Cropp and Gibert 2004, 272–274.

We have two lines in iambic meter preceded by rather more than a line of close paraphrase. The *Alcibiades II* only has words corresponding to the lines that appeared in good iambics in the *Gorgias*, and modifies most of the first of these:

> "allotting the greatest part" in the community
> "to this,
> where he finds himself at his best."

The idea seems to be that each man not only practices hardest at what he himself is skilled at, but also thinks that his own skill is the most important in the workings of the *polis*. The quotation here is more of a literary embellishment than a genuine appeal to the spirit of Zethus' words,[181] and the author is trying to introduce into his present dystopian picture the idea that in such a city no control would be exercised over when and for how long the various skills should be used, so that everybody, in the pursuit of widespread recognition (*philotimoumenon*, 146a4), would think it right that his own area of expertise should have a higher profile in the state than any of the others. It is in particular specified that "to this" would refer not just to the skill, but to the particular aim that is achieved through that skill: what is best according to its own internal criteria.

The result would be that for the most part (*ta polla*, 146a8–9) the skilled individual would miss out on both their own and the community's best interests, because they have put their trust in opinion without intelligence (*aneu nou doxêi pepisteukota*, 146a9). This interesting phrase will be repeated exactly at 146c12–13, and though it cannot be precisely matched in the rest of the corpus the perfect active of the verb for "trust" (*pisteuein*) occurs at *Gorgias* 454c8, d2, and e2 in the course of the distinction between belief backed by mere trust and belief backed by learning.[182] Also present later in a relevant part of the *Gorgias* (467a5) are the words "without intelligence" (*aneu nou*), which is otherwise

181 Zethus had been concerned about the effect of Amphion's studious pursuits on himself and his family, while it seems that Socrates is concerned about the effects of a variety of not-so-studious pursuits on the city as well as on the individual: if anything taking Amphion's side rather than that of Zethus.

182 Other examples are rare, confined to one case each in *Prot.*, *Crat.*, *Laws*, and *Epistle VII.*

found only at *Meno* 88b5 and 99e6, *Republic* 494d3 and 506d8, and *Laws* 644a4, but the phrase is probably responding rather to "without one's knowing" (*aneu tou eidenai*) in the same passage of the *Gorgias* as the perfect of *pisteuein* (454e4 and e7): an expression that could not without confusion be used in the *Alcibiades II* owing to the fact that such persons are thought of as knowing their own craft even if they do not know when it is to be used. The substitution of *aneu nou* from 467a5 is quite appropriate, since it was used there as the equivalent of "without knowledge *of what's best*," as can be seen from 466d9–10:

> SO: Then do you think it is a good thing if somebody does whatever things *seem* to him to be best (ἃ ἂν δοκῇ αὐτῷ βέλτιστα εἶναι) though he is without intelligence (νοῦν μὴ ἔχων)?[183]

Furthermore, the presence in the phrase of the word for opinion (*doxêi*) is also explained by the presence in this passage, and elsewhere in its context, of the verb for seeming so to somebody: for the noun *doxa* is cognate with the verb *dokein*, so that one's opinion is in fact what seems so to one. In fact the key words "without intelligence" at 467a5 occur alongside the verb *dokein*: "and even you admit that to do what *seems* [good] without intelligence is a bad thing."[184] It seems therefore that this phrase, found at 146a9 and repeated at 146c12–13, is constructed consciously in response to a reading of the *Gorgias*, as is so much else in the context.

After drawing the conclusion that such a constitution, with a population of rival craftsmen lacking all guidance as to how the crafts are best used, is full of confusion and lawlessness, Socrates may proceed to recapitulate:

1. We must first either think we know or actually know about anything that we shall readily do or say. [Agreed at 144d7–e2]
2. If somebody tries to achieve what he knows or thinks he knows, and it additionally turns out beneficially, we shall have a profitable outcome for the city and he for himself. [Alcibiades assents]

183 Note also 466e1–2: ὅτι ἂν αὐτοῖς δοξῇ βέλτιστον εἶναι.

184 τὸ δὲ ποιεῖν ἄνευ νοῦ ἃ δοκεῖ καὶ σὺ ὁμολογεῖς κακὸν εἶναι.

3. But if the opposite happens, [there is profit] neither for the city nor for himself.
4. Most people are foolish and only a few wise. [Agreed at 145a6–9]
5. What is best eludes most people, because for the most part they put their trust in opinion without intelligence. [Agreed at 146a8–9][185]

The conclusion to be drawn from this is that it is beneficial for the majority neither to know nor to think they know, given that (a) this will make them more eager to act in these cases, while (b) for the most part they will be harmed rather than benefitted by their actions (146d2–5). Upon Alcibiades' agreement Socrates then reminds him of what he had said a little earlier, asking if it wasn't obviously correct. This dialogue tends to mark its back-references through significant word-for-word repetitions, and here twenty-three consecutive words are repeated exactly, though with two additional words for clarification,[186] with the previous one differing only in that the later reference, following after "I said," substitutes the infinitive *kinduneuein* for the original indicative: a one letter change. The message Socrates wants to drive home is that "there is a risk that the acquisition of other knowledge, at least if one has acquired it without the knowledge of what is best, seldom benefits and for the most part harms the one who has it."

The big difference here from the *Gorgias*, which has been in the front of the author's mind throughout the argument, is that a distinction made there between craft (*tekhnê*) and an empirically acquired knack (*empeiria*), where the former but not the latter takes what is best into consideration, has been transformed rather into one between two kinds of knowledge (*epistêmê*), perhaps more in accordance with popular speech. Our author may possibly think of the *Gorgias*' true crafts as being in fact a combination between a basic field of knowledge and knowledge of what's best, which must be present for the results to be desirable. Another likely influence is the second protreptic digression of

185 One may claim that such an admission was made only for the dystopia depicted there, but it seems clear at 145b that foolish people are in general thought of as acting without knowledge of what's best, and will therefore miscalculate.

186 The simple τοῦ βελτίστου has now become τὴν τοῦ βελτίστου ἐπιστήμην.

the *Euthydemus* (288d–291c), where Socrates reminds the young Cleinias of how they had agreed that happiness depends on the acquisition of knowledge, and that they have to determine which knowledge is responsible for the salutary powers that they seek. As in the *Alcibiades II*, it is going to have to be a knowledge that is not directly concerned with the provision of something as most branches of knowledge are, but which knows above all how and when to make use of knowledge more generally: how to actually profit from it. The *Euthydemus*, unlike the *Gorgias*, was looking for a single type of knowledge that would make all the others useful, whereas the *Gorgias* was postulating at least four types of knowledge that were, in their own right, aimed at what was best. And whereas in the *Euthydemus*, as indeed in the *Charmides* (174b–175a), the actual identity of any such overriding knowledge remained problematic, its identity is largely treated as unproblematic in the *Alcibiades II*, as indeed is the identity of the principal true art in the *Gorgias*. What is happening is not a direct attempt to reproduce the philosophy behind a single Platonic dialogue, but an effort to build upon the foundation offered by the *Gorgias* and other works, at the same time creating a Platonic pedigree for the theory being offered by way of a fairly obvious series of allusions.

The Problem with Tail Winds

"Then it is necessary," Socrates says, "for either a city or a soul[187] that is going to live correctly to grasp hold of this knowledge." We need this knowledge as much as the sick man needs a doctor or the sea-traveler a helmsman. Note that this is not a case of the individual having to acquire for himself the knowledge of what is best, for that will not justify the examples given. Rather, both individuals and cities need to seek out the guidance of an individual who does know what is best so that they will not go astray. Socrates' implied message for the

187 The reference to "soul" here marks the first time the term *psukhê* has appeared in anything like this sense in the *Alcibiades II*, for at 141c1 it had meant "life." The juxtaposition of "soul" and "city" here can hardly fail to recall the analogy between the two that occurs in the *Republic*, and especially in book IV. The term will recur in the same sense at 149e8 and 150e1. It occurs in the MSS only five lines further on, but is there written out of the text by all editors after a hastily accepted emendation.

interlocutor, not an entirely altruistic one, is that Alcibiades too is in need of such an individual to guide him if he is to live as he should.

At this point we are confronted by a sentence that is little more than a modern reconstruction, about which I have protested in Tarrant (2015). The manuscript text reads something like the following:

> However much it does not earlier drive on [like a following wind] the soul's [desire?]—for without this it will concern either the acquisition of property or the strength of the body or some such thing—so much greater are the mistakes that are probably bound to arise from them.[188]

While this sounds in dire need of some correction, the corrections should pay some heed to the vocabulary that one meets elsewhere in the dialogue, and to the general sense required. Accordingly I have rejected the standard emendation of "the soul's [desire?]" to "the [wind] of chance" (τὸ τῆς ψυχῆς to τὸ τῆς τύχης), and prefer "the [object] of one's prayer" (τὸ τῆς εὐχῆς)—an emendation similarly involving only one letter, on the grounds that chance plays no part in the dialogue and that prayer is central to it. I concur with editors in thinking that the negative at 147a1–2 is wrong, but I have tried to rest content with the adverb *proteron* ("earlier"), while editors usually emend it. However, there is one comparative adverb that has occurred in the previous section and would deserve special consideration at this point, *prokheiroteron*. We had met its slightly less regular comparative form[189]

188 ὅσῳπερ ἂν μὴ πρότερον ἐπουρίσῃ τὸ τῆς ψυχῆς—ἄνευ γὰρ ταύτης ἢ περὶ χρημάτων κτῆσιν ἢ σώματος ῥώμην ἢ καὶ ἄλλο τι τῶν τοιούτων—τοσούτῳ μείζω ἁμαρτήματα ἀπ᾽ αὐτῶν ἀναγκαῖόν ἐστιν, ὡς ἔοικε, γίγνεσθαι.

189 I can find 16 different comparative adverbs in -τέρως in Plato, none found in more than two dialogues (not counting ποτέρως or ἀμφοτέρως, which are not comparative in meaning). The *Alcibiades II* has one other such form (ἐνδεεστέρως, 149a5), and no obvious examples of comparative adverbs in -ότερον. One may question whether *any* adverb of this kind should be restored at 147a1–2 apart from those like πρότερον, which is always found in this spelling in the Platonic corpus (also before Plato and in Aristotle—except with καὶ ὑστέρως following it). This might be an argument why πρότερον should be retained, and not replaced by any other comparative adverbial form.

prokheiroterôs at 144d9[190] and the simple adverb *prokheirôs* at 146b6.[191]

It may be enough to omit the negative μὴ or to substitute the particle δὴ for it,[192] as in Tarrant (2015). I there gave the following tentative translation:

> To the extent that it/one[193] supplies a tail-wind[194] to accelerate the operation of one's prayer prematurely (for without this [knowledge] it would be either about the acquisition of property or about physical might or about something else of this sort), to that extent it is in all likelihood necessary that greater upsets arise as a result.[195]

One might more fluently render it "So the earlier that one gives a tail-wind to the object of one's prayer (. . .) to that extent, as is likely, are greater upsets inevitably going to arise as a result." But why should an *earlier* acquisition of wealth, for instance, increase the likelihood of disaster? Its *premature* acquisition, before one knows the good, would increase its likelihood, but involves taking *proteron* in the sense of "too early," which is possible but less natural in this context where the full comparative force is to be expected. Rather, then, I here propose to read *pr<okheir>oteron*, for which LSJ give the meanings "readily," "hurriedly," or "rashly." This might yield: "The more readily one gives a tail-wind to the object of one's prayer . . ." And we know exactly what

---

190 We also met the same idea captured with a different comparative at 146d3: μᾶλλον προθυμήσονται, and one might therefore also consider πρ<οθυμ>ότερον, in addition to πρ<οχειρ>ότερον. The translation would be somewhat similar.

191 It is just possible that this had been glossed μὴ πρότερον ("not 'earlier'") in the margin, and that the gloss as a whole had then ousted the original reading.

192 I note that the combination ἂν δὴ is rare, but it occurs at *Phaedo* 108c1, *Parmenides* 144b4, *Laws* 777a2, and *Alcibiades I* 130b6.

193 I suggested that, as the present sentence seems to be amplifying what had been said at 146d7–e3, one could take the subject to be τό γε τῶν ἄλλων ἐπιστημῶν κτῆμα: the possession of other types of knowledge, which seldom helps but often harms. Alternatively, one might take the individual or city from 146e4 to be subject, or take τὸ τῆς εὐχῆς as the subject rather than the object.

194 The verb ἐπουρίσῃ can be transitive or intransitive, with the latter seemingly more common. In these circumstances τὸ τῆς εὐχῆς may be either subject or object, but it makes slightly better sense that it should be the object.

195 The αὐτῶν might refer to the other ἐπιστῆμαι discussed at 146d7–e3, or (slightly better) to the various bodily and external goods that are the object of one's prayer.

the author thinks will encourage us to set our dream in motion, for it has been clearly stated three times that this is other relevant knowledge, or imagined knowledge (144d9, 146b6, 146d4). And such knowledge is reintroduced in the very next sentence, which has the effect of explaining both this readiness and the nautical metaphor:

> As for the man who has made himself into a so-called polymath or technical genius, but is bereft of *this* knowledge and is driven on by each the others singly, will he not actually deserve to experience "a perfect storm"—because, I presume, he has continued on his ocean course without a helmsman—throughout his brief life (147a5–b1).

The reference to the helmsman at 147a8 recalls the reference to a need for the helmsman at 146e6, framing the problematic passage in between with its extended nautical metaphor. It guarantees that the impetus given by the wind's metaphorical assistance was to be credited to the knowledge or conceit of knowledge that makes people readier to take action that they think will lead to the fulfillment of their dreams. And this gives the confirmation that we need to know not only that some ignorance can be a good thing, but that much knowledge of a non-moral or technical kind can actually have disastrous consequences when divorced from the knowledge of what is best: the kind of knowledge that only philosophy would have been expected to supply. Alcibiades needs a philosopher.

"Homeric" Confirmation

In conformity with this dialogue's policy of illustrating important notions with reference to poetry and its myths, Socrates now argues that Homer had recognized just this problem with certain kinds of knowledge. Homeric examples would normally be drawn from the exalted pages of the two famous epics, but the example used comes from a work in a lower genre about a buffoon. This requires Socrates to credit Homer himself with the composition of the curious poem *Margites* that, like many other "epics," would not normally be credited to Homer today, and might not have been credited to him by Plato himself. Plato does not mention the work in undisputed dialogues and is normally more circumspect about epic cycles other than the *Odyssey* and *Iliad*.[196] Indeed it seems only to be in the latter part of the fourth century that the poem made its mark on extant literature. Aristotle in the *Nicomachean Ethics* (1141a14) does name Homer as the author of the *Margites*, and also in the *Poetics*, where he considers its relation to the true epics as being analogous to that of comedy to tragedy (*Poetics* 1448b28–1449a2). The *Margites*, or at least its primary character, seems to have become something of a talking point in Athens, when, following the death of Philip II of Macedonia, Demosthenes recklessly called Alexander "Margites,"[197] as we learn from Aeschines' speech of 330 BCE *Against Ctesiphon* (160) and from Plutarch's *Demosthenes* (23.2). Hyperides, too, made reference to Margites as "the stupidest of all" in his speech for Lycophron (VI 25–26), and Alcidamas (fr. 5) has an anecdote about Homer relating to the time just after he had supposedly composed it. A little later Zeno of Citium (fr. 274) wrote about the poem, and Dio (53.4) implies that he (Zeno) accepted its authenticity, attributing it to Homer's early career, and praised it accordingly. At any rate, by late in the fourth century, the *Margites* itself was being talked about, and the figure of Margites had become a byword for extreme stupidity. It should by now be less than surprising that Alexander III is linked with this revival.

Extreme examples are indeed a feature of this dialogue, and we have already met Oedipus, Orestes, and Alcmaeon. The tactic seems to be to invite Alcibiades to somehow compare himself with these individuals, as if there might not be so very much difference after all—especially since they shared in ignorance of what is best. Alcibiades will actually show his understanding of the example, by employing the rare adjective *margos* ("ludicrous": Johnson 2003) to his own predicament at 148a9.[198] The realization of even a small similarity between himself and Margites would surely have caused Alcibiades to feel a degree of shame, and

196 When he mentions Homer, we are intended to think of the poet of the *Odyssey* and *Iliad*, as for instance in the *Hippias Minor*, and in the case of the *Cypria* he declines to name the poet at *Euthyphro* 12a.

197 Aeschines is clearly mocking the insult here, as can be seen by the accompanying information that he had said that Alexander would not leave Macedonia and the comforts of Pella. But the insult may have been originally intended as mockery of Alexander's adoption of the true Homeric hero, Achilles, as his model, or again of his appeal to Zeus as father (for Margites was confused about the identity of his parents). See Lane Fox 1973, 60–61, 215.

198 In Plato the adjective is otherwise found only at *Laws* 792e5.

Socrates' speech at 147e5–148a7 takes advantage of this opportunity to be unusually frank with the young man about his condition.

Since part of the argument relies on the premise that the poem is by the wisest of poets, it is essential that it be regarded as Homer's work, and, as often in the Platonic corpus, it does not trouble the author that the interpretation of the passage is "as forced as his interpretation of Simonides at *Protagoras* 339a–348c."[199] It is unlikely that readers would ordinarily have found Socrates' interpretation of the quoted line convincing, especially if they had known anything about the content of the poem itself. What matters here is whether it is plausible that it should help to get Socrates' message across to Alcibiades. Also, that by depicting a quasi-Homeric mock-hero who endures a ridiculous life as a result of his varied but nevertheless limited knowledge, this passage might have provided an example of a man with selective insights into life that give him misplaced confidence in his own wisdom, and yet a woeful lack of the things that were essential for him to know. Certainly, the reference to the poem follows the sentence with the only reference in the dialogue to polymathy (*polymathia*) and multi-skilling (*polytekhnia*), as if it had been prompted by a memory of the problems that precisely these traits could set in motion. The quoted epic line runs "Many were the deeds that he knew, but them all he knew badly," and Socrates' central claim is that this line of poetry could be validly applied "in this case too" (*kai entautha*, 147b2): that is, to that multifarious knowledge without the most important knowledge of all.

Initially, Socrates did not name Margites as the polymath concerned, nor did he name Homer as the poet. He merely suggested the relevance of the line to the problem of potentially harmful polymathy. The controversial part does not occur until Alcibiades has asked what the implication of the poet's verse is, as he does not see how it is pertinent at all. It is doubtful whether he recognized the line, for Socrates makes sure that he gives the details in his next speech, in which he argues for its relevance. He begins with the notion that nearly all poetry speaks in riddles, and requires some expertise to decipher.[200] There is a hint that

199 Johnson 2003, 71.

200 The position taken is reminiscent more of Neoplatonism than of Plato, who normally considers himself under no obligation either to treat poets as requiring allegorical interpretation, or to make philosophic sense of them. In the related case of myth the *Phaedrus* (229c–e) resists a certain kind of allegorical interpretation as being an unprofitable way to spend one's time, and even in the case of his imaginative

in this line the poet might be particularly keen to hide his real meaning. Denying that Alcibiades could imagine that Homer, the wisest and most divine of poets, was ignorant of the fact that it was impossible to "know badly," he now affirms that it had been Homer who wrote this line about Margites. His own belief is that Homer had used the adverb riddlingly, and meant to say that Margites "did know many deeds, but it was bad for him to know all these things." And presumably it was because he was a worthless man (*phaulos*) that it was bad for him. Alcibiades is happy to believe this, because he trusts the overall argument concerning ignorance: not apparently because of anything particularly plausible in the interpretation.

It is now that Socrates turns to the particular situation of Alcibiades himself. The kind of ignorance that he is confronting here is his problem too (his *aporia*, 147e5). In a description of the near-Heraclitean flux[201] of his friend's opinions, Socrates manages to recall not only the *Alcibiades I* (116e–118b) with its diagnosis of Alcibiades' double ignorance, but also the *Gorgias* once again, and its description of his saying different things at different times, in contrast with the steadfastness of philosophy (482a6–7). But within the context of the present work this kind of complaint is insufficiently justified. Socrates is certainly able, through his arguments, to get Alcibiades to take note of factors that he had not previously considered, thus securing a change of perspective that indicates a lack of knowledge. But it is not so clear here that Alcibiades had always imagined that he knew the truth of the matter. Furthermore, we are dealing with a theory in which the only kind of ignorance that receives significant criticism is ignorance of what is best, and then only when one is prompted to action by some other kind of assumed knowledge.

This is where the setting of the work and its principal topic of prayer[202] again become relevant. Alcibiades has been prompted to try and

---

interpretation of Simonides' poem, Socrates immediately does his best to deny that he attaches any value to it—he sees no resolution to disputes about a dead poet's meaning, and thinks that they have more important things to consider (*Prot.* 347b–348a).

201 Note μεταβαλλόμενός γέ τοι ἄνω καὶ κάτω οὐδ' ὁτιοῦν παύῃ: "in nothing at all do you stop changing your position, up and down."

202 Note that I postulate the presence of a general reference to the object of one's prayer in my restoration of the text at 147a2 (above, p. 114), but otherwise there has been no such reference to prayers and praying since 143b5. The resumption of the main topic after the digression on ignorance is now being prepared, and is highlighted by several close echoes of the earlier discussion of prayer.

win the god's support for his endeavors by prayer. Clearly some kind of knowledge, real or imagined, has given him quite a lot of confidence, but has he taken the trouble to ask what is really best for him? At 148a, with a remarkable fifteen-word direct repetition,[203] Socrates imagines the god[204] offering one of the earlier types of tyrannical rule they had discussed (141a–b), or just leaving Alcibiades to make a request for himself. How would he take advantage of the opportunity either by accepting something when offered or by making his own request? Alcibiades couldn't say, and it seems to him a ludicrous thing (*margon ti*)[205]—a situation requiring great care to avoid that process of actually praying for something bad, pausing, offering a palinode, and praying for the undoing of one's prayer—the process that Socrates had referred to at 142d.

So Alcibiades has now returned the conversation to the topic of prayer. That enables Socrates to remark on the wisdom of the poet (whose prayer he had earlier cited at 143a1–3), who had asked Zeus to deliver them from evils even when they prayed for them. The scene is now set for a comparison of Spartan and Athenian prayers and sacrifices.

The Language of 143b–148b

The dialogue that comes between the initial monologue and its continuation at 148b constitutes about five of the twelve Stephanus pages occupied by the *Alcibiades II*. Yet the amount of unusual or surprising language here cannot compete with that of the first dialogic section (138a–141c). Apart from listing five unusual spellings or forms,[206] Neuhausen (2010: 243) lists four words or phrases that might be used as evidence for a late date, and one additional instance of language that is difficult to match. They are:

203 141a6–8 and 148a2–3 have fifteen words in the same order, differing only in the presence of an enclitic nu in the earlier passage.

204 On the continued effort to avoid naming the god here see above, pp. 48, 96.

205 Carlini posits a lacuna here in 148b1, for it is difficult to see the continuity behind this thought.

206 144d8, 148a8: οὐθέν; 144d9–e1: προχειροτέρως; 145d1: οἴδαμεν; 148b5 and c4: πλείων (for πλέον or similar in either T or BCD traditions). While the third of these, involving a *-terôs* rather than *-teron* ending, is somewhat rare (exceptions being the recurrent *poterôs* and *amphoterôs*—6 and 10 times respectively in undisputed dialogues), one cannot affirm that Plato could not have written it. In the final two cases it remains unclear what the author wrote.

143e9: παρεσταίη
144b9: ἐπίθοιο
145d2: κατὰ ταύτην τὴν τέχνην
145e7: πολιτικὸν φύσημα φυσώντων
147e5–6: τὴν ἀπορίαν . . . κεκοινωνηκέναι

The first of these may be somewhat unusual in the applicable sense, the second in its form (*thoio* for *theiês* in *tithêmi* and compounds being unparalleled in Plato). I do not see the problem with the third; the fourth seems a colorful but satisfactory literary expression ("blasting out political bluster"), while the fifth involves no grammatical difficulty when the intervening words are inspected, even if the sense of *aporia* strikes one as somewhat psychological. Hence in this passage it is mostly the non-Platonic word forms that seem to betray non-Platonic material.

As for the expression "The entire poetic art . . . is by nature enigmatic" (ἔστιν . . . φύσει ποιητικὴ ἡ σύμπασα αἰνιγματώδης) at 147b9 there appears to be a notable parallel, both in diction and in thought, in the Derveni Papyrus, VII.4–5: ἔστιν . . . πόησις καὶ ἀνθρώποις αἰνιγματώδης. I hope to explore the implications of this parallel with the early interpretation of Orphic poetry elsewhere.

Chapter Five
Socrates' Later Monologue

Clarification

By "later monologue" this chapter means the extended speech that begins at 148b9, and ends when Socrates, at 150b3–4, turns directly to Alcibiades and invites him to offer his opinion on what has been said. There have of course been speeches of around half a page since the first major monologue ended at 143a4, where Socrates again seeks to re-engage Alcibiades in discussion, but, as we have previously observed, Socrates only temporarily breaks off his theme there with the quotation of an unknown poet's prayer. The "later monologue" resumes the theme of the initial monologue just after Socrates reminds Alcibiades of that poet's lines, particularly the part that requests the god to avert evils even if he and his friends pray for them. This occurs at 148b5–6, following Alcibiades' observations at 148a8–b4 that serve to remind the reader of Socrates' memorable words from 142c7–d4. The poet's lines were supposed to offer one example of how we might alter the way we handle our requests to the gods, particularly for the individual but also for the group, while the resumed monologue will go on to offer an alleged oral story that suggests other modifications, particularly for the city and only secondarily also for the individual. The advice that is contained in the later monologue is supposed to be backed by the authority of a particularly insightful deity, the Egyptian Ammon, in some brief advice to the Athenians as a community, who were complaining about excessively favorable divine protection enjoyed by the Spartans.

The Egyptian Story: Athens and Sparta

One thing that we should not expect is for "Socrates" to be telling us a story with any historical truth to it. After all, Phaedrus had remarked in the *Phaedrus* that Socrates could "easily construct tales from Egypt and from wherever" he likes (275b3–4), but for Socrates the issue is whether the message conveyed by the story's authoritative character is true. There it was King Thamous who had reproached Theuth for failing to realize that it was for one individual to make advances in technical knowledge, and for another to recognize the degree to which they have the power to help or harm the user—a distinction that was similar to that which Socrates drew in the *Alcibiades II* between knowledge of how to achieve a goal and knowledge of what is best. Thamous was the authoritative figure within the story, equivalent to the philosopher-king, and it is for Phaedrus to evaluate the truth of his claims rather than whether any such figure had actually said such a thing. Messages of wisdom could come from Egypt, but Egyptian stories would remain historically suspect.[207]

A second reason why one should not expect historical truth here is that a group of doubtful dialogues within the corpus contain monologues that are of a contentious nature, often a revisionist nature, and opposed to what one would expect to hear from an Athenian or even from a Greek. Undoubtedly, these monologues are more important for the innovative, sometimes radical, ideas they present than for any purpose relating to the author's desire to give factual information—and arguably also for any internal purpose within the dramatic structure of the dialogue. I have treated the monologic sections of both *Alcibiades* dialogues, the *Hipparchus*, the *Theages*, and the *Minos* together in this regard.[208] They are meant to challenge the addressee in much the same way as the monologic address in which Socrates develops his interpretation of Simonides' poem in the *Protagoras*, where Socrates afterwards compares such examinations of the meaning of poetry to the entertainment of lesser men at symposia—who rely heavily on the sounds of flute and lyre rather than on their own voices—and seems intent on diminishing the importance of what he had said before (347c–d, on 342a–347a). In the doubtful dialogues such passages show a clear pattern of differing linguistically from their dialogic surrounds

207 See on Egyptian stories Johansen 2004, 39–41.

208 See Tarrant 2018.

in ways that are obvious when computer analysis of vocabulary is applied,[209] and there is a strong tendency towards pro-Spartan or other un-Athenian sentiments. Sparta is also idealized in the monologue of the *Protagoras*, here in the *Alcibiades II*, and along with the Persians in the *Alcibiades I*, while Crete and its hero Minos are idealized in the *Minos*. The *Hipparchus* paints a remarkably positive picture of Athens' internal enemies, the Pisistratid tyrants.[210]

We begin with remarks about how the Spartans emulate the poet who has been quoted, or had perhaps discovered the same thing for themselves, because both in public and in private matters they regularly offer up more or less the same prayer, requesting the gods to grant them splendid as well as advantageous outcomes. That is as far as their acts of prayer will go. They have therefore been as fortunate as any human beings, and even if not everything has turned out well for the them, at least their failure is not due to what they prayed for, because it is presumably up to the gods whether they actually grant what is asked or something contrary to it. Offering the appropriate kind of prayer still does not give any assurance of success,[211] but in practice it has served the Spartans well over a long period.[212] So the beginning of this speech is closely linked with the end of the earlier monologue (141c–143a).

What Socrates now offers is an account he has heard from certain older persons[213] of a time when the Spartans were winning the gods'

---

209 Tarrant 2018, 398–400.

210 While the monologue of the *Theages* is not without contentious material, it does not appear to have comparable political significance.

211 As emphasized by Zeller 2002, 167: ". . . les Lacédémoniens sont aussi heureux que les autres qui ont réussi, à la différence des Athéniens qui, à cause de leur culte inacceptable, n'eurent pas de chance dans les combats. Le dialogue présuppose une relation vérifiable entre prière et fortune. Seulement, elle ne fonctionne pas forcément." I would qualify the statement about presupposition: the rhetorical force of *the monologue* presupposes one's acceptance of *some* relation, *suggested by empirical evidence*, between prayers and success.

212 One might observe that the force of this claim would have been somewhat weakened as early as its defeat by Thebes at the battle of Leuctra in 371 BCE, which could explain the strange phrase "up until the time that has just arrived" (εἰς τὸ παρῆκον τοῦ χρόνου). It would have been even more problematic once Philip II took control over most of Sparta's sphere of influence by the creation of the League of Corinth in 337 BCE.

213 I cannot think why, with Burnet, one would wish to exclude τῶν πρεσβυτέρων, in which case the story would just come "from certain persons"; Carlini retains it, as does Brisson, suspecting an echo of the *Critias*.

favor and constantly prevailing in battle, while the Athenians, as a state, consulted the oracle of Ammon in the Egyptian desert because they were unhappy about the way they were faring in conflict with the Spartans in spite of the multitude of rich offerings they made to the gods. For the story to be true, the following points would have to have been operative at some period of Greek history prior to the dramatic date of the dialogue:

1. The Athenians and Spartans were engaged in a conflict involving both land and sea engagements.
2. The Athenians were losing regularly on both fronts.
3. The Athenians were the most extravagant of the Greek in all their dealings with the gods including the provision of temples and sacrifices, while the Spartans were correspondingly mean in this regard.
4. The Spartans had as much wealth as the Athenians.
5. The Athenians collectively imagined that they could find the answers to their problems by consulting a non-Greek oracle such as that of Ammon.

The only period, or the only one that Socrates could have spoken of, during which the Athenians might indeed have worried that they were constantly losing by land and sea in an on-going struggle with Sparta was in the closing years of the Peloponnesian War, well after Alcibiades' youth. Eventually, in that same period, the wealth of Athens, which had according to Pericles been far superior to that of their opponents in its earlier stages (Th. 2.13.2–5), became seriously depleted, so that one might by then have spoken of the Spartans as being just as rich—but surely the extravagance of the Athenians had by then diminished also. However, given that Pericles is supposed to be still alive at the time of the present encounter between Socrates and Alcibiades, the wealth of Athens must still have been a formidable asset. Perhaps we are meant to be looking back to an earlier time before the Athenian empire had become established, but when could this have been? The earlier the date that we consider here, the less likely it is that Athens would have gone beyond the confines of Greece to consult an oracle. Ammon had been consulted by leading Athenians privately by the middle of the fifth century, as by Cimon (Plut. *Cimon* 18.7),[214] and it was consulted later by Alcibiades just prior to the Sicilian Expedition (Plut. *Nic.* 13.2).[215] But the public sphere was slow to follow the example of private individuals, and we know of no state that would consult the oracle until the fourth century.[216] While Pausanias (3.8.3) talks of the Spartans having been the earliest to consult the oracle of Ammon in Libya, the actual example given is that of Lysander who (as was claimed) dreamed of the god's advice concerning the termination of the siege of Aphytae, and then made it an excuse for a *private* visit to the shrine (Plut. *Lysander* 20.5–6).

The oracle obtained for Alcibiades and predicting a favorable outcome for the Athenians if the Sicilian Expedition went ahead must have made an impact at Athens, for Ammon then receives a high profile in Aristophanes *Birds* (619, 716), written just before the expedition collapses. This distant oracle is the only one mentioned alongside Delphi at 619, where it is said that Athenians will no longer sacrifice at these sites. While the birds, having their own long-standing association with prophecy, declare at 716 that for humans they now take the place of Ammon, Delphi, Dodona, and Phoebus Apollo. So while it is highly likely that Athens had not yet publicly consulted Ammon when this conversation takes place, the author is almost certainly aware that Alcibiades would consult it later in his own life. Assuming that the story is just an imaginative fiction aimed at supporting Socrates' case against specific requests when praying to the gods, the choice of Ammon is probably natural enough simply because of that god's later involvement in Alcibiades' career and his complicity in the hawkish promotion of war against Syracuse. This would be a case when Alcibiades had indeed obtained the backing of a god, and in consequence was instrumental in bringing about disaster for his city. Might it be a case of his not having known what he should pray for?

This means we should not hastily assume that the monologue was only written after the more famous consultation of Ammon by Alexander III. Even though I suspect there is an on-going tendency in

214 The indirect consultation by Cimon's delegation provides a parallel for the refusal of the oracle to give a straight answer in our passage (149a8–b1).

215 We are given the impression that Alcibiades' delegations to consult oracles might have gone to a number of oracular sites, but it was the response of Ammon that was of most use to him in his promotion of the war, and Plutarch informs us that it predicted the Athenians would take all the Syracusans.

216 See Sommerstein 1987, 237.

this work overall for its content to have as much to do with Alexander as with Alcibiades, it seems the reference to Ammon cannot be used to prove this, and it does not entail that Plato was not ultimately responsible for this monologue.[217] However much the dialogic parts and any transitional passages may offer us language and content that does not strike us as Platonic, we should not rule out the possibility that the monologic sections originated in some kind of semi-serious speech of Plato, possibly designed for delivery at the intellectuals' equivalent of a symposium, where inventiveness and literary allusion or quotation were esteemed.

The important message of the story of the visit to Ammon, after the priest's failure to give the Athenians the kind of answer they wanted, comes when the priest then calls to them and tells them that the god preferred the respectful language (*euphêmia*) of the Spartans to the sum total of the Greeks' sacrifices (149b1–4). Though the priest says no more, the response is interpreted as referring to the type of prayer that the Spartans offered, which was importantly different from that of the rest of Greece. The rest tended to offer lavish sacrifices and dedications in support of whatever it came into their heads to pray for, whether good or bad. And hearing this unseemly language the gods turned down their expensive processional offerings and sacrifices. The response is taken to confirm the great caution and consideration needed in any supplicant's utterances.

Pseudo-Homeric Lines

At this point Homer's alleged authority regarding communal acts of piety is adduced. This time "Homer" means the poet of the *Iliad*,[218]

217 Rather, what I should claim is that if Plato was the author of the monologue, then the reference to Ammon might have suggested to one of his followers that a dialogue on prayer should be composed, with suggestive comparisons between Alcibiades and Alexander.

218 Though only part of the material belongs to the *Iliad* it does belong to the *Iliad in particular*, and nothing is to be gained from attributing the lines to any of the lesser epic poems. Note that Zeus had acted in support of the Trojan side in the *Cypria* too (fr. 1 *ad fin.*), thus conflicting with 149d5–6 (lines 850–851), and that his motivation for bringing about the war was to reduce the human population *in general* (fr. 3). That his role is the crucial one (as is to be expected) is suggested by fr. 20 (= *Euthyphro* 12a). A connection is made between the Trojans and Ares in the second line of the *Little Iliad* (fr. 2), so that the gods in general could scarcely have felt Trojan conduct disrespectful, while the outrage of Athena at the conduct of the Greeks is what we are told about in the *Sack of Troy*.

for it is acknowledged that 8.549 is closely paraphrased, while the line the author inserts before the paraphrase and the three dactylic lines thereafter are lacking in the manuscripts. They have sometimes been added in editions and translations, where they are known as lines 548 and 550–552, and their status remains unsettled. However, if we look at the differences in 8.549 they are little more than is required to place the content within a sentence that reports Homer's word in the accusative and infinitive, adding articles before three of the four nouns.[219] The preceding line is even closer to a line of the *Iliad* for it is merely 2.306[220] with the verb (ἔρδομεν) turned into the infinitive (ἔρδειν), again so that accusative and infinitive construction can be employed. The three lines that follow the paraphrase of 8.549 present greater problems. While it is conceivable they were present in some alternative early version of the poem that has not otherwise been preserved, and barely even conceivable that they have been transferred here from a different epic, I think it more probable to see the hand of the author of this speech behind them. The final line and the final two feet of the preceding one are used as a formula early in the *Iliad* but not in other epics, and they occur three times there (4.46–47, 4.164–165, and 6.448–449). The speakers vary (Zeus, Agamemnon, and Hector), and the only context where the words have any bearing on the present topic of state supplication of the gods by prayer and sacrifice is the first. Here Zeus declares that he would personally be sorry to see the demise of the city of Priam *because his altar had never been lacking in any of the due offerings* (4.48–49), indicating that he appreciated the proper sacrificial practices of the Trojans. In book 4 of the *Iliad* Zeus is certainly not among the gods to whom Troy was hateful, nor among those who would refuse his share in Trojan offerings. This means that the first line and two thirds after the paraphrase of 2.306 and 8.549 are actually incompatible with the only relevant context of the next line and a third.

One must therefore consider the possibility that these three lines have been added here to manufacture Homeric evidence that did not in fact exist. The gods were always divided in their support for Greece or for Troy, and there is no justification within the *Iliad* for the notion

219 κνῖσαν δ' ἐκ πεδίου ἄνεμοι φέρον οὐρανὸν εἴσω in Homer has become τὴν δὲ κνῖσαν ἐκ τοῦ πεδίου τοὺς ἀνέμους φέρειν οὐρανὸν εἴσω.

220 As recognized by Aronadio 2008, 227n25. Like Carlini and Brisson, Aronadio refers to the very brief discussion of Labarbe 1949, 410. Modern commentaries on Homer, e.g. Wilson 1996, 206, and Kirk 1990, 340, are worth consulting, as is Erbse 1971, 387.

that the Trojans were hated by all of them.[221] Material has been cobbled together out of three different books of the *Iliad*, with the greatest adherence to meter, except for the last line and a third which were used by Homer three times, coming in the part that most conflicts with Homer's view of the gods, his understanding of sacrifice, and even his language.[222] The author uses an eclectic combination of quotation, paraphrase, and invention to suggest, contrary to all the evidence, that Homer's gods paid attention to the virtues of those who approached them and ignored their rich offerings as being tantamount to bribes. The falsification of such lines would merely add to the contentiousness that to my mind is an expected feature of this kind of monologue. The alleged evidence, whether a false story from the Athenian past (cf. the Atlantis story) or some purely invented Homeric lines, is justified in terms of the appropriate nature of the overall message, and may have been an accepted feature of this kind of instructive entertainment;[223] it might be the kind of noble lie that is sanctioned at *Republic* 414b–c.[224] What is certain is that this speech has no concern whatever for the truth of the alleged evidence for the view that it offers.

What the falsehoods have done is to enable Socrates to introduce his conclusion, which will be as serious as anything he ever said: that the gods are not swayed by our sacrifices and offerings, but by the justice and holiness (149e8) within us. Both gods and men of good

221 Kirk 1990, 340, finds "the idea that the gods in general were hostile to Troy . . . absurd."

222 Again see Kirk 1990, 340, for the view that οὐκ ἤθελον is not Homeric language, and that δατέονται is inappropriate as it presupposes a different model of sacrifice in which the gods divided up the meat itself rather than inhaling the savor.

223 If I am correct in suspecting an origin in the style of symposium favored by intellectuals, then one should heed Socrates' words at *Symposium* 198d3–e2: "I in my stupidity thought that one should speak the truth about each of the things being praised, . . . If [the claims] are false it simply does not matter."

224 *Phaedrus* 261e–262d demonstrates Plato's own interest in the mechanisms by which deceit may be achieved, and that it involves the use of what is similar to that which is actually so. It is in effect the prerogative of the philosopher who can distinguish degrees of similarity. Centrone 2011, after careful consideration of this passage and of the "deception" theme in the *Hipparchus*, is able to remark: "È dunque possibile interpretare molti dialoghi come esempi di retorica filosofica sotto questo particolare aspetto, nel senso cioè di uno sviamento che avviene a piccoli passi, di un "inganno" positivamente orientato alla conversione dell'interlocutore." I owe this reference to my collaborator François Renaud.

sense regard justice and wisdom as worthy of the highest honors, and those who possess them are precisely those who know what is to be done and said both in our dealings with the gods and in our dealings with men. There seems to be a nod to ideas in the *Euthyphro* here, with the reference to dealings with gods and men reminiscent of the idea that holiness is that part of justice that involves our relations with the gods (12e9), while the role of knowledge (cf. *Euthphr.* 14b2–d2) is also affirmed by bringing in *phronêsis* as practical knowledge—knowledge about what obligations we are under. One might even detect a reference to the idea that holiness is what is dear to the gods and unholiness what is unwelcome to them (cf. *Euthphr.* 6d11–7a1), indeed to *all* the gods (8b7–9), in the notion that all the gods had hated the Trojans because of failings in the area of holiness and justice (149d5–150a1).

One should also note here that we are no longer referring to knowledge of what is best (*tou beltistou*), but simply of what must be done and said. The sentiment may appear to differ little, but the wording is suggestive of *absolute duties toward others*, rather than *the most favorable of various options for the individual.* Coupled with the fact that even *the most favorable of various options for the city* had become *kratiston* rather than *beltiston* at 148e2, this suggests there is a discontinuity between the central epistemological section and the monologues.

The Language of the Egyptian Story

After the words "both towards gods and towards men," Socrates turns to Alcibiades and asks him what he thinks, thus initiating the closing episode of the dialogue. Before we consider that, we should briefly review the supposed linguistic irregularities within the resumed monologue. Neuhausen (2010: 243) singles out for attention nine spellings, words, or phrases for attention:

148c4: πλείον
148e8 and 150a4: ἀν' ἕκαστον ἔτος
149a8: οὐθέν [attic in T]
149a8: use of aorist passive infinitive ἀποκριθῆναι apparently in middle sense.
149b2: τάδε λέγει Ἄμμων
149c2–3: ἀναθήμασιν δωρούμενοι
149d1: ἔπαυλιν ποιουμένους
149e5: τοκιστήν

At 148c4 Carlini (1964: 307) reports "πλείω Par. 1813 (coniecerat Burnet): πλεῖον T: πλείων BCD." We cannot be certain what had been written, but oddly, just before the monologue at 148b5 where the singular is certain, BCD had reported the expected form πλέον, T giving πλείων. It is as if BCD and T were correlating the same marginal correction with different points of the text.

As for the repeated phrase ἀν' ἕκαστον ἔτος ("each year") there is only one other instance of this phrase prior to the sixth century CE, and that is in Theophrastus (*Hist. Plant.* 4.4.4), who I would suppose to be roughly contemporary with our author. Theophrastus also uses καθ' ἕκαστον ἔτος (*Hist. Plant.* 6.5.4) as do Ps.-Demosthenes (*against Phaenippus* 14.4.6) and Aristotle (*HA* 517a26). Plato, whose preference is for the simple κατ' ἐνιαυτόν, uses no similar phrase with ἔτος,[225] but does twice use καθ' ἕκαστον ἐνιαυτόν (*Menex.* 249b4, *Laws* 926e7), a phrase present in many of the orators, Aristotle (*HA* 547b9, 611b9), and Theophrastus (*Hist. Plant.* 4.12.3, etc.). In fact, outside the etymological discussion at *Cratylus* 410c–e, the singular ἔτος is found only at *Alcibiades I* 110a5, *Republic* 615c9, and three times in the *Laws* (and always with ordinal numbers).[226]

At 149a8 the spelling οὐθέν in BCD, corrected to οὐδέν in T, suggests only that the ultimate author was not trying to mask the presence of post-Platonic material, and the aorist passive infinitive there is abnormal if one can rely on the following text being correct and "the prophet" being its subject.[227] While I have no problem with 149b2, there is a cluster of language here that has added to suspicions of lateness.

The construction at 149c2–3 (with "the gods" in the accusative and the "dedications" in the dative) is the reverse of what one might expect in Plato, as seen particularly at *Laws* 955e6, where Plato interestingly says that the moderate man should make offerings by setting up only modest dedications to the gods. Here, however, it is hard to say

225 But note *Phd.* 58b2: ἑκάστου ἔτους θεωρίαν.

226 This applies also to the dative singular (*Phdr.* 249a4, *Meno* 81b9 in quoted verse, *Minos* 319c5, *Laws* 760d3), though not invariably to the genitive singular.

227 For an author so conscious of undertaking a literary task this non-Attic form seems little short of extraordinary. Rather than accept that this is what was written I suggest removing τὸν προφήτην as a gloss: "no other answer was given; for obviously the god did not allow it, but calling the Athenians he said 'Ammon speaks as follows.'"

whether the verb δωρεῖσθαι or the participle ἀνατιθέντα was more responsible for determining that the dative should be used for the dedications and accusative case for the gods to whom they are offered. It is also the reverse of what might have been expected from 148e7–8, where the gods are in the dative as normal, and the processions offered in the accusative, so there is internal inconsistency here.

At 149d1 the noun ἔπαυλιν with the middle of ποιεῖν looks Hellenistic, as the earliest occurrences elsewhere are in Polybius (5.35.13, 16.15.6, fr. 145). However, the noun itself is found in Aeschylus (*Persae* 870) and Herodotus (1.111), so one cannot say that it would not have been available to Plato. One has to look at whether there is anything similar in the lead up to the material about the Trojans' unsuccessful sacrifice in *Iliad* 8, and one finds the phrase ἀγορὴν ποιήσατο in line 489. So the middle of ποιεῖν, if not the noun it goes with, is explained by the Homeric context. One simply has to explain why ἔπαυλιν has replaced ἀγορὴν at 149d. It perhaps tends to signify a more long-term military "encampment" outside the city than Homer's word would have implied, but given the normal Attic meaning of ἀγορὰ it would not have been attractive to simply atticize the epic form: the Trojans were not setting up a trading center.

At 149e5 the term used for a "money lender" is a colorful choice, reminiscent of New Comedy, in which the *tokistês* is a stock character. But the transition towards New Comedy was well under way by Aristophanes' late play *Wealth*, and the application of comic touches is not foreign to Plato. This too sounds like a post-Platonic touch, even though it cannot be proven.

Overall, there is more problematic language in the resumed monologue than there was in the earlier one, and fewer literary excuses for it. If there is Platonic material behind both parts of the monologue, the language is in this case unlikely to be pure Plato.

The Poet's Prayer Reconsidered

Since the two principal monologues of the *Alcibiades II* must be considered as one, with the former placing the emphasis on the value of cautious, non-specific wording in prayers offered by the individual, and the latter extending that to the context of the *polis*, we should return here to the quotations at the end of that monologue. Here we note that the author has partly quoted and partly paraphrased words given to Zeus at *Odyssey* 1.32–34. He has done so with a degree of accuracy and no obvious deceit. The authority of Homer goes unmentioned here, for the lines would have been well known. It seems, in fact, that the name of Homer is only adduced when we are asked to believe something that we are not so familiar with and are not used to accepting as in accord with Homer. The appeal to the *Odyssey* had come immediately after the suggestion that mortals have brought troubles upon themselves by praying for things destined to turn out badly, whereas the gods cannot be blamed for answering our prayers. The Homeric context has nothing specifically to do with prayer, but refers rather to the folly of Aegisthus in seducing Clytemnestra and slaying Agamemnon, even after Hermes had been sent to him to warn him of it. There is not even any mention of the ruling power that Aegisthus would thereby obtain. So it is the message of the quoted words alone that can be legitimately used, and it is no evidence of the correctness of Socrates' concerns about prayer. One might even claim that the passage is the very evidence one needs to counter Socrates' claims about the gods' disregard of rich sacrifices after the resumption of the monologue, for immediately after Zeus' words Athena seizes the opportunity to remind Zeus of the undeserved sufferings of Odysseus, and in establishing his merits she refers directly to his generous sacrifices, for which Zeus himself then expresses his own appreciation (*Od.* 1.60–61, 66–67).

More worrying for those who seek to read the monologue at face value is the reference to the poet who wrote the lines:

> King Zeus, both when we pray for them and without
> our prayer
> Give us good things, and ward off wretched ones even
> when prayed for.[228]

This prayer is again in the hexameters used by epics, but it has been claimed that the address "King Zeus" is not elsewhere found in this meter.[229]

---

228 Ζεῦ βασιλεῦ, τὰ μὲν ἐσθλὰ καὶ εὐχομένοις καὶ ἀνεύκτοις
ἄμμι δίδου, τὰ δὲ δειλὰ [MSS δεινὰ] καὶ εὐχομένοις ἀπαλέξειν.

229 See Scrofani 2009. The address Ζεῦ βασιλεῦ is actually found in hexameters—and moreover in a prayer—in the prefatory prayer to the *Orphic Hymns* (Prologue, Orpheus to Musaeus, 3). In this case the second line claims that the prayer is something of a model, and the final two lines ask the huge list of divinities only for the benevolent presence at Orphic rites. It therefore appears to conform broadly to the requirements of the *Alcibiades II*, and could indeed have the dialogue in mind.

It occurs twice in Aeschylean choral songs,[230] and more often in indelicate exclamations in Aristophanic comedy,[231] and no such precedents make it an expected part of a prayer in hexameters. In Roman imperial times it occurs in a prayer of the Persian king reported by Arrian (*Anab.* 4.20.3),[232] and at the commencement of Aristides' *To Zeus*. The prayer from the *Alcibiades II* is reported in Julian fr. 170b, in Proclus (*in Remp.* I 188.6–7), and in the *Anthologia Graeca* (10.108) with some important textual variants from what has been reported in our manuscripts.[233] One might therefore think there must have been a different text in the poem itself, but both Proclus in the passage cited and a *Textus Theosophiae Tubingensis* from late antiquity report the two lines from our dialogue *as being Plato's*[234] using the variant text (40.1–3), suggesting strongly that some ancient texts of the *Alcibiades II* had the variant reading rather than that of our manuscripts. Nor is it unlikely that the quotation from Julian, which comes to us without any context, had been taken from Plato. Furthermore, nobody in antiquity can be said with certainty to have known the lines from a different source.[235]

Given, then, that we do not have the exact text that editors print anywhere, that what they print is only supported, given a one-letter "correction," (i) in the manuscripts and (ii) in a witness from the thirteenth century at best,[236] and that some ancients found the variant

---

230 See *Persae* 533 and *Agamemnon* 355, neither of them prayers. With such addresses one might compare the inscription of the Messenians referred to by Callisthenes (*FHG* 23.9) and reported by Polybius (4.33.4) and Pausanias (4.22.7).

231 See *Clouds* 2, 153; *Wasps* 624; *Birds* 223; *Frogs* 1278; *Wealth* 1095. With these exclamations we may compare Hippocrates *Ep.* 17.65. Note that at *Clouds* 2 and *Frogs* 1278 the tone is clearly mock-Aeschylean.

232 One scarcely needs to add the Persian king is unlikely to have broken into a formal Greek prayer, so that the expression originates with Arrian or his sources.

233 The words δεινὰ and ἀπαλέξειν in the MSS appear here as λυγρὰ and ἀπερύκοις, with little change of meaning.

234 Proclus' quotation occurs within a wider citation of the dialogue beginning at 142e1.

235 Orion the grammarian from the fifth century CE cited the two lines with the variants *and a different vocative* (Ζεῦ Κρονίδη) as being "from the Pythagoreans" (*Anthologion* 5.17). But it was common to find material in Plato attributed to the Pythagoreans in late antiquity, and the problem caused by pseudo-Pythagorean writings that drew on Plato or Aristotle and were taken to be genuine is well known. It is improbable the different vocative had its origin in a pre-Platonic source.

236 Maximus Planudes (*Compendia e Platonis dialogis*) finds our text already in a manuscript of the *Alcibiades II*. I take the date suggested by TLG, and have not researched this matter independently. To judge from Orion (previous note), there may be a suspicion here that the lines had a Pythagorean source, as Maximus thinks that they mean "Even

texts in their copies of Plato, it seems likely that the variant reading does not derive from a pre-Platonic text after all, but that it was the original reading in the text of the *Alcibiades II*, and ought to be restored.[237] If that is the case, there is no independent verification of the claim of "Socrates" here to be following a wise poet, any more than there is independent verification of his alleged lines from the *Iliad* at 149d5–6. Therefore it seems to me entirely reasonable to suspect that the "wise poet" is none other than whoever composed this two-part monologue.

But is there any evidence that this is so? There are, I believe, three indications, none conclusive in themselves. First, this hypothesis best explains the address to King Zeus that probably did not belong in epic hexameters at this stage, and is first found in Aeschylean choral passages, and then only after the particle ὦ that is often added to vocative expressions. It was perhaps most familiar to Athenians in the fourth century when used as part of an exclamation, and as debased rather than elevated diction.

Second, our discussion of the diction of the first monologue has already drawn attention to the presence there of two rather imaginative adjectives that employ the alpha privative. They were ἀνήκοος and ἀστρατήγητος, on which we have already commented (above, p. 95). Therefore, when we find the similarly unusual ἄνευκτος that is found only in the *Alcibiades II* and other texts that record the prayer, it is hard to resist the conclusion that it has been invented by the same author as had employed the other two. One might of course choose to derive this adjective from the prepositional prefix ἀνὰ rather than the alpha privative, but then it would recall the similarly unusual ἀνεύχομαι at 142d3, offering much the same argument that the monologue and prayer have been composed by a single individual with a taste for a certain kind of vocabulary.

Third, it should be further observed that this kind of prayer, one that asks the god for no specified benefit, lacks obvious precedents. The

if we are silent favor us with what you know to be best; and if we pray for something inexpedient in our ignorance of the future, prevent it in your goodness." But they surely do not refer to any institutional silence.

237 δεινὰ and ἀπαλέξειν could easily have arisen through the incorporation of marginal glosses into the text. They should only be preferred to the readings that were present in texts used by our earliest witnesses if they are superior, but the fact that editors emend δεινὰ while a second person singular of some kind is clearly preferable to ἀπαλέξειν makes it hard to argue for such superiority.

one person we can name who adopted the same policy on prayer as does this passage of the *Alcibiades II* happens to be Socrates, who is said by Xenophon to have prayed only for what was good on the grounds that the gods knew best what that was, while people who asked for gold and silver or for tyranny were essentially gambling on things of which the outcome was uncertain. And the "Socrates" of the *Alcibiades II* says nothing to exclude the possibility that he himself is the relevant poet, just as he does nothing to exclude the possibility that he himself may be the educator who will teach Alcibiades how he should behave towards gods and men (150d), and who indeed encourages Alcibiades to believe that he is that person (150d–151a), as he had also done in the *Alcibiades I* (105e2–5, 124c5–10).

I therefore tentatively conclude that the lines of the poet are in fact the invention of the author of the monologue, who has likewise supplied, in the same meter, much of the alleged quotation from the *Iliad*. The identity of the author is of course more difficult to ascertain, but it seems that there is a certain playfulness over questions of authenticity and of the authority of his material. That playfulness, however, cannot be allowed to hide the greater seriousness with which the ethical and epistemological philosophy of the dialogue is being taken, nor can it rule out polemical intent.

Chapter Six
Reversion

The overall structure of the *Alcibiades II* can be argued to be that of three dialectical passages separated by two monologues. However, I have already shown reasons for believing that the two monologues in fact form a single integrated study of how one should pray, with the earlier emphasis on what one should say and do as an individual and the later one on what states ought to ask for and be doing. The intervening material primarily treats the positive value ignorance may have if one is unaware of what is best, and its relation to the beginning and to the end of the dialogue is comparatively tenuous. Hence I would postulate a structure roughly along the lines of Introduction (A1), Monologue part 1 (B1), Digression on ignorance and knowledge (C), Monologue part 2 (B2), and Conclusion (A2).

This does not quite conform to the arrangement of this book, because I suspect that 141a5–c8 is best viewed as a preface to the first part of the monologue. If we examine Socrates' only sympotic monologue in Plato, the account of his education in erotic matters with Diotima at *Symposium* 201d–212c, we find that unlike other speakers' monologues, it is prefaced by a dialogue with Agathon from 199c3 to 201c9 that is closely related to the eventual narrative. Alternatively, if we look at the monologue that Socrates later (347c3–e1) compares with sympotic entertainment at *Protagoras* 342a6–347a5, we find that it has been prefaced by a conversation on the same topic from 338e6–342a5, from which the monologue naturally emerges. The central monologue in the *Alcibiades I* lasts from 121a3 to 124b6, but it follows naturally on from Socrates' marked change of topic at 119a8, and the whole passage of about five Stephanus pages was regarded by Olympiodorus (*in Alc.* 12.1–4) as the central "protreptic" phase of the dialogue, following elenchus but preceding a final section in which Socrates is practicing his intellectual midwife's art.[238] So there too we can see a contentious but entertaining central monologue preceded by prefatory material of about two Stephanus pages that leads into it. The prefatory passage I postulate in the *Alcibiades II* may only be about half a Stephanus page, but then the whole dialogue is on a much smaller scale.

The A1:B1:C:B2:A2 arrangement indicates that the dialogue returns at the end to the same kind of material we had encountered at the beginning. The emphasis shifts back to Alcibiades' impending action. He now needs to make an immediate decision whether he should proceed with his prayer and sacrifice to the unnamed god, and if so what he should actually pray for. How much influence has this conversation had upon him, and what will be the consequences both for him and for Socrates? Socrates reminds him of the dangers that prayer involves for anyone unable to distinguish between what will be good and what will be bad for oneself. What might the god's reaction be if he is heard making inappropriate requests? It seems that Socrates still recommends the kind of prayer the Spartans uttered, but he does not think that Alcibiades could bring himself to do this on account of his "high and mighty nature" (*megalopsukhia*). In that case his advice will be that he should do and say nothing (*hêsykhian ekhein*).

It is important that *hêsykhia* is not just a word for silence, but for inactivity as well. Strictly speaking there seems absolutely no reason why Alcibiades should not simply have gone to the temple or shrine and offered the intended sacrifice, dedicating his wreath to the god, but not making any request in return—in much the same way as he could simply have prayed for what's best for him. But the dialogue ends with him having decided that the whole of the ritual should be postponed. It is difficult to know whether the dialogue is advocating that an admission of ignorance should lead not just to indecision but to inactivity as well—but from the point of view of situating the dialogue that issue is important. There was much debate between ancient skeptics and their opponents as to whether it was really possible to live one's skepticism, given that the skeptic could not resign himself to complete inactivity on all the issues upon which he was bound to suspend judgment. That issue may not so easily arise when one is committed to making no decision on one issue only, but ignorance of what is best might be

238 On the commentators' division of the dialogue see Renaud and Tarrant 2015, 170, 180, 199–200.

reasonable grounds for suspending all beliefs regarding what to do and how to do it. Perhaps Alcibiades did not ought to be doing anything at all with his wreath, for instance, but instead he will give it to Socrates. His ignorance here entails only limited inactivity—and inactivity only until the time when he should know what's best. That, of course, is why he acts so positively towards Socrates here, Socrates being his only acknowledged hope of discovering what's best in the future.

In the text we have just covered we meet a number of unmistakable verbal echoes of earlier work, which tie the second monologue to much earlier material, thus binding the dialogue together. They might best be presented as follows:

Reference	Topic	Echoes
150b8–c1	Not noticing imagined good things one asks for are bad	143a8–b2
150c3–4	Praying in ignorance is not safe	141c9–10
150c4–5	Gods don't accept *blasphemiai* (unholy utterances)	149c4–5
150c7–8	The Spartan prayer	148e2–4
150c8	Grand aspirations (*megalopsukhia*) as folly	140c9
150d1–2	Knowing right conduct towards gods and men	150b2–3

We can now see the effect of the whole conversation on Alcibiades. He wants to know how soon the time might come when he knows what is best for him. This is because, as in the *Alcibiades I* (especially 118b) he wants to set out on the road to achieving his political ambitions as soon as possible, and realizes that he is in need of an educator (compare *Alcibiades I* 119b). So he also asks, confirming the pleasure it would give him to discover this, who this educator could be. While Socrates and Alcibiades continue to talk of this educator in the third person (150d6, e5–7, 151a1), Socrates' initial reply ("That man who is concerned for you") leaves no real room for doubt, whether for Alcibiades or for the reader, that it will be Socrates himself. So as in the *Alcibiades I* again (135d–e), Socrates will be the chosen educator by the end of the dialogue.

Agreeing on Education by Socrates

Socrates affirms that in his view the process will be a two-stage one, one removing the mists that are engulfing Alcibiades, the other applying the remedies that will promote his knowledge of good and bad. In so doing he employs another Homeric quotation, this time *Iliad* 5.128 with the justifiable alteration of a second person singular subjunctive to a third person optative to fit the grammar of the wider sentence. There is no deceit in this case. Socrates must first act for Alcibiades like Athena had done for Diomedes, lifting the mist from his eyes "so that he might easily recognize both god and man." The early theme of sight and blindness, introduced first with the mention of Oedipus at 138b–c and continued with the use of eye disease as an example at 139e, had just now returned at 150d4 where Alcibiades expresses his desire to *see* his educator, so that the removal of mist from the eyes and the act of recognizing gods and men are themes that Socrates can raise naturally in response.

This act of recognizing "both god and man" is clearly not something that was only supposed to apply to the Homeric situation, and must somehow apply to Alcibiades' situation as well. We can scarcely ignore the fact that knowing how to deal with gods and with humans had already become a theme at the end of the preceding monologue (150b1–3), where the "wise and just" people (*phronimoi kai dikaioi*) are identified with those who know how to act and to speak in their dealings with both gods and humans. Picking up that passage, Socrates has shortly afterwards affirmed (150d1–2) that anybody like Alcibiades must, if he is to offer *specific* prayers as opposed to the generic one of the Spartans, "wait until he learns what attitude he should adopt towards gods and towards humans." Obviously Alcibiades would need to know the correct way of dealing with the gods if he is serious about praying to them, and about how he should deal with men if he will pray to rule them.

It is a reasonable inference that Alcibiades must also know the *difference* between the divine and the human, and hence "know himself" *qua* member of a certain non-divine species—a rather different form of self-knowledge from the one that has so far been relevant to the dialogue: knowing whether what one is doing is good or bad for oneself. After listening to the close of the monologue, Alcibiades has responded positively to the view of prayer adopted by Socrates and the god (Ammon), adding that it would not be reasonable for him to be casting his vote against the god—here employing one of only two words in the final section that Neuhausen (2010: 243) considers relevant to studies examining the date of the work.[239] This seems already to show a consciousness of the limitations of human cognitive ability, not only his own but also Socrates', for there is no suggestion here that it would be unreasonable to disagree with his companion. Whereas a reader fresh from interpreting the *Alcibiades I* might argue that *even within Socrates* one should distinguish the divine from the human, basing the distinction on 133c1–6 and 134d4–e7,[240] one is not encouraged to make that distinction in this dialogue. After Socrates' second reference to gods and humans at 150d2, obliquely implying that Alcibiades is in need of a teacher,[241] Alcibiades responds that he would love to see the identity of *this human being* (*touton ton anthrôpon*) who will educate him, and Socrates has no hesitation in identifying (obliquely again) that educator as himself: "This person who cares about you." It is not Socrates *qua* divine inner person who will educate Alcibiades, it seems, but Socrates *qua* human being. At this point both Socrates and Alcibiades "know themselves" insofar as they are aware that they are human and understand that the human is inferior to the divine. Soon afterwards even this limited self-knowledge will be called into question.

As we have said, Socrates is envisaging a two-stage education. It is made quite explicit that Alcibiades' would-be "educator" must first remove the mist from the pupil's eyes, and then at that point (*to tênikauta*)[242] apply remedies by which the pupil would be able to tell "both good and ill." This phrase is made to sound Homeric in a way that matches the Homeric meter in the phrase "both god and man,"

239 The words are ἀντίψηφον here at 150b6, which is not found elsewhere in the Platonic corpus, and προσαπολαύσῃς at 150c6, which I find quite natural in the context. But Neuhausen should perhaps have mentioned τυχόν at 150c5, seeing that he mentioned it at 140a2. Also relevant is τὸ τηνικαῦτα at 150e2.

240 Given the shift of focus towards the personal relationship between Socrates and Alcibiades, it is possible this is what the reader should momentarily expect, even though that expectation will be put right.

241 The word for learning, *manthanein*, is in ordinary circumstances used of learning *from a teacher*.

242 There seems to be real doubt whether this expression, involving τηνικαῦτα with the article, is earlier than the second half of the fourth century BCE. It is found in book II of the Aristotelian *Problems*, but nowhere in undisputed Aristotelian works. Even without the article the adverb is found only once elsewhere in the Platonic corpus, at *Laws* 792b8.

so that one might deduce that this, the knowledge of good and evil," is the equivalent lesson that Alcibiades must be learning—as might indeed have been anticipated from the whole course of the dialogue so far. So had the knowledge of god and man not been relevant to him after all? Or can the two be somehow reconciled? At the close of the monologue the precise knowledge that was identified with wisdom and justice was knowledge of how we *should* behave and speak both in relation to gods and in relation to men (150b1–3). That would surely involve recognizing *how it is best to act and speak* to either group. That same "should" (*dei*) is present at 150d1 as well. It would certainly be useless to be able to distinguish between god and human, and indeed to identify any particular god or human, if that had no bearing on how we are best to address them or act towards them. It has already been established that it would be harmful for Alcibiades to recognize Pericles if he was utterly mistaken about the best way for him to act towards him, and likewise for Orestes with regard to Clytemnestra (143e8–144c8).[243] One ought also to note that, speaking of Orestes, the author even at that point had virtually identified the wise (*phronimoi*) with *those who know how it is best for them to act* (143d7–8).

All this confirms the dialogue is not interested in prescribing the knowledge of some absolute Good that can never in any circumstances prove harmful. Instead it recommends what is good relative to a number of determining factors. What Alcibiades has been encouraged to think about all along is whether any given thing is good for a given individual in a given situation (144c6–11). But, where that given thing is an action carried out by one individual towards another, one must also take into consideration the identity of the person acted upon as well as the person acting. Much of the craziness of Oedipus' curse was due to the identity of those cursed—Oedipus' own household. Orestes' act of murder might have been justified if he had been avenging his father's death by murdering somebody other than his mother, for nobody talks about the horror of his murdering Aegisthus. Both acts were used as examples because the horror of either depended upon who was committing it and against whom. Only by recognizing who it is who will be affected by our actions can we make sure that they are best for us. None of us can dice with the fate of those who are naturally our friends without detriment to ourselves. We must recognize all who

243 Note 143e9 and c6 (βέλτιον) and 143d8, 144a5 and 144a6 (βέλτιστον).

enter into our lives for what they are if we are to act as is best *for us*. Alcibiades must therefore recognize Socrates for what he is. And he ought also to have recognized that god to whom he was intending to pray, for how else would he know what is an appropriate prayer to be addressed to him, and what the chances might be of its being answered?

Love's Effects

Alcibiades now invites his educator to take away from him the mist or do anything else he wants, since he is ready to take that person's instructions (whoever he is), making no exceptions just as long as he is going to be improved as a result. As we learn from "Pausanias" at *Symposium* 184d–e, these are the very circumstances in which it is considered honorable for a lad to gratify his lover, with the former aiming for his own improvement in wisdom and virtue while the latter makes a genuine contribution to his intellectual and moral well-being. If a normal homoerotic relationship between Alcibiades and Socrates were to be justified, then popular morality would have required it to be along these lines. While it is of course far from certain that they had such a relationship, the account given in the *Symposium* (217c–219d) has Alcibiades clearly intent on one for just those allegedly honorable reasons, even if Socrates had resisted.

Socrates' response to Alcibiades' submissive attitude at this point certainly did not lack enthusiasm. He declares that "he [*houtos*] too" is tremendously keen about his friend, suggesting reciprocation but without of course giving any clear indication of what the relationship would entail. Even so, "keen *about* you" is not quite the same as the English "keen *on* you." The enthusiasm could mean he is keen that Alcibiades should be educated in this way, that his career should move successfully forward, or that the two should experience a loving relationship. It is mostly the intensity of his words that suggest this is love, and what he says is enough to make Alcibiades immediately anxious to postpone his intended sacrifice until a later stage,[244] winning

244 I am unsure whether the καὶ in the text at 151a3 is strong enough to warrant translating "the sacrifice *too*," as if it had not been the whole ceremony but only the prayer that he had previously been asked to forego. However, it has not been explained why the sacrifice on its own should constitute "so great a danger" in that case. I tend to believe the καὶ indicates that Alcibiades' mind is simply shifting to the physical aspect of the intended ceremony rather than the verbal one, without his really suggesting that the two could be entirely separate.

approval from his so-called lover, who in turn emphasizes how this is much safer than running the risks involved.

Alcibiades' next speech begins with a slightly odd "But how, Socrates?" The simple "But how?" (ἀλλὰ πῶς;), with or without an added vocative, is found only twice more in the corpus,[245] and with it the interlocutor poses the genuine question of how something could be the case. But what can Alcibiades be asking? He is not questioning how the postponement could prove safer, or continuation of the ritual a real danger. Rather, I believe he is asking how it could possibly be the case that he would carry on with the ritual given the arguments he has considered. But there is still a question over whether Plato himself would have used the words in this way.[246]

It is at this point (151a7–b3) that Alcibiades announces he will, since he thinks Socrates has given good advice, give the wreath in his possession to him rather than to the god, adding he will give wreaths and all other customary offerings to the gods (now plural!) when the promised day of enlightenment is *seen* to come.[247] If the gods are willing, he suggests, it will not be long. The switch to considering his obligation to the gods in general is rather unexpected, given the dialogue has so far been keen to confine its discussion of prayer and offerings to one special divinity that Alcibiades is now visiting (141a6, 148a2). Why should he not declare that he will return to this same god and make the offerings due?[248] Another feature of this speech is Alcibiades' unrealistic idea of how long this knowledge of what is best for him will take to be communicated. Signs of Alcibiades' impatience had already been evident at 150d–e, and one might have expected a cooler-headed Socrates to try to dampen Alcibiades' hopes of an early enlightenment. This he does not do, and exactly what he does say needs careful investigation, as the dramatic impact of the dialogue depends on our interpretation of his last speech, which is by no means straightforward.

---

245 *Tht.* 153e3 and *Rep.* 529a5.

246 Johnson 2003 translates "But what's next?" while Kenny 1997 has "Here's an idea." I find neither attractive, in both cases because what *follows* begins καὶ μήν, itself a phrase that typically introduces a new consideration. Brisson 2014 has "Comment faire autrement, Socrate?"

247 On the verb for seeing here, see below on 151b5.

248 No doubt many explanations are possible, but if as I have supposed he had been going to Poseidon at Potideia then it might prove impossible to visit his temple there in the future, and it would be to whichever gods he had access to that the offerings would have to be made.

Socrates' Final Words

There is no hesitation on Socrates' part: "Well (1) I accept this, and (2) I should be glad to *see myself*[249] accepting another of the gifts that come from you." I have used the numerals to try to capture something of the force of "both . . . and . . ." (καὶ . . . καὶ . . .), which is difficult to combine with an accurate translation of the rest of the sentence.[250] Let us remind ourselves of what was said earlier (141c9–10): "So you see how it is not safe either to accept things on offer spontaneously[251] or . . . ." If Socrates was concerned to give a good example to Alcibiades he could easily have said, "After weighing up the likely consequences . . ." or something similar, but it is clear he is not thinking so much about the effects of acceptance as about who the gift is coming from. There is quite a lot of emphasis upon "gifts that come from you." Socrates would love to think that Alcibiades might make him other offers he could accept. These are emotional words,[252] coming after the clearest

249 Strictly speaking, Socrates might just have said: "I should be glad to accept . . . ," so exactly why is his *seeing himself* introduced? It may be tempting to suppose the reflexive cognition of the *Alcibiades I* is somehow being recalled, but I doubt this is the explanation. It seems that the intense desire now felt by each of the speakers for some act of reciprocation by the other has caused both to talk of what they would gladly see: Alcibiades at 150d4–5 (cf. the verb of seeing at 151b3); Socrates here at 151b4–5. For a more sinister desire on the part of Alcibiades, similarly expressed, see *Symp.* 216c1.

250 Note that neither Johnson nor Kenny include "both," nor does Brisson seem to include any equivalent. Carlini's "io accetto questo dono, come accetterei con piacere . . ." is quite neat.

251 The term is εἰκῇ, often in other contexts "at random," is translated "without thinking" by Kenny 1997 and "simply" by Johnson 2003. I take it that both come close here, and that the term strongly suggests the lack of any rationale.

252 While the privileging of what he would see "with pleasure" (ἡδέως) might seem to suggest emotion rather than reason (cf. what Alcibiades would see ἥδιστα at 150d4, where "see" is again a vivid way of saying "discover"), not too much should be built on this alone. I judge as much from the "amazing enthusiasm" of 151a1, from the words which will follow, and from the employment here of ἄν + optative (again see 150d4, where the aorist infinitive stood for the aorist optative). The only comparable example in the corpus is actually at *Symposium* 216c1 (πολλάκις μὲν ἡδέως ἂν ἴδοιμι αὐτὸν μὴ ὄντα ἐν ἀνθρώποις). It is more usual in Plato to find ἡδέως ἂν with the first person singular of the aorist optative of the verb "to hear," which occurs nine times (but only once, at *Lysis* 204b2, of what Socrates wants to hear). With ἡδέως ἂν we occasionally find Socrates using the verb πυθοίμην ("I should gladly learn by inquiry"), but, as with "I should gladly hear" in the *Lysis*, this only ever happens at the beginning of the dialogue before the serious conversation starts (*Tht.* 143a2, *Hp. Mi.* 363a6, *Rep.* I 328e4).

sign so far of Alcibiades' affection for him, and we are not encouraged to believe that Socrates is giving due consideration to his acceptance. He has successfully restrained Alcibiades' impulses towards acquisition of what he had presumed (wrongly) to be advantageous, but he seems to have done so at the expense of his own capacity for making rational decisions.

One should pause to consider the image that this act of acceptance creates in the mind of the reader or listener. One may easily suppose that Socrates, in accepting the garland, allows Alcibiades to place it upon his head as he intended (151b1: *perithêsô*). What could this possibly symbolize? Perhaps one is reminded of Pentheus' receipt, from the god Dionysus, of the oriental *mitra* appropriate to his worship in Euripides' *Bacchae* (833; cf. 929). That *mitra*, so carefully placed upon his head by the god known in Sophocles (*OT* 209 with scholia) as "him of the golden *mitra*," would shortly feature in the description of Pentheus' death (*Ba.* 1115). The parallel may not be perfect, but we are now invited to recall another scene from tragedy in which the symbolism of the crowning garland is famously misread by the central figure.

"And as Euripides depicted Kreon, on seeing Teiresias crowned with garlands and on hearing that he has received them as first fruits from [our] enemy plunder[253] thanks to his skill, as declaring . . . ." These words precede the quotation of *Phoenissae* 858–859. There are three things I need to draw attention to here. First, Socrates is directly comparing himself with Kreon, brother of Jocasta and both uncle and brother-in-law of Oedipus. In Greek tragedy he is seldom portrayed as a desirable figure, and often as a tyrannical one. He is a central figure of many tragic sequences, and typically learns his mistakes too late, especially in Sophocles' *Antigone*. So the comparison is with a tragic figure who clearly falls short of the standards Socrates would like to set for Alcibiades in this dialogue.

Second, in the quotation the person who has received a wreath, Teiresias, is himself blind, yet has the knowledge to make him one of the most successful seers in Greek mythology, and consequently many of the tragedies in which he appears make sight and blindness, knowledge and ignorance, a central theme, rather like our dialogue. He is also a figure who sometimes remarks in tragedy on the uselessness

253 Not from Thebes' enemy, as is made clear in the play, but from the Athenians' enemies, the Eleusinians, with outside help from Eumolpus.

of knowledge. Take, for instance, his first lines in Sophocles' *Oedipus Tyrannus* (316–318):

> Alas, what an awful thing knowing is wherever it cannot undo
> the outcomes for the knower; this is what I once knew well,
> but I forgot; otherwise I should not have come here.

Oedipus demands the solution to the problems of Thebes, but as he is himself the source of the problem there is no solution that he can be offered, only the bad news that he himself must inevitably bear. In the *Phoenissae* itself Teiresias says to Kreon that he wants [to know the means of saving the city] now, yet very soon he will not want it (899). The awfulness of knowing the truth can be excruciating. And since this passage (876, compare 66–68, 475, 765, 1051–1054) also mentions the curse of Oedipus referred to at 138b9–c3, it seems to bring together most of the major themes of our dialogue.

Third, Teiresias has been given a substantial reward by the Athenians for the services of his prophetic art. This cannot simply be for predicting the outcome of their struggle against the Eleusinians and Eumolpus correctly, for in that case his art will not have achieved the result. Rather, it is because he has told them what they must do in order to achieve the desired outcome. His message for Thebes will be of the same kind, for Kreon tells Teiresias at 863–864 that it is his job to learn from him by what act they may best save the city. Teiresias will reluctantly tell him what must be given up in order to achieve the goal that is desired. He will tell Creon that in order to save Thebes he has to sacrifice his son Menoeceus, in much the same kind of prophecy that Calchas made for the Greeks stranded at a windless Aulis. In that case Agamemnon was given no option but to sacrifice his daughter Iphigeneia if the Greeks were to sail to Troy. What such prophets were renowned for is accurately telling what must be given up in order to achieve outcomes upon which a leader's heart is set. In effect, Teiresias tells the price of success, having much the same kind of knowledge that Alcibiades lacks: what will be the price of generalship, what of autocratic rule, what of war, what of treachery. It reminds the reader too, perhaps, of what will be the price of Socrates' closeness to

Alcibiades—suspicion of teaching corrupting ideas that will undermine Athenian democracy, and ultimately the court charges that will lead to his death. Assuming it is to include the price of achieving one's goal, the knowledge of what is best, of which Alcibiades is now so desirous, is not in fact something Socrates can impart, but, rather like the knowledge of what is to be feared and what welcomed at *Laches* 195e, something that only a seer would lay claim to.

In Euripides' play Kreon's words run as follows: "I take[254] your crowns of glorious victory as a [victory] portent, for we lie in the path of a storm, as you know yourself." Socrates appears to mean them in the sense that he takes the gift of the crown as a glorious omen of victory pertaining to the struggle for the attention of Alcibiades that he is about to endure. He thinks he is in no less a storm than Kreon, and he is hoping to win "glorious victory" over his lovers. With declarations to this effect the dialogue ends. But what does it mean? There are two factors here, the nuances of meaning in the original play and how it is likely to have been understood by our author and his readers, and the subtleties of Socrates' meaning.

In the play itself, though Kreon must welcome Teiresias' prize as an indication of the efficacy of his predictions, he can be far from confident. As Mastronarde (1994: 443) affirms in relation to the suggestion of beautiful victory (the adjective καλλίνικος) at 1048: "The context undermines the value of the 'beautiful victory,' and a similar irony attached to other references to victory as a fine achievement." Several other passages are used to document this claim, and the logical consequence is that there would also be at least a suspicion of irony when the very same word was used at 858, where he had used a cross-reference to refer forward to his note on 1048. Craik (1988: 219), in a helpful note on this word's use at 858, makes it quite explicit that it is ironical in the context of this play. How then does this affect Socrates' choice of it for quotation? He is well aware of its dreadful context in the original play, one of the most tragic (in our sense) of all of Euripides' works. Selecting a passage such as this is by no means a sign of confidence, and he surely knows any relationship with

254 It is true the Greek has the aorist ἐθέμην, but Mastronarde 1994 explains this is an "instantaneous aorist as elsewhere in welcoming a good omen." He refers to E. *Ion* 561 and S. *Electra* 668.

Alcibiades must be built on shaky foundations. Is he then aware of the irony underlying the Euripidean reference to "glorious victory"?

Other questions also arise. Is Socrates' struggle really to be compared with that of Thebes against the Seven? Surely that must be an exaggeration. And who are these lovers? The *Alcibiades I* that purports to be the first conversation Socrates ever had with Alcibiades opens with the news that all lovers (in the conventional sense) have disappeared already as Alcibiades reaches manhood (103a, 131d4). One might argue Socrates can still be victorious over them simply by receiving more trust and respect from him, but if they are no longer vying for him then they cannot explain why Socrates thinks he is at a crisis point. Only if the *Alcibiades I* is not being presumed could this be referring to such lovers as that. If the *Alcibiades I* is taken as read then it is obvious Socrates is now thinking rather of impending assaults on Alcibiades' better nature by less scrupulous Athenians, particularly from among the democrats (*Alc. I* 132a). These attempts had been transformed at the close of that dialogue (135e6–8) into attempts from within the city to undermine their relationship. In effect both dialogues would be closing with reference to the same general concern, and this is underlined by the language: Socrates' wishes for an ongoing relationship are expressed in the closing remarks of both dialogues with the first-person optative of the verb for wishing (*bouloimên an*).[255] There is a little more realism, however, in what we presume to have been the earlier dialogue.

While it is easy to deny this closing wish is the same as a formal closing prayer, it is giving expression to what Socrates has set his heart on, and thus it is similar to an informal prayer. It may not constitute a request to the gods in particular, but it is surely not a hope that is being addressed only to his human companion either. Unlike the prayers attributed to the poet and to the Spartans (143a, 148c), it has specific content, being fixed upon one desired outcome rather than simply aiming at what will be best. Even if he has not technically *prayed* too hastily, he has certainly accepted a gift from Alcibiades rather too hastily, and it looks very much as if he would do so again. In the emotional intensity of the moment Socrates too fails to live up to the standards that he would like others to adopt. As the comparison with Kreon makes obvious, he simply does not know enough about the consequences

255 It should be noted that at 151c2 T's ἄν is not included by other manuscripts reported by Carlini 1964 (including the Bodleian B). No variants are reported at 150b4.

of one thing that he wants in order to be able to assess whether it will stand in the way of other things that he wants more. And he has offered himself to Alcibiades as the means whereby the young man can achieve knowledge of what is best for him without showing any real sign that he knows what is best for himself. If Alcibiades has made a little cognitive progress already, it is hard to see how further cognitive progress is going to be made, because it is unclear whether Socrates is far along the road to the relevant knowledge himself. Certainly it is thanks to Socrates that Alcibiades has become more reflective about what he does and what he wants, but Socrates seems not to have any knowledge or quality to guarantee he can make such progress himself.

It is tempting to recall here the "unbelievable but true" assertion of the young Aristides in the *Theages* (130d4–6): "I never yet learned anything from you, as you yourself know, but I made progress whenever I was with you, even if I were only in the same house but not in the same room." We can believe that Socrates' company is beneficial for Alcibiades, but it is hard to pinpoint why. Alcibiades is now highly conscious of the knowledge he lacks, but it is only the sense that there has been progress up to this point that makes it plausible the next stage can be achieved. Socrates does not know what's best. If he did he would not be comparing himself with the highly vulnerable Kreon who *sees* the wreath that is worn, but rather with its bearer—Teiresias the blind seer with exceptional cognitive powers (cf. *Meno* 100a). He can never become a Teiresias since Teiresias is a figure who walks into and out of episodes in tragedies, into and out of the tragic events others are left to experience. Socrates remains deeply embedded in the tragedy that was Alcibiades' life. He cannot walk away.

Yet it is not quite true that he does not compare himself with Teiresias. At first sight it is with the tragic Kreon that Socrates is compared here, but as the wearer of the garland he also resembles Teiresias, and his reading of the "portent" and his sense of an impending storm remind the reader that Socrates too is a prophet. The final lines show a Socrates who is himself endowed with Teiresian gifts, somehow aware not just of the dangers that lie in wait for others, including the young Alcibiades, but also for himself and his city. Perhaps he too knows the price that is to be paid if the city is to be saved, just as Teiresias had known the price to be paid by Thebes. As Will Altman has pointed out to me, Socrates the prophet is observing Socrates the tragic lover—the wiser Socrates seeing his counterpart accepting gifts, yet still allowing those gifts to be accepted. It may be that this two-fold nature actually *explains* why Socrates, as servant dedicated to Apollo (cf. *Phaedo* 85b), fails to assert explicitly that he himself will be the educator. The educator will be his more fallible twin, Socrates the deeply involved lover. It may also be that this rift between the supremely human Socrates and his divine counterpart is what *explains* why the author chose a Homeric line that spoke of the recognition of both god and man following the removal of the mist (150d9). As the mists blow away at the end of the dialogue, Alcibiades captures a glimpse of the divine side of Socrates, as promised at *Alcibiades I* 133c and recalled at *Symposium* 222a, placing the garland intended for the god upon his head. Momentarily, it seems, there are two faces of Socrates. The tragedy is they have to exist within the same human body.

Chapter Seven
How "Academic" is the Alcibiades II*?*

The Dialogue's Epistemology

While there is much more of interest in the *Alcibiades II* than a casual reading is likely to reveal, and much more skill has gone into its composition than its relative neglect might cause one to believe, I am writing above all with the conviction that it will ultimately offer us insights into the so-called "New Academy" of Arcesilaus, or into the developments within the Academy that contributed towards the changes that we associate with Arcesilaus. Since those changes are concerned primarily with epistemology, I intend to reflect further upon all material within the dialogue that seems to have much bearing upon epistemology. Issues that have arisen include:

a. the relation between madness, folly and wisdom;

b. the concept of the wise man (*phronimos*);

c. self-deception;

d. a particular kind of self-ignorance, ignorance of what is best for oneself;

e. the evaluation of knowledge;

f. recognition of "humans and gods";

g. the process that will yield the knowledge that prayer requires.

There appear to me to be two further issues about the type of Platonism we find here: how the dialogue is responding to the self-knowledge that had been idealized in the *Alcibiades I*, and how far it takes a relativist approach to knowledge that owes something to Plato's discussions of Protagoras and Heraclitus. Let us now review these issues.

It has not been widely recognized just how important the concepts of folly (*aphrosunê*) and wisdom (*phronêsis*) are in this dialogue. Insofar as they were by now largely associated with *practical* folly and wisdom, they are obviously relevant to any work dealing with practical decisions. But the *Alcibiades II* employs the terminology of folly[256] almost *four times more frequently* than any other dialogue.[257] The relevant adjective and adverb for "wise" and "wisely" (*phronimos*, *phronimôs*) actually occur more than four times more frequently than in any other dialogue.[258] By contrast, the term for "wisdom" occurs three times more frequently in the *Philebus* and twice as frequently in *Epinomis* and *Meno*,[259] and this seems due in part to there being far more emphasis on the instantiation of these qualities in the person or her deeds than in the abstract concept or anything akin to the Platonic Idea. If the terminology had been confined to the one passage at 138d1–140e5, then this might have been less remarkable. But in actual fact the terminology recurs at several points,[260] with a comparable concentration also at 145a–d. This goes a long way to confirming that epistemological concerns run right through this dialogue. We shall examine the passage on madness and wisdom first.

When Alcibiades suggests Oedipus' case should be regarded as one of madness at 138c, Socrates first establishes that being wise is the opposite of being mad, and then immediately introduces the distinction between being wise (*phronimos*) and being foolish (*aphrôn*). It is agreed that everybody must be one or the other, with no third intermediate possibility, partly it seems because one might see *phronimos* as roughly equivalent to "with one's wits about one" and *aphrôn* as being "witless."

256 Here I include not only "folly" (*aphrosunê*), but also the corresponding adjective and adverb for "foolish" and "foolishly" (*aphrôn, aphronôs*).

257 In every thousand words the terminology occurs 4.07 times, as opposed to 1.10 times in the *Epinomis*, and 0.66 times in the *Protagoras*; in other dialogues there are a maximum of 0.5 cases per thousand words. In absolute terms the figures are *aphrosunê* 6 (behind 7 for *Protagoras*) and *aphrôn* 12, ahead of 9 in *Gorgias* and 8 in *Laws*.

258 The rate is 3.84 times per thousand words, while the next highest rates are those of *Crito* (0.92) and *Gorgias* (0.65).

259 My figures are *Philebus* (2.10), *Epinomis* (1.41), *Meno* (1.35), *Alcibiades II* (0.68). Figures for other dialogues are all lower than this.

260 See 142d7/e1, 143d8, 145a6–d9, 146c3/c9, 150b1, and 150c9.

One either possesses this good quality or one does not, and so these two are polar opposites. But where there is no third possibility, as there had been in Aristotle's theory of moral virtue as a mean,[261] then any given quality can only be the opposite of one thing. Assuming that both being mad and being foolish can plausibly be regarded as the opposite of being wise, this makes the two concepts essentially the same. Yet there soon follows a counter argument, based on the obvious difference between living in a society of foolish people and living in a society of lunatics. In order to explain how they might have missed something, Socrates returns to the example of physical health and finds that all sorts of diseases deviate from the healthy state—being species of unhealthiness. This allows him to postulate several species of folly, of which madness is just one rather extreme kind. *Qua* foolish Oedipus and Alcibiades may not differ, even though Alcibiades suffers from a species of folly different from Oedipus' madness.

So Alcibiades needs to replace his folly with wisdom, which would seem to imply some knowledge. But what kind of knowledge would this be? The *Alcibiades II* is quite explicit about what it means to call people "wise" (*phronimos*): it is a matter of knowing (*eidenai*) what one must do and say (140e1–2). In the case of Orestes the same overall concept is employed, although speaking is dropped as it has no bearing on the matricide (143d7–8), and at the end of the final monologue (150b1–3) the wise and just are identified with those who know what to do and to say "in their dealings with both gods and humans." The addition here does not in theory add a lot, but prepares the way for further discussion of gods and humans at the close of the dialogue.

More important clarifications occur at 145a–c. One would not call an orator who knew how to advise "wise," without him knowing whether something was the better course and when, nor would one call an expert on warfare "wise" without him knowing when and for how long war is the better course. Nor indeed would one use that word for an expert on punishment who did not know who and when to punish them in a given way. Central to the concept of "wisdom" here is the belief that actions and words are appropriate only at certain times or in certain situations or for certain people. So when Socrates goes on at 145c1–7 to identify the knowledge needed for the appellation "wise" with the knowledge of what's best (*tou beltistou*) or

261 See also Chapter 2 above. *EN* 1108b13–15; *EE* 1220b30–32, 1222a19–21, 1227a37–38.

what's beneficial (*tou ôphelimou*), there is no hint of an intuition of some immaterial and ideal Form, only of what will be of benefit in any given situation. This practical wisdom belongs to the here and now; it is, as we have already emphasized, relative. And at 145d9–e1 it is confirmed that no amount of expertise in other matters will suffice for somebody to be called "wise."

This knowledge that is required, being relative to the situation and thus tied to this world's changes, might not be anything that would meet an exacting definition of knowledge such that it conformed precisely with the theory of the *Meno*, *Republic* V–VI, or Stoic theory. However, it is taken to be something that goes beyond mere opinion, as indeed any Hellenistic philosophy would have required. The trouble with craft-like knowledge that fails to determine what is best is that it "has come to trust in an opinion (*doxa*) without intelligence (*nous*)" (146a9, cf. c12–13). While there is little to further clarify the meaning of *doxa* in this dialogue, and no hint of a process that might convert correct opinion into knowledge, it is worth noting that the cognate verb *dokei* occurs regularly and seems to suggest the relevance of a *personal* perspective, and that *doxa* too may come close to indicating a personal perspective. Though there are a few other uses of the term *nous* in the dialogue, all seeing it as something positive, they are mostly rather unhelpful for working out precisely what it means for the author. One might make an exception of 150a7, where it is said that justice and wisdom receive special honor from the gods and those men who have intelligence. It is something, then, that aligns our judgment about what is to be valued with the judgment of the gods, and might be thought of as offering the complete or divine perspective. It seems it is something far closer to intuition than to reasoning, but there are no clues as to how it might arise, not even as much as the *Seventh Epistle* (344b3–c1) suggests as the origin of "wisdom . . . and intelligence." It would seem to be reserved for the especially gifted, as the *Meno* says of those politicians who have real excellence, endowed with something akin to the insights of Teireias (99e6–100a7). One cannot avoid asking the question whether such intelligence is supposed to be humanly explicable, but no answer is found in this dialogue.

And what of the status of ordinary knowledge such as is associated with the crafts and other kinds of expertise? Since the foolish are clearly thought to outnumber the wise (139c6–9, 145a6–10, 146b11–13), the majority of those who possess this sort of knowledge are surely going to fall into this category. But, whereas what is done with wisdom is presumed to have good results, it does not follow that the results of these people's efforts will automatically be bad. According to 146e2–3 their limited knowledge sometimes assists but is for the most part harmful. The state without that additional knowledge is rather like a ship with nobody in charge (146e–147a), facing all sorts of dangers but not necessarily failing to arrive. When Socrates first questions Alcibiades' censure of ignorance it is made plain that some ignorance can be helpful for some people in some situations (143b6–c3). It is also suggested that such knowledge can easily be the source of harm if it leads one to presume one has the most important kind (146b–d). As often in Plato, awareness of the limitations of one's cognitive powers is a most important asset: thinking one knows something one does not know is treated as a likely recipe for disaster. To judge from the criticism of the *polis* in which everybody thinks his own craft supreme (146a3–b3), the author believes all of us need to know the limitations of craft, and that if it is to yield the best results it needs to be under the guidance of a knowledge of what is best, and when, and for whom.

In this context one needs to consider the theme of self-deceit, which has already been treated in Chapter 1.[262] The verb *lanthanein* ("escape one's notice") occurs with a reflexive pronoun at 138b7, at 140e7, and at 150c1 in Socrates' words, and at 143a8 and 148b1 in those of Alcibiades. Most examples are concerned with praying for something that one assumes to be good for oneself, but is actually bad. There is minor variation at 140e, which concerns doing and saying what one should not, taken to be the outcome of some kind of folly. As we have seen, the issue is whether something that one wishes for is good for that given individual in a given situation. Hence, whatever other mistakes one might make in the process of deceiving oneself, the individual's own self-assessment must play a part, so that self-ignorance seems to play a part: more obviously in mistaking what is good for oneself than in doing and saying things that one should not do and say. While we have seen little to suggest that knowing oneself *qua* human being is relevant, the late theme of recognizing gods and humans, discussed in Chapter 6,[263] seems to be more than just incidental. It may possibly color the ending of the dialogue, though this is less than

262 See above, pp. 58–60.

263 Above, p. 142.

certain. Alcibiades had earlier been conscious of the wide range of evils that ignorance had caused *for us human beings* when it leads them to fail to realize (*lelêthamen hêmas autous*) that what they are working towards is actually very bad (143a–b). Alcibiades was aware that, as a human being, he was vulnerable to errors of considerable magnitude, so what he needed to know at the end of the dialogue was to distinguish good from bad rather than god from man (150e3).

So how will he come to tell them apart? It had been merely the lifting of the mists that Diomedes had needed in order to be able to recognize gods and men. His eyes would then tell him all he needed to know. But the "lifting of mists" from his soul's eye was simply the first of two steps for Alcibiades. He was ready not only for this, but also for other prescribed remedies. He needs what seems to be that initial elenctic step, but it appears the vision of his soul will not then be enough. He needs further education. But what will he learn? Whatever it is, the reader knows Socrates will not successfully impart it. Like Clitophon in the dialogue bearing his name, we may suspect that Socrates cannot move on to the next step. Why can he not do so? Is Socrates too making some cognitive mistake?

Language and Protagoreanism

The constant signs that it is always a personal viewpoint that is relevant, from the limiting *egôge* ("I at least") to the unusual frequency of expressions indicating what "seems to me" or "seems to you," cause one to ask whether this is a sign of the epistemology, only partially stated, with which the dialogue is working. The first thing that comes to mind when we consider such a trait is that the author may incline towards a Protagorean view of cognition—not necessarily of all cognition but at least of that part which is grounded in sensation.

This in turn makes one wonder about the background relevance of particular dialogues, first and foremost the *Theaetetus.* The close examination of Protagorean and related theory here, which occupies a substantial portion of the dialogue (151e–186e), most obviously rejects the idea that what stems from our personal sensations and our immediate reflections upon them should be termed "knowledge." It rejects the idea that any human being can be the measure of *all* things, but it does not reject the notion that we are the appropriate measure of those experiences we ourselves are undergoing. In brief, it can seem to be saying that we cannot be the measure of what is so, but we might be the measure of what is so *for us*. The Heraclitean view of the world, which is used there to bolster Protagorean theory, had always interested Plato, as long as it was applied only to this world of sensations we experience. Certainly, Plato was searching for something more stable than this, but did he actually find it?

The *Theaetetus* is not alone in highlighting Protagorean theory. It may be ethics that dominate in the *Protagoras* itself, but the epistemological theory, rejected by Hermogenes (386c, 391c), also receives attention in the *Cratylus*, where Heraclitean theory is at the center of the main debate. *Euthydemus* 286c is perhaps also relevant. It is natural, therefore, to consider as we go along the question of whether such dialogues are central to the world in which the *Alcibiades II* was written.

Now Protagoras was famously not trying to deny the existence of truth, for his book was (at least sometimes) known as *Truth*. Rather, he was trying to revise the concept in such a way as to make it less demanding. But since we are claiming to have found a dialogue that abounds in the language appropriate to one's personal viewpoint, it is worth asking whether the *Alcibiades II* gives one any clues as to whether its author was operating with any particular theory of truth. However, on inspection, this dialogue—along with several others of doubtful authenticity—seems distinctly lacking in the very language of truth (all words starting with *alêth-*).[264] One can compare the rates of all dialogues across the corpus, but one does need to remember that some of them discuss issues in which the language of truth is bound to occur, while others contain lengthy monologues giving no opportunity for an interlocutor either to challenge the truth of what is being said or to intervene with an innocent "True!"

The ten dialogues in the corpus with the lowest rates of this vocabulary of truth per thousand words are as follows: *Theages* 0.55; *Clitophon* 0.63; *Menexenus* 0.81; *Hipparchus* 0.82; *Alcibiades II* 1.13; *Erastae* 1.24; *Laws* 1.31; *Timaeus-Critias* 1.41; *Epistles* 1.45; *Protagoras* 1.77. If we ignore *Clitophon*, *Menexenus*, *Timaeus-Critias*, and *Epistles* on the grounds that they are mostly monologue, then examine what is left with lower rates than *Protagoras*, there remain four works of doubtful authenticity, with adjacent positions in the corpus, plus the *Laws*,

264 For this analysis it was important to allow neuter forms of the adjective that join with the article in *crasis* (*taleth-*).

which is also much less dialogic than the Platonic norm. The *Alcibiades II* has in fact five examples of such truth terms, four of which are put into the mouth of Alcibiades ("truly" at 143b5, 145a1, and 148b; "very true" at 146d6) and therefore do not reflect Socrates' stance, and the other is rather revealing, because it occurs in the words "I myself worry (*aporô*) that people really blame the gods in vain . . ." (142d4). In this case "really" (*hôs alêthôs*) comes close to meaning "in actual fact," with the implication "contrary to their belief."[265] Socrates remains aporetic, very far from making a statement of certainty, and simply expresses his own personal worry that is to be contrasted with the presumptions of others. Certainly, he thinks his own view is superior to the unreflective views of the masses, but that is quite compatible with Protagoras' claim to use discourse to promote healthier views in other people, replacing previously deficient ones (*Theaetetus* 166e4–167a6).

The avoidance of truth claims is naturally associated with skepticism, but relativism too has at times been linked with it,[266] and possible links between the *Alcibiades II* and the New Academy and Arcesilaus have often been discussed.[267] Such issues are quite problematic, first because the term "New Academy" does not seem to have preceded Antiochus of Ascalon, so that there is no evidence that the Academy itself recognized any major change of direction. Second because it is fundamentally unlikely that any change that did occur was as sudden as is usually presumed, or that it was totally due to the accession of Arcesilaus in the mid-260s, which is supposed to have erased all trace of the plausibly Platonic doctrine that preceded.[268] Thirdly, because even if the dialogue had been written by an Academic after 265 BCE, there is no guarantee it would have been intended simply as a vehicle for the New Academic point of view ("doctrine," of course, is scarcely the

265 Kenny (1997) translates "I wonder then if humans are not wrong . . . ," otherwise ignoring *hôs alêthôs,* while Johnson (2003), apparently with a different interpretation of the μή after ἀπορῶ, has "I can find no way to deny that it is truly vain for men . . . ," which in my view makes Socrates seem far too certain.

266 Sextus Empiricus includes Protagoreanism among the philosophies that need to be carefully distinguished from skepticism at *PH* 1.216–217. The eighth of the ten skeptic modes (*PH.* 1.37, 135–140) and the third of the five modes (*PH.* 1.164, 175–177) appeal to relativity, and thus owe something to Protagoras. Seneca *Ep.* 88.42–46 attacks various philosophies considered to be sophistically skeptical, and Protagoras is one of the individuals attacked. And anon. *Tht.* LXI–LXIII understood that the views of Pyrrho needed careful distinction from those of Protagoras and of Theaetetus.

267 Beginning with Bickel 1904, and continuing particularly with Carlini 1962.

268 See on this Tarrant 2020, Snyder 2018.

appropriate word). Rather, any dialogue written in such circumstances would be expected to reflect a New Academic view of how Plato writes and of how the Platonic Socrates operates. The proper question to ask about the *Alcibiades II* is whether it is the kind of dialogue that reflects the New Academic view *of Platonic writing.*

How Plato Wrote: The New Academic View

As outlined both in Cicero and in the anonymous *Prolegomena to Plato's Philosophy* (10), the New Academic picture of Plato does not make ridiculous claims, but merely exaggerates certain aspects of the dialogues, and privileges them over others. Take Cicero's account at *Academica* 1.46, which talks of Plato's support for investigation involving argument on both sides of the question:

> Platonem . . . cuius in libris nihil adfirmatur et in utramque partem multa disseruntur, de omnibus quaeritur, nihil certi dicitur.
>
> Plato . . . in whose books nothing is affirmed and many questions are argued on both sides, there is a search into everything, nothing is stated for certain.

That Plato communicates through the voices of others, often allows doubts about his conclusions, and is prepared to discuss just about any subject of philosophy, goes some way to justifying the majority of these claims. The claim about contrary arguments, though, is not that Plato *always* used argument on both sides of the question, but that he frequently did so. It is enough that he should sometimes have given it his imprimatur.

It is important to know which dialogues were prominent in establishing this portrait of Plato, for one can then go on to establish if there were linguistic affinities between all or any of these dialogues and the *Alcibiades II.* There are six dialogues regarding which antiquity discussed the issue of argument on both sides of the question: *Lysis*, *Charmides*, *Euthyphro*, *Theaetetus*, *Phaedrus*, and *Parmenides.*[269] Of these some at least came under attack quite early from other schools. Already

269 It could be argued that Olympiodorus (*in Phd.* 1.5.3–16) also involves the *Phaedo* in this, but he does not claim the *Phaedo* actually *argues* both sides of the question, but that it contrives to *suggest* both answers may be valid, especially when taken in conjunction with statements in the *Republic* and the *Laws*.

in the fourth century BC the Peripatetic Dicaearchus had attacked the *Phaedrus* for being crude and juvenile (D. L. 3.38), and comparison with Hermias (*in Phdr.* 10.14–18) suggests that arguing on both sides of the question (over whether the lover or the non-lover was to be preferred) was here a factor. The *Lysis*, a dialogue in which Socrates draws attention to the way in which the discussion had considered opposite cases (222e3–4), was the subject of an early hostile anecdote claiming that Plato misrepresented Socrates (D. L. 3.35, anon. *Proleg.* 3), and was attacked by the Epicurean pamphleteer Colotes in a papyrus of which we have significant remains.[270]

Hence there is an excellent chance that argument on both sides of the question had become a controversial feature of some dialogues and was being defended by Academics at some time during the headship of Polemo, that is, in the latter years of the fourth century and the first three decades of the third. It would not be surprising if the Academy had already been mounting a defense of this strategy, though this did not yet need to involve the "suspension of judgment" that Arcesilaus introduced, and that gives its name (*epochê*) to the "suspensionists" (*ephektikoi*) whose picture of Plato the anonymous *Prolegomena* reports in Chapter 10. Here the *Charmides* and *Euthyphro* were used in addition to the *Lysis* to support the view that Plato employed contrary arguments (*Proleg.* 10.18–20). Fragment B of the anonymous *Theaetetus* commentator shows Plato could be regarded as arguing for and then against Protagoras' epistemology in the *Theaetetus*, while the late Neoplatonist Proclus offers considerable discussion of Plato's contrary arguments when examining the dialectic of the *Parmenides*. Here he compares both the *Lysis* (*in Parm.* V 989.10–23 Steel)[271] and the Protagorean section of the *Theaetetus* (*in Parm.* I 654.11–23 Steel).[272]

---

270 See PHerc 208; see Cronert 1906, Philippson 1938, Concolino Mancini 1976, Vander Waerdt 1989, Kechagia 2012.

271 Note also I 654:19–22: ζητῶν τί φίλον ἐστί, καὶ τοτὲ μὲν ὅτι τὸ ὅμοιον τῷ ὁμοίῳ φίλον ἀποφαίνων, τοτὲ δὲ ὅτι τῷ ἐναντίῳ τὸ ἐναντίον, καὶ τοτὲ μὲν ὅτι τὸ φιλοῦν, τοτὲ δὲ ὅτι τὸ φιλούμενον), διὰ πάντων τὰς ὑποικουρούσας τοῖς δόγμασιν ἀπορίας προβάλλων.

272 The *Theaetetus* was central to two further arguments listed by the author of the *Prolegomena*: one arguing the dialogue did away with every definition of knowledge, and one based on Socrates' remarks about his own intellectual sterility at 150c–d, so that it was clearly important to the Academic case. On the importance of the *Theaetetus* in Hellenistic philosophy see Tarrant 2013.

Proclus shows how even for those who had no time for skepticism, pairs of opposite arguments had a proper place in Platonist education.

Overall, any dialogue written in imitation of Plato that emanated from the New Academy could certainly be expected to depict a protagonist—presumably "Socrates"—who explored a number of questions without much strong affirmation or denial, and who might resort to argument on both sides of the question to the extent that this was done in *Lysis*, *Charmides*, and *Euthyphro*. All this need imply nothing more dramatic than arguing first for and then against the identity of madness and folly, so that in this respect the *Alcibiades II* already displays a degree of agreement with the New Academic picture of Plato. And while the dialogue offers the reader a clear message on the dangers of prayer, that message emerges mainly through a sustained questioning of our ability to know what we should be praying for. Alcibiades is persuaded by the strength of Socrates' case and by his own resultant doubts, not by any strong claims on the part of Socrates to know anything beyond their own present situation.

Finally, we have to ask whether there is anything in the New Academic picture of Socrates that will assist us. Socrates was seen as sharing Arcesilaus' renunciation of knowledge in all but one respect. In Cicero (*Acad.* 1.15–16), when "Varro" had been speaking, Socrates' method is said to be similarly depicted by nearly all his auditors, and it allegedly involved affirming nothing, refuting others, and claiming that he knew nothing except that very fact [that he knew nothing].[273] Later, when "Cicero" replies regarding Socrates' profession of ignorance at *Acad.* 1.44–45, Arcesilaus is said to have maintained that nothing could be known, not even that very exception that Socrates had allowed for himself (*ne illud quidem ipsum quod Socrates sibi reliquisset*). In the Antiochean account of "Varro" Socrates is seen chiefly to be making claims about his own knowledge, but in "Cicero's" New Academic reply the claim that nothing could be known applies to people in general, while it is to himself alone that Socrates allows that one exception.

So Arcesilaus did not adopt Socrates' alleged position.[274] Presumably he did not believe Socrates' stance was superior to his own, hence if

273 *Nihil se scire dicat nisi id ipsum*. Cf. Diogenes Laertius' *Life of Socrates* (2.32), where Socrates' claim is "to know nothing, except that he knew this very thing" (εἰδέναι μηδὲν πλὴν αὐτὸ τοῦτο εἰδέναι).

274 To the extent that the *Academica* attributed to Socrates the *knowledge* that he knew nothing it was probably misjudging Socrates' position in the light of *Alcibiades I* 117b–118a; see Kurihara 2012.

his view has determined Cicero's report then at some time he would have judged this Socratic position to be mistaken, perhaps even incoherent. While we should certainly not expect the *Alcibiades II* to provide definitive evidence of a Socrates who claimed to know that he knew nothing, it does give us hints about what wisdom (*sophia*) Socrates might have allowed himself—*sophia* being the term applied in both of the main Platonic sources for Socratic ignorance, the *Apology* (21a–23b) and *Theaetetus* (150c–e).[275] The relevant terminology is unsurprisingly used of Homer (147c4 and c6), and of the anonymous champion of ignorance's merits in certain situations (143b7): "more wise than you or I." Socrates is less wise than this objector,[276] it seems, but he does not explicitly deny that he is wise, and he promises some more positive lessons for Alcibiades by the end of the dialogue. In spite of his promises, he shows no signs that he can actually deliver them. This Socrates does not look like somebody who knows that he knows nothing, but then according to the *Apology* he had not come to this conclusion until after the process of testing what the Delphic Oracle had meant (21b3–d8). When Alcibiades was young and Pericles still lived, Socrates might have at least entertained more hope that he would be able to know something worthwhile, and in our dialogue he seems to believe that both he and Alcibiades could benefit cognitively from the wisdom of others. All we can affirm for certain is that our dialogue does not depict Socrates as having the same reserve about human wisdom that he expresses in the *Apology*.

How "New Academic" is the Language?

We should explore further the New Academic picture of Plato as presented in the *Prolegomena* (10.1–71) and elsewhere to see what other assistance it might offer in situating the *Alcibiades II*. We have

275 It is clear from the anon. *Commentary on Plato's Theaetetus* (LIV) as well as anon. *Prolegomena to Plato's Philosophy* 10 that *Theaetetus* 150c4-d2 influenced the Academic picture of the Platonic Socrates as well as the *Apology*.

276 I cannot exclude the possibility that this objector might somehow stand for the author, and hence believe that all things are relative in such a way as to exclude the possibility of knowledge as normally understood, while also requiring that individuals are the only competent judge of what is relative to themselves. I have also asked whether the author is in some way attributing epistemological error to Socrates that hinders him from applying his own principles regarding the acceptance of gifts at the end of the dialogue.

to bear in mind the report in the *Prolegomena* cannot be linked with any particular phase of New Academic activity, but it does at least show how Plato could be enlisted among the supporters of the New Academic cause. After argument on both sides of the question, the next feature mentioned was the frequency in Plato of adverbial expressions indicative of doubt or hesitation, such as "as is likely," "possibly," or "perhaps as I think."[277] A parallel passage of Elias, also from the school of Alexandria, helps to clarify the actual expressions that were thought to have supported the New Academic case, and the extant Plato commentaries of Olympiodorus give us further insights into which expressions the Alexandrian Platonists discussed in this context. If they were broadly correct in thinking that New Academics had believed limiting or doubtful expressions were a pronounced feature of Platonic style, then these Academics would have been likely to imitate the practice if they ever tried to compose or revise a dialogue of the Socratic-Platonic type.

At first sight the expressions listed in the *Prolegomena* (εἰκός, ἴσως, τάχ' ὡς οἶμαι) do not seem to have much influenced the writing of the *Alcibiades II*—at least not these exact three examples. But we must ask whether those three expressions have been accurately transmitted to us in any case, or whether they reflect an approximation of something expressed in greater detail in whatever source the Alexandrian school had drawn their information from. Elias' version will help us resolve this question, as will reflection on which Platonic expressions could plausibly have influenced the New Academy. The simple *eikos* (εἰκός) as a positive response formula ("that's reasonable") occurs only eight times in Plato, while its most prominent use as an adjective, with important consequences for epistemology, is in the *Timaeus*,[278] where it seems to place restrictions on the accuracy one can expect from theorizing about the physical world.[279] While this can only have legitimately restricted our expectations about Plato's commitment to theories about the physical world, this was the only world that was much debated in Hellenistic philosophy. The main reason why the New Academy needed to include *eikos* among the expressions of uncertainty was the prominence of the

277 Anon. *Prolegomena to Plato's Philosophy* 10.7–12.

278 The *Timaeus* remained central to the study of Plato from the time of Plato's second successor Xenocrates until the end of antiquity.

279 See 29c2–d2, 30b7, 40e1, 48d2–3, 53d5, 56a1, 56b4, 56d1, 59d1, 67d1, 68b7, 68d2, 72d7, 90e9.

Timaeus in early Academic debate, involving Speusippus, Xenocrates, and Crantor on the Academic side and Aristotle and Theophrastus among their Peripatetic opponents.[280] This was the *only term* that could justify the attribution of doubt to the author of the *most important* dialogue of all, hence it had to appear among the terms of uncertainty. The *Alcibiades II* uses only the neuter singular of this word, and then only once at 150b6, but in the Platonic corpus the word is actually at its commonest in the *Alcibiades I*.[281] One can say with some confidence that it is not the most important expression of cognitive limitations for Olympiodorus, who does not raise the question of uncertainty in his commentary on the *Alcibiades I* even though he draws attention to other features of this term's negation.[282] However, at *in Phd.* 6.14.1 (on *Phd.* 67a7–8) he does insist that the word *eikos* in that context implies no hesitation.

Within the corpus the lone *isôs* (ἴσως: usually "perhaps") occurs as a stand-alone response some thirty-two times, but it is only found integrated into full sentences in the *Alcibiades II* and then only twice (143b6, 144d2).[283] This word too is relatively common in the *Alcibiades I*.[284] Again, Olympiodorus misses several opportunities in the *Commentary on the Alcibiades* to comment on any suggestions of hesitation the term might imply in his lemmata (*in Alc.* 46.10, 93.22, 135.4, 176.2, 189.3, 194.18, 228.4; cf. *in Grg.* 8.7), but he does

280 See here Tarrant, Layne, Baltzly and Renaud 2018, 15–18; Baltussen 2003.

281 See 104d6, 112d7–10, 114c11, 117a7, 120d12, 126d11, 131d3, 134d3, 134e9, 135a9; for the neuter plural see 120d10, 134e5. The rate is 0.097 per hundred words, rather more than the rate in *Cratylus* (0.088) and well ahead of other dialogues. Many of the so-called "Socratic" dialogues have lower rates than the *Alcibiades II* (0.023) (e.g. *Apology* [0], *Hippias Major* [0.011], *Lysis* and *Gorgias* [0.014], *Euthydemus* [0.015]) while *Phaedo*, *Republic*, *Phaedrus*, *Theaetetus* and all acknowledged "late" dialogues have higher rates. One feature of the *Alcibiades I* is the occurrence of εἰκός γε five times (out of a total of 38 in the corpus), as many as in any dialogue. The rate is 0.044 per hundred words, barely rivaled by even the most epistemologically relevant dialogues of the corpus (*Crat.* [0.026], *Hp. Mi.* [0.022], *Phil.* [0.021], *Tht.* [0.017] being the next highest). However, the brief and spurious *De Virtute* has three examples and the surprising rate of 0.230 in spite of its close relation to part of the *Meno* (which has only one example in all).

282 οὐκ εἰκός at 112d10: see *in Alc.* 98.14–16 and 101.1–2.

283 But note that in the former case the word is used to express such grave doubt about an idea that Socrates will embark on the refutation of it.

284 See 104c7, 105c7, 110d5, 118c1, 123c6, 124d2, 127a1, 130b10, 130d5, 133d1; the rate of 0.088 per hundred words is mid-range.

comment on the reserve implied by it at *in Grg.* 11.5 and *in Phd.* 6.14.2; on its ironical use at *in Grg.* 18.15; on a time-limited use at *in Grg.* 39.8 and *in Phd.* 1.8.5–6; and on its non-demonstrative (mythical) context at *in Phd.* 1.16.1–2 and 1.18.1–2. Hence the commentaries on the *Gorgias* and on the *Phaedo* do show Olympiodorus trying to explain this word for "perhaps" carefully, as if to counter any suggestion it might offer support for a New Academic reading of Plato. So far, it seems, the author of the *Alcibiades I* had a greater attraction to the alleged New Academic vocabulary than that of the *Alcibiades II.*

There is clearly something wrong with the transmission of the text that follows in the *Prolegomena,* either in his source or in the manuscript tradition, for the phrase *takh' hôs oimai* (τάχ' ὡς οἶμαι) simply does not occur in Plato, however common its three components may be. Fortunately, assistance is available from Elias' commentary on Aristotle's *Categories* (110.12–16), which produces a comparable list of the expressions of hesitation some had used to suggest Plato belonged to the school that suspended judgment (the *ephektikoi*). Elias' list begins with *dokô moi* ("I seem to me": δοκῶ μοι), which seems an odd choice given these exact words are found only seven times in the corpus, mostly on the lips of interlocutors or narrators.[285] Of principal speakers, they are given to Parmenides at *Parm.* 136e, and to Socrates only at the very end of *Hippias Major* (304e8–9) and at *Republic* 583b (in both cases of what Socrates thinks he has learned). However, if we recognize it is the *meaning* that is important and allow the transposition of the two words (to μοι δοκῶ or in three instances ἐμοὶ δοκῶ) we find 34 cases spread across much of the corpus, including a highly significant example of Socrates' hesitation at *Meno* 98b3, where Socrates says he does not seem to himself to be guessing that right opinion and knowledge are different.[286] Any equivocation over basic epistemological theses was indeed likely to have been noticed by the New Academy. Another case of μοι δοκῶ is found at the close of *Hippias Major* (304e6), just before the example of δοκῶ μοι, giving the strong impression that Socrates is here judging what good he has gained from his encounters with Hippias and his own *alter ego* from his *personal impression.* So there are reasonable

---

285 Alcibiades (*Alc. I* 135c), Apollodorus (*Symp.* 172a), Aristophanes (*Symp.* 190c), Hermogenes (*Crat.* 391a).

286 There is also an "at all" to be fitted in. Depending on the way this is construed it could mean that he does not "seem at all to himself to be guessing" or that he does not "seem to himself to be guessing at all."

grounds for the New Academy to appeal to the frequency of expressions such as "I seem to me" as the indication of a refusal to claim absolute truth. However, rather than demonstrating one's inability to reach any conclusion, it is more accurate to see this first person expression as an indication that the individual is judging *by his own impression* what is so *for him*. Hence it seems to be more accurate to regard it as a Protagorean rather than a genuine Skeptic trait.[287] There are two cases of μοι δοκῶ in the *Alcibiades II* (144b3, 150d4), uttered by Alcibiades rather than Socrates, and as the following table will confirm this is enough to give the dialogue the highest rate of μοι δοκῶ (including ἐμοὶ δοκῶ) of all dialogues that use it (table 6).

Dialogue	Examples	Rate per hundred words %
Laws	2	0.002
Republic II–X	2	0.003
Philebus	1	0.005
Symposium	1	0.006
Phaedrus	1	0.006
Phaedo	2	0.009
Cratylus	2	0.010
Sophist	2	0.011
Parmenides	2	0.012
Theaetetus	3	0.013
Euthydemus	2	0.015
Euthyphro	1	0.018
Meno	2	0.019
Republic I	2	0.021
Hippias Ma.	2	0.022
Crito	1	0.023
Apology	3	0.034
Alcibiades II	2	0.045

Table 6: Rates of *moi dokô* in dialogues where found

287 In this case one should notice how Elias (*in Cat.* 109.31–110.3) actually views the final refutation of Protagoras (170a–171c) as a refutation of skeptics (*ephektikoi*) rather than of Protagoreans, reworking the argument in terms of cognitive grasping rather than in terms of wisdom. For him Protagoreans believe in the *truth* of what the individual assesses to be the case (for himself), while the suspenders of judgment follow this without claiming it to be true.

So once again the *Alcibiades II* seems to have a greater claim to be working within a Protagorean epistemological framework, taken by New Academics to be supporting their reserve, than any other dialogue.

Elias goes on to mention the two ways of saying "perhaps" also listed by the *Prolegomena*, *isôs* and *takha*, before adding a fourth expression, *hypolambanô* ("I assume": ὑπολαμβάνω). This gives a strong indication that the expression "perhaps as I think" (τάχ' ὡς οἶμαι) in the *Prolegomena*'s list should have read "'perhaps' and 'I think'" (τάχα καὶ οἶμαι);[288] for "assume" and "think" differ only marginally *in meaning*. Olympiodorus does comment on possible hesitation implied by "I think" at *in Alc.* 37.16 making its relevance clear. In actual fact the New Academics and any later skeptic allies were more likely to have appealed to the frequency of "I think" than of "I assume," since the latter (*hypolambanô*) is found only ten times in the corpus, and then usually in a rather different sense.[289] The transition in the tradition from the simple "I think" to "I assume" is natural in the light of the later debate over skepticism and dogmatism, where the key issue is what one securely grasps (*katalambanein*), while "assume" (*hypolambanein*) implies a less-than-secure grasp of whatever one would ideally know. Put simply, "I think" is just one of the verbs that would be taken to express the kind of assumption that would more accurately be rendered by "I assume."

Given what we have seen, it seems clear that Alexandrian Platonists held that the New Academy had regarded both *takha* (τάχα, usually with ἄν) and *oimai* (οἶμαι, with or without ὡς) as indications of Plato's (or where relevant Socrates') hesitancy and uncertainty. While *takh' an* as a stand-alone response occurs just five times, it occurs sixty-nine times in all uses; and while the stand-alone τάχα occurs only in the *spuria* (*Virt.* 376d6), it too is found about twenty times within sentences that contain no ἄν, but many of these examples are in the sense of

288 Less likely, in spite of greater palaeographic plausibility, is "perhaps as I think" (τάχα καὶ ὡς οἶμαι).

289 It sometimes indicates the way one interprets words (*Crat.* 401b7, *Gorg.* 477a5), usually the words of another (*Gorg.* 458e5, *Tht.* 198a9, *Theag.* 122c1, *Rep.* 349a6) or his look (*Soph.* 265d2) or some phenomenon (*Ap.* 40b6, *Phil.* 51b1); it is roughly in the required sense at *Euthd.* 278d4 (and also at *Eryxias* 406a2, excluded from the ten examples).

"soon." The *Alcibiades II* contains no examples either with or without ἄν, and the *Alcibiades I* offers only two (129a–b).

The full expression *hôs oimai* (ὡς οἶμαι "as I think"), if that had been intended by the *Prolegomena*, occurs before a stop only at *Philebus* 25b7, and just eleven times elsewhere. However, if we examine the simple *oimai* we find it occurs with considerable regularity in the corpus, and thus constitutes a common Platonic expression of hesitation or mild uncertainty; it is particularly frequent in the two *Alcibiades* dialogues, and most frequent of all in the *Second*, as may be seen from table 7:

Dialogue	Words	οἶμαι	Rate οἶμαι %
Erastae	2,424	0	0.000
Tim.-Criti.	29,144	1	0.003
Epinomis	6,389	1	0.016
Minos	3,078	1	0.032
Laws	106,298	44	0.041
Epistles	17,213	8	0.046
Parmenides	16,434	9	0.055
Menexenus	4,908	3	0.061
Sophist	17,414	14	0.080
Crito	4,329	4	0.092
Symposium	17,530	17	0.097
Protagoras	18,077	18	0.100
Meno	10,396	11	0.106
Phaedrus	17,221	19	0.110
Hippias Ma.	8,911	10	0.112
Euthydemus	13,030	15	0.115
Charmides	8,410	10	0.119
Statesman	18,592	23	0.124
Phaedo	22,633	28	0.124
Cratylus	19,201	25	0.130
Hippias Mi.	4,505	6	0.133
Theaetetus	23,803	32	0.134
Theages	3,650	5	0.137
Ion	4,091	6	0.147

Apology	8,854	13	0.147
Lysis	7,319	11	0.150
Philebus	19,054	30	0.157
Laches	8,021	13	0.162
Hipparchus	2,426	4	0.165
Gorgias	27,824	50	0.180
Republic II–X	79,907	145	0.181
Clitophon	1,575	3	0.190
Euthyphro	5,464	12	0.220
Alcibiades I	11,317	26	0.230
Republic I	9,451	33	0.349
Alcibiades II	4,422	21	0.475

Table 7: Rates of *oimai*—lowest to highest

The *Alcibiades II* offers a much higher rate of this non-technical expression of personal belief than any other dialogue.[290] Though the *Alcibiades I* is third on the list, the rate is less striking, and not quite half that of its shorter cousin. The *Hipparchus* and *Theages* have moderately high rates, but the figure for the first book of the *Republic* (and indeed for the whole *Republic*) is still so high that one must not use high figures directly as an argument against authenticity. Rather, we are investigating the possibility that the author of the *Alcibiades II* believed writing in Platonic style involved imitating Platonic ways of conveying the speaker's uncertainty.

The signs are that he did so with respect to both "I think" and "I seem to me," but at first sight he did not have the same view of all expressions that we have discussed, since the dialogue is not rich in either of the ways of suggesting "perhaps" that are recorded in the *Prolegomena* and in Elias: ἴσως or τάχα. However, another way of capturing this uncertainty is to use the verb κινδυνεύειν, usually in the third person singular of the present tense. This occurs five times (139c1, 139d5, 142e1, 144d4, 150a6), enough to give this dialogue the highest rate per hundred words for any work in the corpus. In several

290 For all inflections of the verb the *Alcibiades II* displays a rate of 0.91 percent, rivalled only by the *Hipparchus* at 0.80 percent. The average would appear to be about 0.38 percent (using methods outlined below, p. 191).

dialogues it is not found at all, and others have fewer than one case for every 3,000 words. That leaves the following rates per hundred words:

Dialogue	Rate *kinduneuei* %
Apology	0.034
Alcibiades I	0.035
Cratylus	0.036
Euthyphro	0.037
Statesman	0.038
Sophist	0.040
Parmenides	0.049
Republic I	0.053
Theages	0.055
Lysis	0.082
Alcibiades II	0.113

Table 8: Percentage rates of *kinduneuei*

So while we have examined, beginning in Chapter 2, (i) language suggesting the relevance of a *personal perspective*, we have now gone on to consider (ii) language suggesting what is likely, (iii) three words suggesting what might "perhaps" be the case, and (iv) the verb "I think." Nine principal tests were carried out, all of them suggesting a degree of "New Academic" flavor. The top ten performers in each case are listed in table 9:

Test	I	II	III	IV	V
Place	*eikos*	*isôs*	*takha*	*kinduneuei*	*oimai*
10th	*Ion*	*Laches*	*Charmides*	*Alcibiades I*	***Philebus***
9th	*Menexenus*	*Clitophon*	*Phaedrus*	*Cratylus*	*Laches*
8th	*Clitophon*	***Philebus***	*Erastae*	*Euthyphro*	*Hipparchus*
7th	*Republic* I	*Gorgias*	***Statesman***	***Statesman***	*Gorgias*
6th	*Republic* II–X	*Minos*	*Hippias Ma.*	***Sophist***	*Republic* II–X
5th	***Tim.-Criti.***	*Euthyphro*	*Apology*	*Parmenides*	*Clitophon*
4th	*Minos*	*Meno*	***Philebus***	*Republic* I	*Euthyphro*
3rd	***Laws***	*Charmides*	***Sophist***	*Theages*	*Alcibiades I*
2nd	***Epinomis***	*Cratylus*	*Clitophon*	*Lysis*	*Republic* I
1st	***Epistles***	*Apology*	*Minos*	*Alcibiades II*	*Alcibiades II*

Test	VI	VII	VIII	IX
Place	*soi/dokei*	*emoi dokei*	*moi/dokei*	*egôge*
10th	*Protagoras*	*Laches*	*Phaedo*	*Republic* I
9th	*Ion*	*Phaedo*	*Republic* I	*Laches*
8th	*Hippias Ma.*	*Lysis*	*Hippias Mi.*	*Gorgias*
7th	*Euthyphro*	*Euthyphro*	*Menexenus*	*Charmides*
6th	*Minos*	*Meno*	*Lysis*	*Alcibiades I*
5th	*Cratylus*	*Euthydemus*	*Ion*	*Euthyphro*
4th	*Gorgias*	***Epistles***	*Laches*	*Alcibiades II*
3rd	*Meno*	*Cratylus*	*Cratylus*	*Theages*
2nd	*Erastae*	*Erastae*	*Meno*	*Meno*
1st	*Alcibiades II*	*Alcibiades II*	*Alcibiades II*	*Hipparchus*

Table 9: Top rates on each of nine tests—late dialogues in **bold**

If one allocated 1 point for any tenth place, 2 for any ninth, and so on up to 10 for a first place, one might be able to offer a crude working criterion for conformity with the "New Academy Plato." The top results (ten points and above) would be as follows:

Dialogue	Points
Alcibiades II	57
Meno	38
Cratylus	33
**Euthyphro*	30
Republic I	23
Erastae	21
Clitophon	20
**Lysis*	17
Minos	17
Epistles	17
Theages	16

Table 10: Dialogues scoring well on nine "New Academic" criteria —doubtful works in **bold**

*dialogues held to be arguing opposite theses

However, in view of the strong emphasis on acknowledged late dialogues[291] for the first test (*eikos*), which appears to be aberrant, there

291 The situation regarding the *Clitophon* is unclear, since while it carefully avoids hiatus it is principally concerned with a Socratic approach to philosophy, being in some way

are doubts as to whether its use is warranted. In the case of either of the *Alcibiades* dialogues, which clearly aspire to belong to what might be broadly termed the "Socratic" tradition, it is obvious they would not deliberately set out to imitate those dialogues in which Socrates played a minor role or no role at all. One of the principal questions in this chapter is whether the *Alcibiades II* sets out to imitate the language of uncertainty that New Academics ultimately found in Plato, and since we may take it for granted that it was particularly concerned to follow Plato *as he emerges in dialogues of a Socratic type*, what counts is the language of uncertainty in such dialogues as that. It is preferable, then, to use only tests II–IX giving the following order:

Dialogue	Points
Alcibiades II	57
Meno	38
Cratylus	33
**Euthyphro*	30
Erastae	21
Republic I	19
Clitophon	17
**Lysis*	17
Apology	16
Theages	16
Minos	15
Alcibiades I	14
Gorgias	14
Sophist	13
**Charmides*	12
Laches	12
Philebus	11
Hipparchus	10

Table 11: Top dialogues on eight "New Academic" criteria
—doubtful dialogues in **bold**
*dialogue held to be arguing opposite theses

related to *Republic* I; in any case its authenticity is under challenge, so that it may not conform with expected Platonic patterns. While it does not avoid hiatus in the same way, the *Minos* too may be both "late" and in some sense "Socratic."

Eleven of these eighteen dialogues are widely agreed to be genuine, and most of these are generally considered to be fairly early. The exceptions, *Sophist* and *Philebus*, are not high on the list, and the character "Socrates" plays a minor role in the former, which would have been important for its depiction of the role of *elenchus* (230b–e), and returns in the leading role in the latter. However, since the *Alcibiades II* did not uniformly display high rates in the eight tests, this list may only be used as an *approximate* reflection of linguistic proximity to our target dialogue. It gives only a general idea of which dialogues may have inspired one facet of the New Academic picture of Plato. It does not include the *Theaetetus*, for instance, which clearly inspired other aspects of that picture, both with regard to Socrates' profession of ignorance and with regard to the failure to arrive at a satisfactory explanation of knowledge.

By including *Euthyphro*, *Lysis*, and *Charmides* it does contain the three examples given in the *Prolegomena* of works employing *argumentum in utramque partem*, though by omitting *Parmenides*, *Phaedrus*, and *Theaetetus* it fails to include every dialogue that antiquity believed to have done so. But surely it would not have escaped proponents of counter-balancing arguments that the *Meno* had argued first for and then against the teachability of virtue (87c–89c, 89c–96d) without any clear resolution; that the *Cratylus* made an elaborate case for a Heraclitean world-view accurately reflected in our names for things, and then went on to cast doubt upon any such name's ability to offer enduring insights into how things are (439b–c); that *Republic* I argues tenaciously against Thrasymachus that justice is the better and wiser course, but then *Republic* II (up to 366d, once part of the same book)[292] has Glaucon and Adeimantus argue the opposite thesis powerfully, even though neither of them do so out of personal conviction; and that *Laches* (194c–199e) seems to argue both for and against the idea that courage can be correctly explained as a kind of knowledge. It seems most of the dialogues that come close to the *Alcibiades II* on these linguistic tests could plausibly be regarded as indulging in the propounding of opposite theses, and as sanctioning New Academic practice to that extent. Hence there is an argument that the list given above includes most of the genuine dialogues that the author of the *Alcibiades II* has been most influenced by.

---

292 On the six-book *Republic* see Tarrant 2012.

Vocabulary Reminiscent of Arcesilaus and of Skepticism

The *Protagoras* (348d1) cites a Homeric line, *Iliad* 10.224, for the justification of a cooperative inquiry in which Protagoras will partner him:

> *sun te du' erkhomenô kai te pro ho tou enoêsen.*
> σύν τε δύ' ἐρχομένω καί τε πρὸ ὃ τοῦ ἐνόησεν.

The *Symposium* (174d2) quotes the same first four words, and then, after a parenthetic "he said," seems to misquote humorously the words πρὸ ὃ τοῦ:

> *sun te du' erkhomenô . . . pro hodou . . .*
> σύν τε δύ' ἐρχομένω . . . πρὸ ὁδοῦ . . .

In this case we are no longer talking of a joint inquiry, but of a joint journey (as had been the case in Homer). The *Alcibiades II* (140a1–2) again uses the line to justify cooperative inquiry, but in a situation where it is made quite clear they will not be equal partners, but that Socrates will take the lead and Alcibiades will learn by paying attention to him. In this case only the first three words are quoted without change, but the participle is replaced by one from a different middle verb, again in the nominative dual:

> *sun te duo skeptomenô . . .* (σύν τε δύο σκεπτομένω)

There is no doubt the reader had good reason to notice this substituted participle. Though superficially it seems the verb scans the same as the one it ousted, its two initial consonants mean that the previous syllable is not only not elided, but also lengthened. The effect is somewhat jarring, disappointing any expectations of dactylic rhythm. It is also an unexpected form in the Platonic corpus, since all present and imperfect tenses of this verb are ordinarily avoided,[293] because its active companion verb *skopein* is preferred. However, the Homeric middle participle *erkhomenô* naturally demands the substitution of

293 The exception is *Laches* 185b11, where modern editors follow Ast in deleting it, along with the preceding καί.

another middle participle, and that present middle participle is also without parallel in the Platonic corpus except in the cited passages of *Protagoras* and *Symposium*.[294] Hence, besides the substitution itself, both the unusual form and the jarring rhythm will ensure that original readers took notice.

While one may quickly dismiss the idea that the substituted term *skeptomenô* was meant to suggest the author was in any recognizable sense a "skeptic," one cannot so lightly dismiss the possibility that it was somehow being used to suggest a process that might ultimately transform the verb into what we know as its "skeptic" sense. There are also cases of the verbal form *skepteon* (σκεπτέον) at 140d7 and of the imperative *skopei* (σκόπει) at 144d7;[295] but more remarkable is the repeated use of the verb's *epi-* compound (ἐπισκεψώμεθα 138d4, 143e8; ἐπισκοπεῖν 144d1; and ἐπεσκεμμένοι 148c1). This constitutes 0.9 cases of these two closely related compound verbs per 1,000 words, a rate that exceeds that of any other dialogue,[296] and the dominant meaning seems to be "examine *further*," as can be seen from 144d1, where it is coupled with ἔτι ("further") and τὸ μετὰ τοῦτο ("what comes after"). Another case with ἔτι is 143e8, where reinforcement comes from καὶ τόδε ("the following point too").[297] The case at 138d4 talks about examining a further matter after the last one has been agreed, while 148c1 refers to the extra consideration that the Spartans might give to an issue over and above the authority of a poet. While nothing suggests the author is a hardened skeptic, this dialogue might justifiably be seen as one that keeps finding the need to *go on examining an issue from a new perspective*. If its author did so regularly, then he would have been liable to the mocking suggestion that he was "always examining," a suggestion he might in due course

294 Plato prefers ἰών to ἐρχόμενος. At *Laws* 654e10 the indirect tradition has the correct ἐχομένης.

295 One should also mention the occurrence of the noun σκέψις at 149c7, where it is closely coupled with φυλακή ("caution"), so that its sense is that of a worrying kind of investigation.

296 Closest are *Charmides* (0.83), *Cratylus* (0.73) and *Theaetetus* (0.67). In dialogues usually thought spurious the verb is found in the *Hipparchus* (230d10) and *Eryxias* 400c7.

297 In the rest of the corpus there are examples with ἔτι at *Tht.* 184b4, *Phlb.* 33b11, *Euthd.* 282a1 (also with τὸ λοιπὸν), *Hp. Mi.* 367e8 (with τὸν τρίτον), *Rep.* 509a10, and *Laws* 696c12; also in Aristotle: *Top.* 106b29, 145b21; *Phys.* 260b15; *Met.* 1074a29–30; *EN* 1152b4; and *Pol.* 1316b39-40. Note also πρὸς δὴ τοῦτο τόδε ἐπίσκεψαι (*Phd.* 87b2), and cases with μετὰ τοῦτο at *Phd.* 78b7–8 and *Rep.* 598d7.

have willingly embraced. Ancient skepticism was said to have been so called because its practitioners *always* examine[298] (D. L. 9.70) and never actually discover.

That naturally leads us on to the other terms applied in the same passage to skepticism: "inquisitive" (ζητητική) from its making inquiries (ζητεῖν) on every occasion, "suspensionist" (ἐφεκτική) from its resulting in suspension of judgment (ἐποχή), and "aporetic" (ἀπορητική) from its reducing the champions of doctrine and its own practitioners to *aporia*. Of the relevant verbs that for "searching" is not found at all in our dialogue,[299] and that for being in *aporia* three times, none of them very significant.[300]

However, the verb *epekhein* (ἐπέχειν) for suspending judgment or actions is found twice in a potentially relevant sense ("hold back"), and only another twenty-five times across the corpus,[301] often but not always in a similar sense. In the *Alcibiades II* it occurs at 142d3 and 148b2 in an almost identical context since Alcibiades is depicted as deliberately recalling Socrates' earlier words—a device by which the first monologue is linked closely with the second.[302] In either case *oligon* + the aorist participle *episkhôn* seems to mean "after waiting a little while"; people pray for something unwise,[303] they hold back for a while, and then change their tune (παλινῳδεῖν) and reverse their prayer (ἀνεύχεσθαι). The repetition underlines the importance of this sequence, but does the holding back involve anything like Arcesilaus'

298 ἀπὸ τοῦ σκέπτεσθαι ἀεί.

299 By comparison it is found thirteen times in *Tht.* and six in *Alc. I.*

300 While the verb for being perplexed is encountered at 139e9, 142d4, and 148d8, only the first applies to Alcibiades, when he is not quite sure what answer he should give; the second applies to Socrates, and introduces a suspicion that he entertains, while the third applies to the Athenian experience when they are unsure how to obtain divine assistance in their military ventures. The noun is more crucial as will shortly be seen.

301 This includes two cases in *Theages* when Socrates, at the instigation of his *daimonion*, twice manages to persuade a young friend to abandon his plans, and gets them to hold back (129b8, c3), but is finally unsuccessful.

302 See above, pp. 96, 120, 123.

303 This is the scenario envisaged by Alcibiades at 148b; earlier Socrates had indeed considered this possibility (142d1–4)—but also that of a pre-emptive offer by the god before a prayer is made (141a7), which the individual would then in almost all cases accept in spite of the dangers (142c5–d2). But the "change of tune" and "reversal of the prayer" would seem to apply particularly to the cases where an original prayer had been made.

epokhê (ἐποχή: "suspension of judgment") or merely an absence of any relevant action? If one affords strict respect to the context, it must refer to the gap between one utterance, the initial prayer, and another utterance negating that prayer. This is in fact confirmed at 142c6–7, where we find a reference to the few people who "cease praying when about to obtain something by prayer." But the initial prayer and its reversal both follow decisions about one's tactics in life, and the changing of tune is in fact the second of these decisions. The sequence is:

1. Decision to strive for X
2. Prayer for X
3. Holding back: cessation of prayer
4. Decision that X is not after all desirable
5. Reversal of prayer

The "holding back" would naturally involve ceasing to promote one's initial object of desire, without actually trying to prevent its realization. Perhaps it also involves pondering whether or not one has been saying the right thing; that would involve not just inaction but also a new cognitive state. In the cases where a pre-emptive offer has been made by the god, there is talk of people's failure to "hold off from" acceptance (142c6 and c8), with a slightly different compound of the verb "to hold" twice being employed for declining an apparent benefit: not *epekhein* but rather *apekhein*.

However, this type of "holding back" is not what the dialogue advocates. Alcibiades is being urged *not to pray for any particular thing at all*, or in other words to avoid doing anything towards the implementation of his initial preference. He must rather acknowledge his tendency to waver (147e–148b) and his own ignorance of the correct attitudes towards gods and men (150d1–2), so as to seek the removal of the metaphorical mist from his eyes (150e); he must wait (*perimenein*, 150d1) for that moment and postpone (*anaballesthai*, 151a3) his prayer. In such cases it is clear the delay is the direct consequence of doubts, and accompanies a cognitive condition—a state of perplexity (*aporia*) within Alcibiades (147e5–148a9, 150b8–c2),[304] entailing suspension of judgment about what will be good for him and what will be bad.

The skeptic holds back from making decisions of all sorts; given that he discovers nothing, he does not finally make the decisions he has postponed. At first sight there is a considerable difference. Alcibiades does seem to entertain some hope that he might eventually learn what he needs to know, and Socrates is in no hurry to disillusion him, and, rightly or wrongly, sees *himself* as the person who can educate Alcibiades after removing the mist from his eyes. Until that time comes, the young man seems obliged to suspend judgment (and action) on all matters requiring accurate knowledge of what is good and what is bad. It is just one branch of knowledge he lacks, but it is fundamental to every decision in the ethical and political arenas. The dialogue is quite explicit about the way this knowledge is essential, for without it we are all rudderless (146c–147b). The centrality of the knowledge that is needed to make any other knowledge beneficial means that anybody who lacks that knowledge has no way forward. No course of action can finally be decided unless that basic knowledge can be somehow acquired. The dialogue tells us nothing about Alcibiades' ability to discover psychological, mathematical, technical, or theological truths, for instance; it tells us much more about his inability so far to assess his own interests or those of his city. And it tells us little about Socrates' knowledge and abilities, except that he can remove the "mist" that can prove obstacles to the cognitive progress of others. He never explicitly promises to "teach" Alcibiades anything.[305] Rather, his role is that of mentor and facilitator, acting as midwife and as purifier of false doctrine.

The result of this investigation is to make the *Alcibiades II* largely *compatible with* what one might take to be the New Academic view of Plato's "Socrates" and of Platonic writing; it does not establish that the dialogue would support suspension of judgment in any sphere beyond ethics and politics (precisely the field in which Socrates operated), or for all time, but only for as long as one is ignorant of one central ethical question: the identity of good and evil. Whether the author (or authors) believed one could ever know the answer to that question must remain unclear. There are hints in the language of the dialogue

304 Both cases of the noun at 147e5 and 150b8; the verb seems less relevant.

305 In sharp contrast with the *Alcibiades I*, I can find no instance of the verb διδάσκειν in the dialogue, while the verb often used rather like its passive, μανθάνειν, occurs only at 150d1, where it functions rather as a passive of παιδεύειν, "educate."

that the author at least *inclines towards* Arcesilaus' kind of skepticism, and among these hints we may include the prominence given to the participle *skeptomenô* in an adapted quotation from Homer; the prominence of the language of *skepsis* more generally and especially that of *epi*-compounds signifying "further consideration"; and the prominence of the verb *epekhein* in a repeated theme about those who pray for something unwise and then change their minds. Whether any of this should carry any weight depends upon one's wider view of how the New Academy under Arcesilaus came into being, and our evidence on this is unfortunately thin.

Chapter Eight
Finding a Context

Introduction

This investigation has certainly tended to suggest that the *Alcibiades II* as we have it cannot have been written by Plato, regardless of whether there may have been some Platonic core from which it started. We have found elements of language that appear to be Hellenistic and many others that are not matched in Plato, some carrying more weight than others. Its idiosyncrasies discourage us from postulating the identity of its final author with that of any other work within the corpus. And even though, as we shall see, there are ways in which its vocabulary is reminiscent of two dialogues from the *spuria*, not even they provide many parallels for the more remarkable elements of language. Nor do they show a comparable level of engagement with classical Greek literature, including Homer and the tragedians. Nor do they exhibit comparable complexity of structure. No decision we reach about the authorship of this dialogue, therefore, can have much bearing on the authorship of other dialogues in the corpus. Questions of date, however, are interlinked.

Alexander III[306]

One of the most curious features of the dialogue is the way much of the material in the section on matricide and patricide seems to have more relevance to the kind of machinations that went on in the

306 The relevance of Alexander has been postulated since at least Brünnecke 1912, 179–182. Various authors since then have seen fit to give it serious consideration, among them most recently Timotin 2017, 65–66. I presume that Thesleff 2017, 213, has the same theory in mind, where he says that a "date at the time of Alexander the Great is arguable, but far from certain."

Macedonian monarchy than it does for the case of Alcibiades or any of his contemporary Athenians. When we also read the historically implausible material about how the Athenians had consulted the oracle of Ammon, we cannot help being reminded of Alexander's famous consultation of the oracle at Siwa (Arrian, *Anab.* 3.3.1–3.4.5) before continuing his campaign against the heartland of the Persian empire. The consultation is famous for having apparently confirmed Alexander's suspicion that he was related to a divinity comparable to Zeus himself, and therefore had the same status as Perseus and Heracles. Whatever Alexander had heard at the oracle (and we are not told of the exact response), he is said to have desired to find out more about his divine lineage (3.3.2), and to have received the answer he had hoped for (3.4.5). In any case, he went on to expect from his followers a form of lowering themselves (*proskunêsis*) that was normally reserved for a divinity.

Plausibly, then, this consultation resulted in what many a Greek would have regarded as a failure to distinguish "both gods and men," making the quotation of *Iliad* 5.128 at 150d9 more obviously relevant to Alexander than to Alcibiades, who was not affording himself divine status like Alexander (150b5–6) and probably never did. Again, when wisdom is identified with knowing how to behave and speak "both before gods and before humans" (150b1–3), there would seem to have been a clear implication that the two should be treated differently—something that Alcibiades understood but Alexander did not. Furthermore, the response of Ammon to the Athenians implied the real gods did not worry so much about the sumptuousness of their worship as about the appropriateness of the prayers that accompanied it (149b2–c6).

In this context we should consider the details of one rather important prayer uttered by Alexander before the battle of Gaugamela (hence after visiting Siwa), and reported by Plutarch (*Alex.* 33) on the authority of the contemporary source Callisthenes (fr. 36), the great-nephew of Aristotle who had accompanied Alexander, only to be killed by him in 327 BCE. The Macedonian monarch is about to enter battle with the Persian forces when he raises his right hand and calls upon the gods to defend and give cheer to "the Greeks,"[307] *if he really had been born from Zeus*. An eagle is then seen overhead guiding them straight into the

307 Here including the Macedonians.

enemy forces. The prayer is specific, is conditional upon Alexander's partially divine origins, and is answered by the appearance of the eagle—giving plausible confirmation of divine lineage, and in so doing giving an enormous boost to the morale of Alexander's forces who are about to encounter a huge force and a range of less familiar weapons of war. So this, too, confirms the relevance of questions concerning the recognition of god and man to the career of Alexander.

Alexander would not for long enjoy the empire he was about to conquer. It was certainly open to our author to regard this prayer as among those that had been answered, but had ultimately worked *against* the interest of the young petitioner. So Alexander may also be behind Socrates' cautionary remarks to Alcibiades at 141c about his unwillingness to obtain empire if it meant the premature loss of his life. It is not that the remark makes no sense if we do not think of Alexander, but rather that, in the years after his death, it would have been difficult not to think of him.

In fact the combined effect of the material to which this section has drawn attention is that, for many years after news of Alexander's death had reached Athens, readers would inevitably have been reminded of his career. Several of these details, therefore, are more readily intelligible if the author had been writing after the 320s. The point of introducing small details throughout the dialogue that might cause the reader to think of recent events involving Macedonian monarchs and the career of Alexander is that it encourages regular comparison between Alcibiades and Alexander, and hence between the different philosophic education they had enjoyed: the former under Socrates, the latter under Aristotle. In this way it contributes to the attack on Aristotelian theory.

The Peripatetics

It is hard to resist the notion that the revisionist concept of "high-and-mightiness" (*megalopsukhia*), more often translated "magnanimity" but here more like "megalomania," is not a conscious decision to challenge the status of one of Aristotle's most prominent and exalted moral virtues, discussed in several Aristotelian works, most prominently the *Eudemian* and *Nicomachean Ethics*.[308] This was perhaps the Aristotelian virtue most easily associated with Alexander the Great, and Plutarch employs the term twice in his *Life of Alexander* (30.11 and 42.10), and

308 See above, pp. 72–73n127, cf. p. 136.

the adjective describing his attitude (*phronêma*) at 4.8. While the very nature of the *Lives* would suggest that many of those he wrote of might have been described in such terms, he there used the terminology only thirty times in all,[309] including just once in the *Life of Pericles* (36.9), and never in the *Life of Alcibiades*. In the treatise *On the Fortune or Virtue of Alexander the Great* it occurs three times (327e, 328a, and 343b), and indeed in the last of these passages Alexander is said to have been "more magnanimous than Achilles." This is enough to show that Alexander was an excellent example of somebody thought to have this quality.

Another way in which the *Alcibiades II* might be seen to differ from the teachings of the Peripatetics is in the dialogue's apparent refusal to see knowledge as an end to be pursued in its own right. It is obvious to any reader of the opening of Aristotle's *Metaphysics* (980a21–28) that the pursuit of knowledge was considered natural to humankind in the same way as the pursuit of sight and visual experiences; we do not have to act upon any of the information gained by sensation or other cognition in order to value them extremely highly. The result, of course, is that the Peripatetics sought to advance knowledge in a huge range of areas, without necessarily having any other end in view. The scientific life led them into a range of studies, most of them having no immediate benefit for the well-being of the community, but all offering quiet satisfaction to the researcher. By contrast it seems (from the little information we have) that the Academy moved away from scientific studies and concentrated almost exclusively on ethics under Polemo, who had replaced Xenocrates as scholarch in 414/3 BCE, as under his successor Crates. One can readily understand such an attitude if its leader had at that time believed, with the author of *Alc. II* 146d7–e3, that the *only thing* that would make the majority of knowledge offer more benefit than harm to its possessor was a knowledge of what was good, whether for the individual or the community. Moral knowledge was the one thing that really mattered. Philosophy did not require one to be a polymath, but for all one's activities to be grounded in the knowledge of what is best.

Accordingly, it should come as no surprise that not only a small portion of this dialogue (147a–b), but also most of the *Erastae*

309 The *Life of Dion* has four examples, the most of any of the lives.

(133c–139a), should seem to attack those who confuse philosophy with the breadth of one's learning (*polumathia*) or the breadth of one's skills (*polutekhnia*).[310] Both likewise see a kind of moral knowledge as supreme, but the *Erastae* places more emphasis on its application in the political sphere. The *Erastae* is also more explicit in connecting that knowledge with our knowledge of ourselves as human beings (138a), making self-knowledge depend particularly on recognition of good and bad human beings. I do not suggest it is likely our dialogue has the same authorship as the *Erastae*, but it seems to me not unlikely that they date from roughly the same period.

After the deaths of Aristotle and Alexander Theophrastus became the scholarch of the Peripatetic school. Some indication of the range of his writings can be gleaned from the catalogue of his works in Diogenes Laertius (5.42–50), and we are told of a disparaging quip that the Academic Crantor made about his *Theseis* (D. L. 4.27). The story is also told of Crantor's having attracted the young Arcesilaus away from the Peripatetics, a loss that Theophrastus had apparently resented (D. L. 4.29–30). As for Polemo, however, who was the Academic scholarch in the final years of the fourth century, there is little evidence he was inclined to indulge in the same kind of inter-school rivalry.

Multivariate Analysis of Relevant Vocabulary

Multivariate analysis enables one to capture the same overall effect as one would by conducting multiple comparisons of particular words. Here each word becomes an independent variable, and makes its own contribution to the final result. It is not the case that all count to the same extent, but either (1) the potential to discriminate is proportionate to how common the word is, or (2) each word has equal potential to discriminate, and the weighting that it is given depends upon factors determined by the program. I use the latter methods here, employing principal component analyses and cluster analyses *with standardized data*.

Previous work with Terry Roberts has shown by multivariate analysis that a degree of similarity exists between the working vocabularies of the *Alcibiades I*, *Alcibiades II*, *Hipparchus*, and an early

310 *Erastae* does not employ the word *polutekhnia*, but *tekhnai* become the primary focus at 135b–136a, cf. 139a5.

portion of the *Theages*.[311] There was also a suggestion that the *Minos* fell into the same general group. Few conclusions were drawn at that stage, as the findings applied particularly to the more *dialogic* passages of these dialogues, and the *Erastae* did not appear to follow this pattern. In subsequent work I went on to suggest that the tetralogical order sometimes captures linguistic similarities between dialogues, and specifically in respect of tetralogies four and seven—except that the *Theages* and *Erastae* somehow came to be switched, something that may be due to their having sometimes been known by the same subtitle, *On Philosophy*.[312] Subsequently I have paid more attention to the differences in style between the primarily dialogical and more monological passages of these dialogues, and discovered that the differences here tend to be considerably greater than in genuine Platonic dialogues where such distinctions in presentation can be made (e.g. *Crito*, *Ion*). The monological passages on the whole seem far closer to what one expects of a Platonic style, leading me to suspect they may constitute a surviving Platonic core.[313]

One of the problems of the earlier work is that some of it was based primarily on words that were common across the relevant group of dialogues (*Alcibiades I*, *Alcibiades II*, *Hipparchus*, and *Theages*), and the much greater length of the *Alcibiades I* caused it to dominate in the choice of those words. At this point, with the focus being the *Alcibiades II*, it is preferable to allow the target dialogue to have a greater say in which words are analyzed. Accordingly I determined its two hundred most common words, and opted to include only those that were used a number of times in the *Alcibiades II* (136), going on to exclude all those words I believe are as much indicative of the subject matter as of the style of the work: primarily nouns, verbs, and adjectives. While I might otherwise have excluded first and second person personal pronouns

311 Tarrant and Roberts 2012.

312 See Tarrant 2013, including, on the question of a switch, pp. 21–22. The *Theages'* correct subtitle is probably *On Wisdom* (περὶ σοφίας rather than περὶ φιλοσοφίας), as manuscript F suggests at D. L. 3.59 agreeing with Plato T.

313 See Tarrant 2018. The idea is that these were passages intended to be the highlight of Plato's sympotic contributions, to which he would have added framing material of a dialogical type, whether by reporting a conversation or by interrogating one of those present. Something of the nature of these framing conversations may have been preserved orally.

and verbs such as "to seem" and "to appear" (since they can occur most frequently in discussions of certain metaphysical distinctions), they are included here because they seem more relevant to style, and in some cases to be something of a mannerism of the author. The result is a list of eighty-four words selected on the basis that they are common (though not necessarily more common than elsewhere) in the *Alcibiades II*, and unlikely to allow the subject matter of different works to skew the analysis.[314]

I wanted to determine how close the *Alcibiades II* would prove to be not only to dialogues within the corpus, but also to some spurious ones. I had available for these tests *Eryxias*, *Sisyphus*, *On Virtue*, *Axiochus*, and *Halcyon* (also part of the Lucianic Corpus, but perhaps attributable to one Leon). For the purpose of displaying results, any dialogues longer than 14,999 words are divided into blocks of 7,500 with a final block of between 7,500 and 14,999 words. Alongside the listed *spuria*, I included early Plato, most of what may be thought of as "middle Plato" (though only two books of *Republic*, and only the 2,000-word narrative introduction of *Symposium*), together with a selection of late (that is, hiatus-avoiding) Plato (*Laws* I, *Sophist*, *Philebus*, and the first 7,500 words of *Timaeus*).

Cluster analysis[315] placed works in four clusters as follows:

Cluster 1: this centered on both blocks of *Phaedrus*, *Menexenus*, and *Republic* VIII, to which *Epinomis* and *Timaeus* were closest, then *Clitophon* and *Axiochus*, and finally *Halcyon* (quite loosely attached).

Cluster 4: this was most closely related to cluster 1 and contained all remaining late dialogues (*Sophist*, *Philebus*, *Laws* I).

Cluster 3: *Alcibiades II*, most closely associated with the spurious *Eryxias*, a dialogue probably not composed before the final quarter

---

314 The list involves the following words and their inflections (if any): ὁ, καὶ, εἶναι, δὲ, οὗτος, οὐ (with or without -κ or -χ), ἂν, δοκεῖν, αὐτὸς, τις, σὺ, μὲν, ἢ, γε, γὰρ, ἀλλὰ, τε, οὖν, ὃς, οἴεσθαι, ἐγὼ, πολὺς, ἄλλος, εἰ, πρὸς, εἰδέναι, ὡς, ἐκεῖνος, ἔχειν, πᾶς, οὐδὲ, γίγνεσθαι, τυγχάνειν, τίς, οὕτως, μὴ, πράττειν, οὐκοῦν, ἔγωγε, ἡμεῖς, ἕτερος, ἐν, ἆρα, ποτὲ, ἑαυτὸν, ὅστις, μάλα, δὴ, ὥσπερ, τοιοῦτος, μέντοι, ἔτι, διὰ, δεῖν (1), μέλλειν, ὥστε, οὐδεὶς, ὅτι, κατὰ, πῶς, εἷς, δήπου, ἄρα, ὅσπερ, ὅσος, ἕκαστος, δῆτα, περὶ, οὔτε, νῦν, ἐὰν, πάνυ, ὁστισοῦν, ἄνευ, ὑπὸ, τοίνυν, παρὰ, ὁπότε, ναὶ, μήτε, κινδυνεύειν, φαίνειν, εἴτε, ἀπὸ.

315 Ward's method, standardized data, 4 clusters, 84 words as variables.

of the fourth century,[316] and then with *Sisyphus*. Cluster 3 was less remotely associated with cluster 2 than with clusters 1 and 4.

Cluster 2: this contained everything else. Specifically, all that would normally be thought of as "early" and much "middle" Plato. Doubtful or spurious works included were *Alcibiades I*, *Hipparchus*, *Erastae*, *Theages*, *Minos*, and *De Virtute*. It is noticeable that the most significant sub-cluster consists of all *Cratylus*, all *Phaedo*, and all *Theaetetus*, with *Republic* IV and the first 7,500 words of *Protagoras*,[317] nine blocks in all with an overall "middle-period" appearance, while the next most significant sub-cluster grouped the *Ion* and *Hippias Minor* with *De Virtute*, *Hipparchus*, and *Erastae*.

None of these findings should be used directly to date works by Plato himself, nor even to settle questions of authenticity. They are a test of one stylistic feature, namely recurrent vocabulary. Nor should they be used alone. Principal component analysis was also used to compare works, and it is needed to give an idea of how far any individual that might have been placed in one cluster might have been from dialogues that had been placed in others. While one can ask for several "principal components," standard paper graphs are only able easily to map two of these, generally the first and second, which are statistically the first and second most significant of the "components," and thus the two that one ought to pay most attention to.

The principal component analysis[318] based on the same variables placed all the undisputed "late" Plato and *Epinomis* well into the top right sector, indicating positive scores on both principal components. Scores ranged from +3.03 to +10.13 on the first component, and between +1.85 and +6.61 on the second component. Close to *Epinomis* and *Laws* I came the *Halcyon* (+7.06, +0.93), falling outside the late range on the second component. The only other works placed in the positive range on both components were *Theaetetus* (words 7,501–15,000) and *Republic* IV, but their scores were lower than those

316 See Hutchinson in Cooper 1997, 1718–1719.

317 The remainder was placed in the company of *Euthydemus*, *Republic* I, and material from *Gorgias*. Note that this first section contains Protagoras' great rhesis, which might be expected to show distinct stylistic traits.

318 For further details of this analysis, and specifically the influence that the different words (variables) had on the calculation of each principal component, see Appendix I.

of the "late" dialogues on both components.[319] In the lower right sector (positive range on component 1, negative on component 2) came both blocks of *Phaedrus*, *Republic* VIII, *Protagoras* 1, *Phaedo* part 2, *Clitophon*, *Menexenus*, and *Axiochus*—this last at both extremes (+6.52, –4.58). Only just over the line on component 1 came *Symposium* introduction (+0.04, –4.54), with *Protagoras* 1, *Apology*, and *Crito* close by in the lower left. Most undisputed works of Plato that are generally agreed to be early are placed in that sector, and in fact all such works fall between –4.87 and +0.40 on component 1, and between –3.95 and +0.94 on component 2.[320] Many works of doubtful authenticity (*Hipparchus*, *Erastae*, *Alcibiades I*, *Theages*, *Minos*, and the spurious *De Virtute*) also fall within these parameters. There is a tendency for works involving a significant amount of continuous discourse, such as *Menexenus*, *Apology*, and perhaps the *Clitophon* to register a somewhat lower score on component 2 than might otherwise be expected.

The sector that interests us most here is the upper left (negative on component 1 and positive on component 2). In the top left corner is the spurious *Sisyphus* (–10.79, +6.74), and nearest to it is *Alcibiades II* (–5.54, +3.10). Closest to *Alcibiades II* is the spurious *Eryxias* (–3.04, +3.67). The only other text in this sector with a higher score on component 2 are the final 7,523 words of *Theaetetus* (–1.25, +4.50), but all three blocks of *Theaetetus* were fairly close to the zero line on component 1 and within the positive range on component 2 (average = –0.22, +2.19). It is perhaps no surprise that this final block was closest to the late *Sophist*. Apart from the *Eryxias* the nearest dialogues to the *Alcibiades II* were *Alcibiades I* (–4.66, –0.09), *Hipparchus* (–4.47, +0.20), and *Meno* (–4.87, +0.50).

319 0.92 and 1.52 for *Tht*.2, 1.08 and 0.27 for *Rep*. IV.

320 We do not count *Menexenus* as a work *agreed* to be early, and its nature is such that it is not expected that stylistics would fix its date.

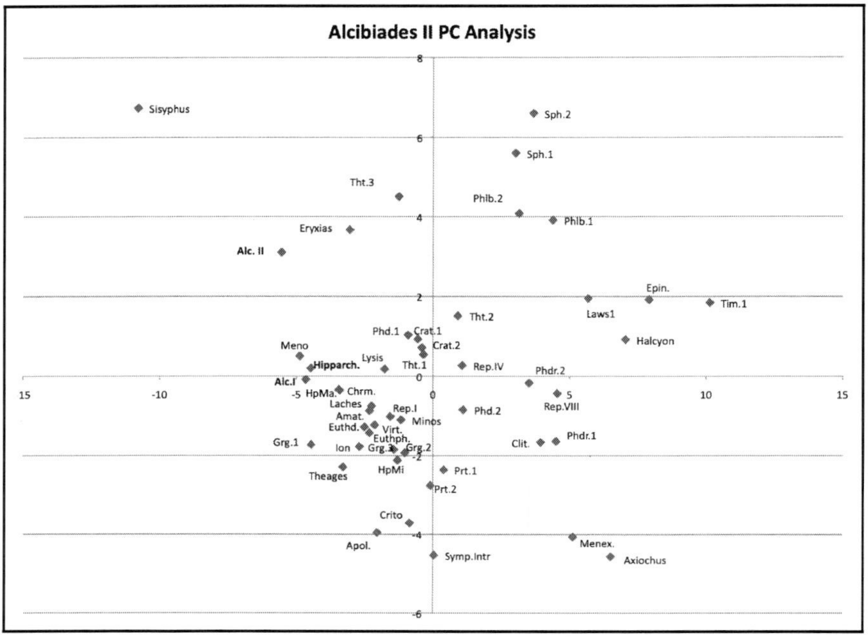

Figure 1: Principal component (PC) analysis

Below is a summary of the values for the *Alcibiades II* and the eight texts that came closest to it on each of three factors:

Dialogue	Score PC 1	Dialogue	Score PC 2	Dialogue	Score PC 3
Alcibiades II	–5.54	*Alcibiades II*	3.10	*Alcibiades II*	–7.20
Meno	–4.87	*Eryxias*	3.67	*Eryxias*	–5.50
Alcibiades I	–4.66	*Philebus* (1)	3.91	*Crito*	–3.32
Hipparchus	–4.47	*Philebus* (2)	4.08	*Apology*	–3.02
Gorgias (1)	–4.45	*Laws I*	1.95	*Epinomis*	–2.53
Hippias Ma.	–3.43	*Epinomis*	1.92	*Clitophon*	–2.41
Charmides	–3.40	*Timaeus* (1)	1.85	*Laws I*	–1.82
Theages	–3.28	*Theaetetus* (3)	4.50	*Menexenus*	–1.79
Eryxias	–3.04	*Theaetetus* (2)	1.52	*Phaedrus* (1)	–1.73

Table 12: Dialogues closest to *Alcibiades II* on each principal component (PC)

The *Eryxias* finds itself among the closest eight texts on all three components, and the closest of all in two out of three cases. While

Epinomis and *Laws* I are in the closest eight on two components, they are not exceptionally close. That apart, we have three very different lists, with the undisputed works in the first list being supposedly early, those in the second list being predominantly "late," and those in the final list being seemingly an eclectic mix. The data discourage us from identifying the author of our dialogue with that of any other work except *Eryxias*, and in particular the *Alcibiades II* finds itself at the opposite end of the spectrum from the following dialogues:

Dialogue	PC 1	Dialogue	PC 2	Dialogue	PC 3
Alcibiades II	–5.54	*Alcibiades II*	3.10	*Alcibiades II*	–7.20
Menexenus	5.12	*Protagoras* (2)	–2.75	*Sophist* (2)	2.36
Laws I	5.68	*Crito*	–3.70	*Sophist* (1)	3.06
Axiochus	6.52	*Apology*	–3.95	*Axiochus*	3.36
Halcyon	7.06	*Menexenus*	–4.07	*Hippias Mi.*	3.43
Epinomis	7.92	*Symp. Intr.*	–4.54	*Hipparchus*	4.88
Timaeus (1)	10.13	*Axiochus*	–4.58	*Minos*	5.15

Table 13: Dialogues furthest from *Alcibiades II* on each principal component (PC)

The spurious *Axiochus* features in all three lists, and of doubtful and spurious dialogues *Halcyon*, *Epinomis*, *Hipparchus*, and *Minos* all feature in one. That *Laws* I, *Timaeus*, and *Sophist* (both blocks) feature in the lists for PC1 or PC3 strongly suggests that the *Alcibiades II* could not be genuine late Plato, while *Apology*, *Crito*, *Hippias Minor*, *Protagoras*, and *Symposium* combine to suggest that it could not be early or early-middle Plato.

Altogether the results suggest that, of genuine dialogues, the greatest influences on the vocabulary of *Alcibiades II* may have come from the dialogues that looked closest to it in figure 1. These were the following (and in roughly this order): *Meno*, *Theaetetus*, *Cratylus*, *Lysis*, *Hippias Major*, and *Charmides*. All of these are placed in the negative range on component 1 and between –0.5 and +4.5 on component 2. These dialogues all show an interest in Socrates and his methods, especially aporetic methods; all are of such a type that antiquity could find contrary arguments within them; and many display a serious interest in epistemology. These are precisely the kind of dialogues we might have expected from either the New Academy, or from those who were inclining in the direction of the New Academy.

How Close are *Alcibiades II* and *Eryxias*?

The proximity of the *Alcibiades II* to the *Eryxias* on all three principal components suggests they reached their final form at around the same time even if they were not actually by the same author. If so then it appears the *Alcibiades II* was likewise written not before, and probably many years after, 337 BCE,[321] ruling out the possibility that Plato could have been wholly responsible for it. So it is worth extending the comparison between the two dialogues a little. To begin with, the three Platonic dialogues that Brisson (2014: 193) thinks especially influential on the author of the *Eryxias* are *Charmides*, *Euthydemus*, and *Meno*, two of which we have just listed as influential on the language of *Alcibiades II*. The *Eryxias* also makes reference to praying to the gods from 398c to 399a, using the simple verb six times and also προσεύχεσθαι once,[322] and there is the same unwillingness to specify any particular god, since the plural is repeatedly used (398c6, d3, e2, e5, 399a1). Relativism is present here, too, for we encounter the theme that wealth is only a good thing relative to its owner's goodness and capacity to make use of it at 395e9–396a2. An anecdote about Prodicus is introduced in which he too pursued that theme (397e). Furthermore, Prodicus, if he were now among them expressing such views, would seem to be mad (μαίνεσθαι, 399a8)[323] because of his adoption of a position on wealth that Critias had taken without damaging his good reputation. What people choose to believe, according to this passage, is *relative to individual speakers*: more dependent on their apparent personal qualities than on the strength of their arguments (399b–c). And though there is a lot more talk of what is or is not true than in the *Alcibiades II*, it can be

321 This is the accepted date of the introduction of the *gumnasiarkhos* at Athens, an office openly referred to at 399a2; the office is also referred to in the spurious *Axiochus* (367a1). It is unlikely the office could have been a novelty at the time when the dialogue was written, for in that case the anachronism would probably have seemed jarring.

322 Cf. *Alc. II* 138a1.

323 For the expression "I should be mad to . . ." (μαινοίμην ἄν . . .) in the *Eryxias* see 395e8 (Eryxias) and 403c8 (Critias). In this dialogue, madness seems to be seen simply as an extreme case of folly, at least by speakers other than "Socrates."

seen from Appendix II this does not imply that the boundary between truth and falsehood is clearly marked—quite the opposite, in fact.

Regarding this relativism, the vocabulary analysis that pointed to the similarity between the two dialogues has taken into account *some* of the language expressing an individual perspective that we have taken to be characteristic of the *Alcibiades II*. For instance, the words "I/me" (*egô/me/eme*, etc.) and "seem" (*dokein*) have been taken into account. Again, it included "I at least" (*egôge*), where a separate count has given the figure of 3.87 instances per thousand words, next highest after the *Alcibiades II* (4.30), which was itself fourth highest after *Hipparchus* (7.01), *Meno* (5.58), and *Theages* (4.66). It does not analyze separately any *combinations* of these words, so the analysis of *phrases* has a separate if not entirely independent validity. Therefore, what the analysis does not show is that *Eryxias*, like *Alcibiades II*, is particularly rich in such combinations as *emoi dokei*[324] and *emoige dokei*,[325] and also in *soi* + *dokei*,[326] though it occurs at less remarkable rates in the bare *moi* + *dokei*.[327] One could repeat a wide variety of tests of words in combination, with some expectation of illuminating results. For instance, when I tested the combination *emoi men* (regardless of what follows it), I found that its two occurrences meant it occurred at the fifth highest rate in *Eryxias* (0.37), after *Alcibiades II* yet again (7: 1.58), *Laches* (7: 0.87), *Theages* (3: 0.82), and *Hipparchus* (1: 0.41). It occurred only 36 times in the rest of the corpus.

In this context we should briefly examine another data set, comparing *Eryxias* with *Alcibiades II*, that of hiatus rates.[328] Our dialogue

---

324 Its 0.37 per thousand words is exceeded only by *Alcibiades II* (0.45) and *Erastae* (0.41). But the figures for the simple *emoi dokei* do not include two cases of *emoi men* + *dokei*, an expression that occurs in undisputed works only a handful of times at rates of <0.13 per thousand, but at 0.37 in *Eryxias*, 0.55 in *Theages*, and 0.90 in *Alcibiades II*. This led to the check on *emoi men* generally in the corpus.

325 This occurs ten times in all in exactly that form, giving the *Eryxias* a rate of 1.84 per thousand, ahead of *Alcibiades II* (1.36) and *Minos* (1.30).

326 The rate for *Eryxias* is 1.66 per thousand words, behind only *Alcibiades II* (3.17) and *Erastae* (2.06).

327 My figures suggest that *Eryxias* is only eighth on the combined figure, 0.92, well behind *Alcibiades II* (2.26) and *Meno* (1.83). The simple fact is that the author of the *Eryxias* has a slight but unusual preference for *emoi* over *moi*.

328 Hiatus occurs when a word ending in a vowel occurs before one beginning with a vowel. Tests are usually reported as the number of occurrences per Didot page. Greater accuracy is achieved by reporting the number per hundred word breaks. Figures are as collected for me some years ago, and there will inevitably be a small error rate.

does not here follow the pattern of either the accepted "late" or the "middle" dialogues on hiatus statistics, falling between the two. Its rate for hiatus where no punctuation was involved was around 12.8 percent (as a percentage of word breaks without punctuation), but where a word ending in a vowel was followed by a word beginning with one *after punctuation*, the rate of hiatus was around 31.3 percent.[329] The first figure is 2.9 percent lower than *Phaedrus*, the most hiatus-conscious of "middle" dialogues, but 6.2 percent higher for cross-punctuation hiatus. In comparison with the "late" dialogues the first figure was 2.9 percent higher than book IX of *Laws*, the book showing least concern for hiatus, and a massive 18.7 percent higher on cross-punctuation hiatus. The *Alcibiades II* was unusual, it seemed, in that its author appeared somewhat averse to hiatus that involved no punctuation, but made little attempt to avoid it where punctuation intervened. It is thus somewhat different on this test from the *Eryxias*, for which approximate figures are around 17.5 percent without punctuation and 36 percent across punctuation, the former figure being a fairly low rate for "early" or "middle" Plato, typical of the *Republic*, and roughly the same as book IX, while the latter is exceptionally high.[330] Again, the author seemed relatively indifferent to cross-punctuation hiatus. Closest of those *spuria* that were tested to the *Alcibiades II* was *Demodocus* (14.3 and 31.3 percent),[331] and overall hiatus rates count marginally *against* identifying

329 To check that the figures for *Alcibiades II* and *Eryxias* were indeed comparable, a second calculation of its rates of hiatus was made following the same procedure as was used to arrive at those carried out more recently, specifically for the purpose for which it is used here. That calculation employed a series of TLG searches, but took no account of the many verse quotations (unlikely to involve hiatus) in calculating the number of breaks between words. The main rate dropped marginally to 12.5 percent, and the cross-punctuation rate became 28.4 percent.

330 Rates of between 34 percent and 36 percent are found in *Lysis*, *Euthydemus*, *Republic* I, and the early part of *Gorgias*. Like the *Eryxias*, the first three involve a reported conversation, which may entail much parenthetic use of expressions such as "he said" and "I said," placed within punctuation, many of which both start and end with a vowel, e.g. ἔφη (40 cases in *Eryxias*, 82, 200, and 120 in *Lys.*, *Euthd.*, and *Rep.* I) and ἦν δ'ἐγώ (9 cases in *Eryxias*, 54, 68, and 63 in *Lys.*, *Euthd.*, and *Rep.* I), facilitating cross-punctuation hiatus wherever there is no tendency to avoid it—and it may be significant that no hiatus-avoiding dialogue employs the reported form. A dramatic dialogue like *Alcibiades II* usually has no use for such expressions.

331 No attempt was made to distinguish the four mini-dialogues that together constitute this work. *Demodocus II, III,* and *IV* are in reported form, and together contain 34 cases of ἔφη but none of ἦν δ'ἐγώ. Note that *Demodocus II* begins with an attack on those who would make up their mind on an issue after hearing only one side of

the author of the *Alcibiades II* with that of the *Eryxias*, but the case of Plato himself demonstrates that rates can vary considerably across an author.

Much the same applies to the tests on vocabulary. The tests we have applied do place several dialogues that have little chance of being by Plato at the extremes, most notably *Sisyphus*, but also *Axiochus* and *Alcibiades II*. But they also place genuine works at extremes, most notably *Sophist* and *Timaeus*. Given the distance between either of these and *Apology* or *Crito*, one cannot affirm that the *Alcibiades II* is so far from *Meno*, *Cratylus*, or *Theaetetus* block 1, for instance, that it must necessarily be regarded as the product of a different author or different period. What we want to claim in this section is that our analyses offer some support for the view that the *Alcibiades II* is not genuine Plato, and that there is much to connect it with the *Eryxias*, a dialogue that was not even included in the ancient corpus, and that cannot easily have been written before the last quarter of the fourth century.

Authorship

It is now time to draw the threads together, and make an informed decision based on the evidence we have considered. We begin with a reminder: even in the ancient world there were people who suspected that the author of this dialogue was Xenophon (Athenaeus 11, 506c). They had surely observed, as most scholars still do,[332] that Xenophon's thought on the subject of prayer is very close to that of the text we have been studying. But this is only of great importance if Xenophon's contribution was a distinctive one, and few would maintain that. It is natural to concentrate on the philosophy of prayer, because that seems to be the nominal subject of the dialogue, a subject closely connected with the dramatic situation. Even so, the topic is more about what we should rationally wish to receive, whether or not we formally pray for

---

a case, for which reason it contains two cases of the adverb προπετῶς. The language of προπέτεια is exceedingly rare in Plato, but an established part of the vocabulary of skepticism, being found 24 times in Sextus Empiricus, mostly in the *Pyrrhonian Hypotyposes*; cf. Philo *Ebr.* 192 in material thought to be somehow connected with *Aenesidemus*.

332 Neuhausen 2010, concentrating on the sources for the work's philosophy, is full of such material. Brisson 2014, 21, mentions Xenophon in the third line of the introduction to the dialogue, marginally ahead even of Plato. Xenophon features prominently in the conclusion of the chapter on our dialogue in Timotin 2017, 79.

it; hence it is also about the risks inherent in all our choices. That in turn raises the question of our knowledge or ignorance of what is good for us and what is bad. It is in this area that we meet the most distinctive themes of the dialogue.

The main philosophic feature we have been able to draw attention to is its inclination to consider everything relative to the individual. This is highlighted by the language of how things are for the persons concerned themselves. The emphasis is on choosing what is best for oneself, and the language of what seems to oneself occurs far more often than in most dialogues. Alcibiades is perpetually encouraged to consider the issues for himself, as if he can be an adequate judge of things as they affect him. After reflection he will then be better positioned to make some choices, even though he will not yet be properly equipped to pray for particular outcomes. We judge this to be evidence of a considerable interest within the Academy (or part thereof) in the Protagorean view of the ordinary world of our senses that is outlined at length within the *Theaetetus*. That does not exclude different attitudes towards other types of cognition, and the *Theaetetus* itself offers us two other types of wisdom or the like: Socrates' own "midwife's art" at 150b–151d and the process of assimilation to god at 176a–c, neither of them obviously involving any cognition of the usual type. So similarly the *Alcibiades II* seems to presume that Alcibiades can be taught the lessons he requires even if it is unclear how it is to come about. Comparison with the *Eryxias* gave us reasons for thinking that our dialogue may have been one of several that illustrate this distinctive attitude towards epistemology, an attitude in which knowledge as normally understood and wisdom are seen as very different.[333]

The "Protagorean" theory of the *Theaetetus* also allows for differences within the status of contrasting viewpoints, other than between their truth and falsehood, such as will justify terms like "wise" and "foolish" (166d–167d). Some opinions are better, others less so, and the wiser people are precisely those who can modify the way in which the others perceive things in such a way as to make their views better. Hence the Protagorean can offer oral or written thoughts that will be beneficial for their audiences and bring about

333 See Müller 1975, 327–329, on possible connections between various spurious dialogues and phases of the Academy, especially of the "New" Academy. That work is to be consulted in particular regarding *On Justice*, *On Virtue*, *Demodocus*, *Sisyphus*, and *Halcyon*. For *On Virtue* and *Halcyon* in particular see also Müller 2007.

reflective opinions rather than unreflective ones. He does not go about telling others that all knowledge is impossible, but holds out hopes of improving one's cognitive ability, whether by "removing the mists from one's eyes" or some other process. What he emphasizes should rather be the difficulties confronting those who want to be able to rely on their cognitive abilities and those who need to make decisions that will be critically important to their lives. Above all, one should pause for thought and take any helpful advice while always seeking to improve one's understanding.

It is easy to see how opponents of the Academy might characterize repeated injunctions to readers and pupils to pause before making any decisions about future actions and prayers as an indication that they simply put off every decision indefinitely, and thus would always be "suspensionists" (*ephektikoi*). It is also understandable that some who had originally been encouraging postponement of decision-making should wear this badge more proudly and seek a more in-depth epistemological foundation, and a more nuanced picture of their predecessors (including Plato and Socrates) to support the image they had embraced. Though we should naturally expect Arcesilaus to be the first to have done this in earnest, we cannot confidently assign such a tactic to any particular phase of his life, and one cannot suppose he suddenly changed direction completely on becoming the Head of the Academy. Before that he was indeed a loyal friend of Polemo and Crates, but never their clone in spite of having trodden for some time in the footsteps of the Old Academy.[334] Afterwards he remained an educator, and would have to have held out the prospect of cognitive improvement, if not of knowledge as his Stoic opponents defined it.[335] Pupils expected philosophy to improve their prospects for whatever life would bring.

However, I do not wish to credit the *Alcibiades II* directly to Arcesilaus. Arcesilaus was the heir of Crantor (D. L. 4.25), and heir in more ways than one. He was supposed by some to have revised or edited some of Crantor's work in spite of having been reluctant to compose philosophical works himself (4.32). The fuller passage in

334 See Philodemus, *History of the Academy* 18.7–14.

335 For my own and similar reassessment of Arcesilaus see Tarrant 2019, and Snyder 2018.

Philodemus' *History of the Academy* (18.34–40) suggests that he also inherited Crantor's *hupomnêmata* (perhaps "notes" or "commentaries") and worked on them further himself, though it is clear there were conflicting versions of the story, some supposing him simply to have authored them, others to have co-authored them, and some to have burnt them before making them available. The result is that some of what Philodemus saw as Crantor's work was supposed by others to have been Arcesilaus'. The exact truth is unlikely to be established, but the very fact that the same writings could have struck some as Crantor's work and others as Arcesilaus' suggests a time close to Crantor's death when there was no appreciable gulf between them. Another thing Arcesilaus was supposed to have acquired when relatively young was Plato's books, and these too could have come from Crantor on his death, a considerable time before he became the Head.[336] On my view, outlined in Tarrant 2019a, the "possessor of the books" (cf. D. L. 3.66) was a recognized role in the Academy, bringing with it some power over the corpus itself. As the first commentator on Plato,[337] Crantor is particularly likely to have held such an office.

It is to Crantor rather than to Arcesilaus that I would first look for an author of the *Alcibiades II*.[338] Crantor was obviously not enamored of the Peripatetic school, and might well have devised the subtle comparison between Socrates' education of Alcibiades and Aristotle's of Alexander. If the argument against the simple identity of madness and folly did serve an anti-Stoic purpose, then Crantor lived late enough to have already seen Zeno propounding his apparently counter-intuitive theses

336 There is disagreement over the chronology of these events, particularly the date of Crantor's death. Dillon 2003, 216, favors 290 BCE, but Müller 2003 and Fleischer 2018 prefer 276/5 BCE in the belief that col. S and col. Q of Philodemus' *History of the Academy* refer to the death of Crantor rather than that of Polemo. New work on the papyrus (PHerc 1021), even if it does not succeed in imaging the reverse of the papyri [the columns marked by a letter rather than a number, and containing opisthographs], is favoring the later date. We are currently reliant on the Oxford disegni for these columns.

337 See Proclus, *in Tim.* I 76.1–2; it is unclear whether Crantor offered exegesis of works other than the *Timaeus*.

338 I allow that Arcesilaus might have edited it after inheriting it, and that he might have been personally responsible for its inclusion with the Platonic corpus, especially if it had contained a modest amount of Platonic material.

around the Academy under Polemo.[339] The anti-Stoic context of the fragment of Crantor's *On Grief* preserved in the Plutarchian *Consolation to Apollonius* at 102d (= Crantor F3a)[340] seems clearly directed at Zeno's Stoic ideal of *apatheia* (immunity from emotions), and the actual fragment is criticizing the kind of psychical insensitivity Zeno might advocate, associating it with savage beasts rather than with sages.[341]

More importantly, the *Alcibiades II* is among those dialogues that most freely use epic and dramatic material to illustrate philosophic argument. Literature is sometimes treated as an *authority*, particularly Homeric literature, while drama, especially Euripides, is used for increasing the dramatic effect of particular passages. A poem recorded by Diogenes Laertius (4.25) makes Crantor especially pleasing to the Muses, and it is then said that he favored Homer and Euripides in particular. As Dillon points out (2003: 225), the most favored authorities in the Plutarchian *Consolation to Apollonius*, which makes extensive use of Crantor's *On Grief*, are Homer and Euripides. The latter is used much more frequently than Sophocles and Aeschylus. Thus one should not doubt that Diogenes' information is in this case correct. Furthermore, the quotation from Crantor at Sextus Empiricus (*adv. Math.* 11.51–58 = Crantor F7a) includes a quotation of Homer and two from Euripides, one of which creatively joins together separate lines from two plays: the *Phoenissae* (prominent in *Alcibiades II*) 558, and *Electra* 944. We have discussed a similar hybrid quotation, this time of Homer, in relation to 149d–e, and there is a striking example in the Plutarchian *Consolation* (114e, omitted from Crantor F6a) of half-lines from different Homeric poems joined together.[342] As for *Phoenissae* 558, both this line and line 555 (with minor modification) appear in the Plutarchian *Consolation* (104a = Crantor F4, 116a), the former with

339 See Dillon 2003, 226n121.

340 All of Crantor's fragments are as given in Mette's 1984 collection.

341 The repeated "pray" in the Loeb translation of this fragment by F. C. Babbitt is potentially misleading, as it represents (reasonably enough) the optative in Greek. It cannot be used as evidence of Crantor's interest in prayer proper, though, as I have emphasized, the *Alcibiades II* was very much interested in wishes, too.

342 The half-line after the third foot caesura matches *Od.* 1.423 and 18.306, which describe dusk. What precedes is from *Il.* 23.109, which refers to men grieving—but at dawn, as the remainder of the line says. Note also that at 117c *Il.* 23.222 is followed immediately by 17.37.

comment from Crantor's contemporary Demetrius of Phalerum,[343] so it is particularly likely to be derived from Crantor.[344]

One can therefore build up a reasonably coherent picture of Crantor's often creative use of quotations from available sources. I freely concede not every quotation in the Plutarchian work can be expected to derive from him, but once a convenient anthology of soothing quotations was available for those wishing to console friends on the loss of their children, they would certainly have searched it for appropriate material, even while adapting it to the particular recipient and enriching it with personal contributions. The picture we have built up agrees surprisingly well with the use of quotation we encounter in the *Alcibiades II.*

The passage of Sextus referred to above (= Crantor F7a) might also have a bearing on the dramatic leanings of the author of the *Alcibiades II*, displayed particularly in the telling of Alcibiades' imagined plot against Pericles (143e–144b), and in the conclusion. Sextus illustrates Crantor's exceptional ability to dramatize a philosophical point, personifying Wealth, Pleasure, Health, and Virtue, and depicting them in a huge theatre, each employing rhetoric laced with poetry to compete for the people's prize. While one may note the part of Virtue seems to rely mainly on courage, it may be significant that Knowledge or Wisdom do not appear in this competition. Such an omission might be expected of one who had written in defense of ignorance.

One might think that Crantor, being from Soli, would have been somewhat more likely to employ non-Attic terms than native Athenians like Speusippus, Polemo, and Crates. However, he could surely write consistent Attic if he desired, since he was highly literate. Rather, he appears to have enjoyed drawing on various types of language, including that of quoted poetic sources and some very innovative vocabulary, as Diogenes Laertius (4.27) makes clear.[345] If we assume our author had

343 Exiled from Athens in 307 BCE after ten years of rule imposed by the Macedonian king Cassander. Another Macedonian snippet in the *Consolation* is the report of a prayer by Philip II after three pieces of good news, one of which is the birth of Alexander (105b). Philip prays the news should be offset by some minor misfortune.

344 Other contemporaries quoted include Arcesilaus (110a), Philemon (102c, 105f), Menander (103c–e, 119e), and Theophrastus (104d). Not all material can have been from Crantor (e.g. Callimachus, and the story that includes Antigonus Gonatas' words, 119c–d).

345 One should perhaps note that the first example given by Diogenes was an alpha privative term (ἀπελέκητος) that may recall the sequence of such terms at 141d6, 142a8, 142c3, and 143a2.

sought to pass off his work as that of Plato, we might think his literary skills would weed out non-Attic prose terms, but that might never have been his intention. The author of this dialogue was clever rather than devious, and it may be he did not regard unremittingly Attic Greek as something that would enhance his work. As we have seen, much of the unexpected language is skillfully used.

As for Crantor's views on prayer, I know no *explicit* testimony. But Mette (1984) understandably includes as F5a and F5b parallel accounts, in Cicero (*Tusculan Disputations* 1.113–114, shortly before the mention of Crantor in 115) and in the Plutarchian text (109a), of two stories where deaths follow a prayer to the gods for what is best for humans: exactly the kind of non-specific prayer that the *Alcibiades II* favors. While the stories come from Herodotus and Pindar and are certainly not original to Crantor, they were almost certainly employed by him shortly before the story of Elysius and Euthynous that follows in both accounts.

Another model prayer is mentioned at *Consolation to Apollonius* 118f–119a, telling of Xenophon's reaction to the death of his son. It is worth remembering here that Xenophon had become associated with the *Alcibiades II* in antiquity, and perhaps partly because of his account of Socrates' prayer that the gods "should simply give what was good" at *Memorabilia* 1.3.2. If this should also be traced back to Crantor,[346] then one can note the approval implicit in his recording of Xenophon's words: "I did not pray to the gods that my son should turn out immortal or long-lasting, for it is unclear whether such a thing is of benefit, but that he should become virtuous (*agathon*) and patriotic—exactly what has happened." Xenophon had arguably prayed for something that could not be bad for anybody in any circumstances, and certainly for a much less specific wish-list than most would utter. He was perhaps among the few who had considered the possibility that it might just have been better, for certain individuals from certain families, to be dead than to be alive. Such a sentiment had also been expressed in the

346 As 118d–119d forms a unity, with a close parallel in Aelian, *VH* 3.2–5, and contains material on Antigonus Gonatus that postdates the death of Crantor, an intermediate source would have to be postulated. However, it is clear that the consolation is a genre in which the same material is likely to be repeated by multiple authors, conceivably because authors had limited time in which to assemble a compendium of suitable material (cf. 121e in the Plutarchian text), and are therefore more dependent upon those who have written similar works before.

last line of the poem presented by the ghost of Euthynous to his father in F5 to which we just referred: "It was more beneficial for him to end this way, both for himself and for you."[347] Cicero's version (*Tusculan Disputations* 1.115) acknowledges Crantor as the source here, and one should notice the element of relativism: the death of some persons is sometimes better for certain individuals.[348]

Though we have tantalizing hints of Crantor's relativism, we are not lucky enough to have much information on his epistemology proper, except for the fact that in his view the Platonic world-soul at *Timaeus* 35a–b (and thus presumably individual souls that were modeled upon it) was composed of precisely the same things that it had to observe, cognition being of like by like.[349] Hence its ingredients were the intelligible and sense-perceptible essences plus sameness and difference. Aristotle's interpretation of Plato's *Timaeus* 35a–b had involved like by like cognition (*De Anima* 404b16–18), and we know from Sextus Empiricus (*adv. Math.* 7.93) that Posidonius' interpretation went into the earlier history of this theory. Though Plutarch does not emphasize it when outlining the position taken by the followers of Crantor, it is still clear that Crantor had assumed like must be observed by like. The precise implications of this are unclear. How, for instance, does self-knowledge occur? Subject and object in that case are not only like each other but actually the same.

A more pertinent question might be how a pioneer of the interpretation of the *Timaeus* could come to espouse some form of relativism. The answer, I think, is simply that if cognition becomes dependent upon the internal construction of the perceiving mind, or indeed the internal construction of the sense-organs employed by that mind, then cognition must become relative to us. Every change in those parts of us that are subject to change[350] has the potential to produce a change in how we view things. Sight in the *Timaeus* is certainly

347 *Sic fuit utilius finiri ipsique tibique* in Latin; in Greek οὐκ ἦν γὰρ ζώειν καλὸν αὐτῷ οὐδὲ γονεῦσι.

348 Cicero had likewise been careful to include datives indicating for whom something is best in his account of the prayers leading to the deaths of Cleobis, Biton, Trophonius, and Agamedes: "the greatest good *for a human being*" (113) and "what is best *for a human being*" (114).

349 Plut. *De Animae Procreatione* 1012f–1013a = F10.

350 The embodied soul is itself subject to many changes, all of which have remedies, *Tim.* 43a6–44b7, 90a2–d7.

explained as an interaction between two similar or related[351] things, but the other sensations also occur as a result of interactions. An interactive model of cognition is likewise supplied as a secret basis for Protagorean relativism in the *Theaetetus* (156a3–157c1). The nature of any such interactions must be dependent upon the condition of the perceiver as well as upon that of the object being perceived. Hence the assessment of all cognitive acts whose origin appears external to us must depend upon our assessment of our own internal condition. In both *Alcibiades* dialogues, Socrates encourages Alcibiades to appreciate the shortcomings of his internal condition as a preliminary to moving further forward along the required cognitive road (*Alc. I* 118b, 124a–b; *Alc. II* 150c3–d2). Once he appreciates his shortcomings, he can begin to tackle them, after which his cognitive abilities will be in a better state.

After that corrective process, perhaps, it should really not be such a difficult thing for a human soul to know its own interests and its own limits just as long as mists did not obscure its vision. Perhaps the kind of knowledge we humans most require is not actually so remote from us as we believe. Just as the world-soul had to be able to perceive the intelligible, the sensible, and their similarities and differences, so too the human soul must be able to acquire cognition of god and man and *their* similarities and differences. Perhaps it was composed of the divine, the mortal, sameness, and difference. But we are now entering into the realm of speculation. The *Consolation to Apollonius* (115f–117a) contains interesting material on self-knowledge and on knowing our limits that can be of interest to those searching for the author of either of the *Alcibiades* dialogues. We must know what is ours and what is not ours, know our boundaries, and desist from blaming the gods for misfortunes we bring upon ourselves. But the name of Crantor is not mentioned here, and the ideas are not atypical of Plutarch or other Platonists of the era. If Crantor is currently my candidate for the author of the *Alcibiades II* it is partly because I have none better; if my career depended upon the avoidance of unfounded opinion then I should surely suspend judgment. As things are, I will merely say this: if we search for the author then Crantor demands our careful consideration.

351 Note "like to like" at *Tim.* 45c4 and also the expression ὁμοιοπαθὲς δὴ δι' ὁμοιότητα ("similarly affected on account of similarity") at 45c7; for a "brotherly" relation note ἀδελφὸν, 45b6.

Love according to Crantor through a Poet's Eyes

Not all the evidence for the thought of Crantor occurs in the form of reports, paraphrase, and quotations. Diogenes Laertius includes in his brief life some lines from a poem by Antagoras of Rhodes,[352] a generation or so after Crantor, and a poet knowledgeable about the Academy under Polemo and Crates (cf. D. L. 4.21). The lines are supposed to represent Crantor addressing Eros, and are thus presumably written in imitation of Crantor. The biographical tradition, at least, had made use of the lines to illustrate what sort of poet and thinker Crantor had been, so even if they were not actually his lines they show how he was perceived. The lines might be translated as follows:

> In doubt stands my heart (for your birth is disputed)
> If I should say, Eros, "first god and immortal,"
> First of all children old Erebus brought forth
> And queenly Night, in the depths of broad Ocean;
> Or son of proud[353] Cypris, of the Earth, or the Winds;
> Such are you who wander, devising for humans
> Both mischief and good things, your body too double.

Most obviously, Crantor is presented as one with a deep interest in Eros, and with views that stand firmly in the Platonic tradition. The same kind of doubts about the birth (and consequent status) of Eros are reflected in Plato's *Symposium*, with Phaedrus (178a–c) calling Eros the eldest of the gods in terms that made him coeval with Chaos and Earth, or at least as among the oldest and generated from a heavenly goddess.[354] Then Pausanias, after Phaedrus had specifically denied Eros had parents in the accepted sense, postulated different parents for two separate gods called Eros, the higher one having Heaven as father and no

352 I follow the Loeb text and translation at this rather problematic point, though Dorandi (1994) has a rather different interpretation, connecting the lines with the poems said shortly before (4.25) to have been deposited by Crantor in Athena's temple at Soloi. For our purposes the more direct the connection with Crantor's own beliefs on Love the better.

353 One might also think of translating *periphrôn* as "wise," "thoughtful," or "cunning." There may in fact be intentional ambiguity, matching the ambiguous nature of her son.

354 The former option follows Hesiod (*Theogony*, 116–120), along with Acusilaos, and the latter appeals to Parmenides (B13), where Eros is the first work of the unnamed goddess of the heavens in B12, who was source of all hateful birth and mingling.

mother, the lower having Zeus as a father and Dione as mother. After silence on such issues from Eryximachus and Aristophanes, Agathon seeks to correct Phaedrus (195b–c) and his authorities by making Eros the youngest god of all but neglects to offer either father or mother. Meanwhile Socrates, who denies he has divine status at all (202c–d), offers Diotima's story that he is the child of Plenty and Poverty, explaining the connection with Aphrodite in terms of his conception at the festival of her birth (203c). This story makes him a paradoxical hybrid of the mortal and the immortal (203d–e). No speaker expresses agreement with any other on the key question of Eros' origin and status, and other dialogues only confuse the issue further, so that Plato himself encourages perplexity.

Antagoras' "Crantor" first asks whether Eros was the oldest of the gods, as argued by Phaedrus in the *Symposium*, but mentions a different account from those there. His version is more reminiscent of Aristophanes' *Birds*, where Night,[355] in the boundless embrace of Erebus, is the source of egg from which winged Eros comes (693–697), while Earth (not yet born) and the winds[356] feature in that same passage. Crucially, in Aristophanes, "there was previously no race of immortal gods, before Eros mingled all together" (700), so that the pre-cosmic beings that produced Eros were no bar to his being the first of the true gods; presumably they were not "parents" as we understand it, in Aristophanes or in Antagoras. The suggestion that Cypris (= Aphrodite) is Eros' mother according to a different story does not directly relate to *anything* in Plato, nor that he is the son of Earth,[357] whom he comes just after in Hesiod's account (*Theogony* 116–120), nor that he comes from the Winds. All that is relevant is the sheer uncertainty about the birth of this ambiguous figure found in Plato and perpetuated in the fragmentary verses. These last two alleged mothers seem to be enhancing this impression, the stability of Earth being contrasted with the instability of the Winds. Instability leads to wondering, deviousness, and the potential to work both good and evil, while the double nature

355 The role of Night and her egg are suggestive of later accounts of Orphic cosmology, so other pre-Aristophanic sources might have been relevant.

356 The egg is described as *hypenemios* ("wind-wafted"?), while the wings of Eros were in some way "like wind-swift eddies."

357 This may originate in the fact that Eros comes directly after Earth in Hesiod's account (*Theogony* 116–120), where parentage seems not to be an issue.

of his body may relate as much to his making both males and females the object of desire[358] as to an ambiguous feature of his iconography. Details are less important than the systematic emphasis on the ambiguities of Eros, ambiguities that prevent "Crantor" from coming to precise conclusions. Love has reduced him to the same perplexity as others experience.

In the *Symposium* only the higher Eros had deserved praise according to Pausanias, so that Eros there was neither unambiguously good nor unambiguously bad. Indeed, it is explicitly stated that the lower Eros is not fine (*kalos*, 181a5), while Socrates will later (202d) deduce from the admission that Eros is not of himself fine the fact that he is not a god either. Correspondingly, in these verses Eros seems to perform good works alongside evil. What might this tell us about the ambiguities at the ending of the *Alcibiades II*, where Socrates finally emerges as a lover and even as the taker of the kind of risks that he actively discourages Alcibiades from taking? The future now seems brighter for Alcibiades, but at Socrates' expense. Socrates must be acutely conscious of the looming danger, for in his own words he is confronting "no less a storm than Kreon" (151b). The differences between good and evil, immortal and mortal, are to the fore of his mind and among the lessons he wants Alcibiades to learn (150d–e). But we are left with serious questions about the wisdom, from his own narrower perspective at least,[359] of Socrates' love. Is he perhaps ready to suffer in the attempt to save his beloved?[360] Is this possibly the way in which his mortal self pursues immortality according to the theories of Diotima (*Symposium* 208a7–e1, cf. 212a)? Socrates is revealed not just as a lover (*erastês*) but as the divine lover (*entheos erastês*) of later tradition,[361] pursuing the love that was described by Crantor's colleague Polemo as "a service to the

358 Note the popular confusion by which Eros is identified with the object rather than the subject of love (*Symposium* 204b–c).

359 The *Alcibiades I* (135e) leaves us with forebodings concerning the future of the relationship, perhaps with an emphasis on Alcibiades' inability to resist the powers of the city rather that Socrates'; but here in the *Alcibiades II* the repeated singulars of Socrates' last speech show that it is all about *himself*.

360 Note the emphasis in Phaedrus' speech on dying for one's beloved (179b4–180b5).

361 See especially the commentaries of Hermias on the *Phaedrus* and of Proclus and Olympiodorus *On the Alcibiades I*.

gods for the care and salvation of the young."[362] Hence his apparent indifference to his own earthly future.

Important though the ambiguities of Eros are in the verses quoted, we should not neglect their first two words: "In doubt . . ." (*en doiêi*). To remain in doubt about matters of mythology accords well with Plato's remarks at *Phaedrus* 229d–e, and it scarcely conflicts with the tendency in the *Alcibiades II* to modify, even purify, ancient tradition before using it as a source of insights. In any case, ignorance on such matters cannot be harmful for those who fail to grasp the knowledge of what's best. One might object here that knowledge of Eros is in fact a facet of self-knowledge—a knowledge of the emotions within us—and that a feeling for human emotions was exactly what enabled Crantor to touch hearts and minds with his work *On Grief*. Yet knowledge of the parentage and thus the origins of Eros is the only thing about which such doubts are expressed, and these doubts actually contribute to "Crantor's" broader understanding in these verses. That Eros is somehow double, and pervades the human race, devising both good and bad experiences for them, is nowhere said to be subject to the same doubts as his origins. The Protagorean may expect to have a grasp of the effects of Eros first upon himself, and second upon those who share their experiences with him. Furthermore, while many of the ancients would have thought it right for some things about the "gods" to remain mysterious, including perhaps their precise supernatural status, Protagoras in particular had disclaimed knowledge about their existence or non-existence (*Theaetetus* 162d–e).

Crantor and Arcesilaus: A Coda

What would be the implications if I am right about the authorship? Postulating Crantor as the author, whether or not the dialogue was one of the documents subsequently revised by Arcesilaus, would mean the latter had been close friends in his younger days with a skilled interpreter of Plato who nevertheless believed Plato had a genuine interest in Protagoreanism, and in the necessity, for most of the management of our lives at least, of arriving at judgments that see things *as they are for oneself*, not as they are in some paradigmatic cosmos. By choosing a mentor who will help us to appreciate our own particular circumstances, including our various human limitations,

362 See Renaud and Tarrant 2015, 109.

we might advance further towards an understanding of how things are in reality. Yet both student and mentor might be better equipped for the task if neither of us insists prematurely that we know we know nothing. Even Socrates, if he insisted that he knew nothing, could only be useful to us—and to himself—up to a given point. So the dialogue ends with a huge question about the consistency of Socrates' judgment in a moment of enhanced emotion.

The theory I would attribute to Crantor (and by extension to Arcesilaus) is by no means a type of skepticism. But Philodemus is quite explicit in his *History of the Academy* (18.7–16) that Arcesilaus first adhered to the dialectical procedures that had prevailed in the Academy from the time of Plato and Speusippus to that of Polemo. Only later did he go further from the accepted practices of Academic education. What he learned from Crantor merely set him on the road to operating in a manner that many held to be without Platonic precedent.[363] But what did he learn from Crantor and when?

How far the polemicist Numenius (fr. 25.15–19, 58–67) really knew the chronology of influences upon Arcesilaus may be disputed, but he seems to claim that Theophrastus came first (ἐν παισί), followed by Crantor, Diodorus, and then (εἶτα) Pyrrho.[364] He sees different teachers as inspiring different traits in Arcesilaus, with Crantor being responsible for his ability to have a persuasive influence on others (fr. 25.17: πιθανουργικός).[365] Clearly the same trait is being attributed to both the mentor and his devotee, and in Crantor's case *On Grief* might well have been thought to demonstrate his persuasive powers. But the word strongly suggests that what is being communicated *falls short of knowledge*, just as "persuasive argument" (πιθανολογία, in conjunction with εἰκός)[366] does when Protagoras accuses Socrates of lowering his standard of proof at *Theaetetus* 162e. Of two Plutarchian discussions of

363 It is pertinent here to mention the study of Magris (1992), that associates the *Alcibiades II* with a turning point early in Arcesilaus' career.

364 For the relative positions of Diodorus and Pyrrho contrast D. L. 4.33, where the famous mock-Homeric line of Aristo given there may influence the order; cf. also Philodemus, *Index Acad.* 19.17–24, improvements to which will soon be published by Kilian Fleischer.

365 The word recalls *Sophist* 222c3–223a2, where the power to control human beings by persuasion (associated with Arcesilaus by Philodemus, *Index Acad.* 19.36–41) is divided into two parts corresponding to erotic (gift-giving) and sophistic (fee-taking) persuasion.

366 For a similar conjunction of πιθανόν with εἰκός see *Phaedrus* 272d–e.

early interpretation of the *Timaeus*, both concerning Crantor among others, one talks of what's both "persuasive" (πιθανόν) and "likely" (εἰκός) as criteria (Plut. *de An. Proc.* 1013b), and the other (1020d) employs what is "arguable" (εὔλογον)—this latter being best known as Arcesilaus' criterion for action.[367] None of this proves that Crantor openly advocated such criteria, let alone that he did so because nothing would yield irrefutable truth, but being largely concerned with the practicalities of philosophy he may have had little personal need of certainty.

I therefore tentatively identify the author of the *Alcibiades II* with Crantor. I allow that Arcesilaus may have had a hand in its revision, but see no good grounds for attributing the dialogue to one who was a reluctant author. I also allow that Plato may have produced some outline for a dialogue that Crantor had reworked. I should be most willing to consider a Platonic hand in the opening and in the two-part monologue, but even in the second monologue there are non-Attic forms one would not normally attribute to Plato, and furthermore the imaginative handling of quotations of epic verse in both monologues suggest Crantor was responsible for some of these at least. The overall result is simply not Platonic, and Plato was not the dominant influence on the dialogue as we have it.

I make these claims knowing well one cannot simply trust in one's own scholarly authority. No less a figure than Giovanni Reale is much more positive about the possibility of Platonic authorship, and would in any case place it during the period of Plato's more youthful and "Socratic" works. From his perspective he has answered the usual arguments for postulating a much later date.[368] While he makes useful cautionary remarks concerning how one might seek to understand a dialogue like the *Alcibiades II*,[369] he tends like many other authors to

367 Sextus Empiricus, *adv. Math.* 7.158: ὁ προσέχων οὖν τῷ εὐλόγῳ κατορθώσει καὶ εὐδαιμονήσει.

368 See Reale 2015, 35–45 in particular.

369 Note especially the words "La corretta comprensione di un dialogo come *l'Alcibiade Secondo* e possible solo se non si parte da convinzioni preconcette, che condizionano dal punto di vista ermeneutico in modo radicale . . ." (Reale 2015, 46). But the problem is precisely what counts as "convinzione preconcette." My own view is that careful study of the language of the dialogue make it *impossible* that the received version of the dialogue derives entirely, or even for the most part, from the very early fourth century.

deal almost solely with what one might call the philosophical issues involved, at the expense of the literary and linguistic issues which must be balanced against them. Arguing as I do for a revival of a kind of Socraticism within the Academy in the time of Polemo and Crantor, I cannot believe the date of the dialogue can be fixed solely with reference to the many signs of agreement with the earlier dialogues or Plato and other Socratics, especially with dialogues and passages that might have provided a model for the work concerned. These questions of authenticity must be settled not only by the nuanced judgments of experienced readers of Plato, which have succeeded in resolving remarkably little, nor only by trying to discern where the philosophy, expressed or implied, really belongs, but also by painstaking study of linguistic details and due assessment of the literary aspects of the dialogue concerned. Vocabulary and literary choices both relate closely to the philosophy, and give it a coloring that must not be ignored. And whereas scholars have mainly sought to show what words or phrases Plato could or could not have used, linguistic methods should also take note of the exceptional frequency of words that Plato did use, but used less frequently or in severely restricted circumstances. Plato's worthier imitators almost always over-imitated certain features they saw as important. My contention is that Crantor was one of these.

Appendix I: The Principal Components

Each of the eighty-four variables can have a degree of influence over each of the principal components (PC). The coefficient for each of the variables determines the degree and the direction of influence. Here I simply give the ten words whose presence in high rates exercises the greatest degree of influence towards negative results on components 1 and 3 (as for the *Alcibiades II*), and towards positive results on component 2, followed by the ten whose absence or presence in low rates does so.

Word	PC 1	Word	PC 2	Word	PC 3
οὐ	–0.209	ποτὲ	0.241	ἄνευ	–0.261
ἔγωγε	–0.204	πῶς	0.240	πράττειν	–0.247
ἀλλὰ	–0.187	ἕτερος	0.237	δεῖν	–0.230
εἰ	–0.179	τις	0.227	τυγχάνειν	–0.221
ἤ	–0.176	ἆρα	0.212	οὐδὲ	–0.201
δοκεῖν	–0.175	τοίνυν	0.211	ὥστε	–0.195
οὐκοῦν	–0.165	γε	0.201	πρὸς	–0.189
ὥσπερ	–0.161	αὐτός	0.177	ἄν	–0.173
μέντοι	–0.151	κατὰ	0.170	δοκεῖν	–0.172
δήπου	–0.151	οὐκοῦν	0.165	εἰ	–0.167
ὁ	0.119	παρὰ	–0.095	γὰρ	0.093
μὲν	0.120	εἰς	–0.097	περὶ	0.098
τε	0.121	ἄλλος	–0.103	πῶς	0.107
διὰ	0.121	ἀλλὰ	–0.119	πάνυ	0.112
δή	0.123	σὺ	–0.135	γε	0.114
δὲ	0.133	ὑπὸ	–0.136	ἀπὸ	0.121
ὅσος	0.133	ὥστε	–0.173	τίς	0.172
εἷς	0.138	ὅτι	–0.186	ἄρα	0.175
κατὰ	0.160	καὶ	–0.205	ὁ	0.180
πᾶς	0.166	ἐγὼ	–0.209	ναὶ	0.237

Table 14: Twenty most significant variables for each component—with coefficients

We have already studied the high rates of ἔγωγε and δοκεῖν, which will serve as a reminder that these analyses are not independent of any other linguistic tests based on vocabulary. However, we have already seen that the *Alcibiades II* shows a high rate of the datives of σὺ and ἐγὼ *when combined with* δοκεῖ, whereas both have contributed significantly to negative results on component 2, where the *Alcibiades II* showed a strong positive result. This is not surprising in itself, firstly because we did not claim the dialogue had high rates for these pronouns overall, and secondly, σὺ and ἐγὼ have both contributed somewhat to negative results on component 1 (coefficients of –0.146 and –0.116, respectively) and very slightly on component 3 (coefficients of –0.021 and –0.031 respectively), so that they do contribute to the negative results for the *Alcibiades II* on these criteria.[370]

370 Note that these are the components to which the variable δοκεῖν has made a substantial contribution.

Appendix II: Truth in Eryxias

The language of truth (all words starting with *alêth-*) is not lacking in the *Eryxias* as it had seemed to be in many potentially spurious dialogues. Of those within the corpus we have mentioned *Theages* 0.55, *Clitophon* 0.63, *Hipparchus* 0.82, *Alcibiades II* 1.13, and *Erastae* 1.24. In the works of the *Appendix Platonica* that were generally agreed to be spurious there are no examples of such vocabulary at all in *On Virtue* or *Demodocus I & III*, but 3 in *Demodocus IV*, 4 in *Demodocus II*, 5 in *Axiochus*, and 7 in *On Justice* and in *Eryxias*. The figure for *Eryxias* gives a rate of approximately 1.48 per thousand words, still below all dialogic works of largely undisputed authenticity except *Laws*, though not too far below *Protagoras* (1.77) and *Euthydemus* (1.84). Unlike the *Alcibiades* II, it also uses the concept of falsehood, though only at 395b6 and c1, both times in contrast with the truth. But the more important question is whether the use of these terms in the *Eryxias* is such as to suggest a Protagorean epistemology of the type that resists identifying any one view as being more "true" or "false" than another. Here are the points at which the terminology is found:

395a3: τἀληθῆ. Spoken by Eryxias, asking what Socrates would say if he "had to tell the truth," seemingly implying the argument he had just used was in support of a falsehood.

395b1: οὐκ ἀληθῶς. Socrates takes Eryxias to be saying that such arguments as one used just before are a joke, as things are "not really" like that.

395b6: ἀληθεῖς. And that such arguments are "no more true than false" . . . .

395c1: ἀληθῆ. . . . and those telling lies can prevail over those telling the truth.

396a4: ἀληθέστερα. How Socrates could resolve a dispute about which of two speaks *more* truly.

397d2: ἀληθῆ. Prodicus was unable to convince anybody that he spoke the truth.

399c1: ἀληθῆ. A jury thinks somebody tells the truth if he is a good fellow.

403d7: ἀληθής. Socrates thinks Critias' professed enjoyment of his arguments is not the result of his believing them to be true.

Eryxias is made to introduce the concept of telling the truth, since he can use the term naively. Socrates in the next three examples seems to have seized upon this word in order to explore Eryxias' assumptions about truth in relation to this type of argument he has expressed problems with. His own concept of truth is not revealed. The comparative at 396a does allow Socrates to go beyond the boundaries allowed by Protagoras in the *Theaetetus*, but does not regard one view as simply true and the other simply false. The remainder of the examples only serve to deepen the problems one might have with recognizing any point of view as simply correct. Socrates does not believe he has not been telling the truth, but he does try to understand Eryxias' point of view, and he does highlight human difficulties in telling which point of view is to be preferred. The dialogue is a useful lesson for the reader, but it seems far from having Socrates distinguish right and wrong beliefs.

Bibliography

Aronadio, F. 2008. *Platone: Dialoghi Spuri*. Torino: Unione Tipografico-Editrice Torinese.

Baltussen, H. 2003. "Early Reactions to Plato's *Timaeus*: Polemic and Exegesis in Theophrastus and Epicurus," *Bulletin of the Institute of Classical Studies*, Supplement, no. 78, 49–71.

Bickel, E. 1904. "Ein Dialog aus der Akademie des Arkesilaos," *Archiv für Geschichte der Philosophie* 17, 460–479.

Brisson, L. 2014. *Écrits attribué à Platon*. Paris: Flammarion.

Brünnecke, H. 1912. *De Alcibiade II. qui fertur Platonis*. Diss. Göttingen.

Carlini, A. (ed.) 1964. Platone: *Alcibiade, Alcibiade Secondo, Ipparco, Rivali*. Torino.

Carlini, A. 1963. "Studi del testo della quarta tetralogia platonica," *Studi italiani della filologia classica* 34, 169–189.

Carlini, A. 1962. "Alcuni dialoghi pseudo-platonici e l'Accademia di Arcesilao," *Annali della Scuola Normale Superiore di Pisa, Classe di Lettere e di Filosofia* 31, 33–63.

Centrone, B. 2011. "Fedro 261e7–262c4, o l'inganno della buona retorica," in G. Casertano (ed.), *Il Fedro di Platone: struttura e problematiche*. Napoli: Loffredo, 39–55.

Cooper, J. (ed.) 1997. *Plato: The Complete Works*. Indianapolis: Hackett Publishing Company.

Craik, E. (ed.) 1988. *Phoenician Women*. Warminster: Aris & Phillips.

Dillon, J. 2003. *The Heirs of Plato: A Study of the Old Academy (347–274 B.C.)*. Oxford: Oxford University Press.

Dillon, J. and Timotin, A. 2015. *Platonic Theories of Prayer*. Leiden: Brill.

Dodds, E. R. (ed.) 1959. *Plato: Gorgias*. Oxford: Clarendon Press.

Dorandi, T. 1994. "Crantor de Soles," in R. Goulet (ed.), *Dictionnaire des philosophes antiques II*. Paris: CNRS Editions, 482–483.

Erbse, H. 1971. *Scholia Graeca in Homeri Iliadem (Scholia Vetera)*, vol. II, books V–IX. Berlin: Walter de Gruyter.

Fleischer, K. 2018. "Crantor of Soli—his Bequest and Funeral in Philodemus' *Index Academicorum* (PHerc. 1021, Col. 16.37–Col. S.10)," *Rheinisches Museum für Philologie* 161, 155–165.

Forderer, M. 1960. *Zum Homerischen Margites*. Amsterdam: Hakkert.

Helfer, A. 2017. *Socrates and Alcibiades: Plato's Drama of Political Ambition and Philosophy*. Philadelphia: University of Pennsylvania Press.

Hutchinson, D. S. 1997. Introduction to *Alcibiades II* in J. M. Cooper & D. S. Hutchinson (eds.), *Plato: Complete Works*, Indianapolis: Hackett Publishing Company, 596–597.

Johansen, T. K. 2004. *Plato's Natural Philosophy: A Study of the* Timaeus-Critias. Cambridge: Cambridge University Press.

Johnson, D. M. 2003. *Socrates and Alcibiades: Four Texts.* Newburyport: Focus Publishing.

Kenny, A. 1997. Translation of *Alcibiades II* in J. M. Cooper & D. S. Hutchinson (eds.), *Plato: Complete Works*, Indianapolis: Hackett Publishing Company, 597–608.

Kirk, G. S. 1990. *The Iliad: A Commentary*. Vol. II: books 5–8. Cambridge: Cambridge University Press.

Kurihara, Y. 2012. "Socratic Ignorance, or the Place of the *Alcibiades I* in Plato's Early Works," in M. Johnson and H. Tarrant (eds.), *Alcibiades and the Socratic Lover-Educator*. London: Bristol Classical Press, 77–89.

Labarbe, J. 1949. *L'Homère de Platon*. Liege: Société d'Édition Les Belles Lettres.

Lane Fox, R. 1973. *Alexander the Great*. London: Allen Lane.

Magris, A. 1992. "Der Zweite Alkibiades, Ein Wendepunkt in der Geschichte der Akademie," *Grazer Beiträge* 18: 47–64.

Mastronarde, D. J. (ed.) 1994. *Euripides:* Phoenissae. Cambridge: Cambridge University Press.

Mette, H. J. 1984. "Zwei Akademiker heute: Krantor von Soloi und Arkesilaos von Pitane," *Lustrum* 27: 7–94.

Müller, C. W. 2007. "*Appendix Platonica* und Neue Akademie. Die pseudoplatonischen Dialoge *Über die Tugend* und *Alkyon*," in K. Döring, M. Erler, S. Schorn (eds.), *Pseudoplatonica*. Stuttgart: Franz Steiner Verlag, 155–174.

Müller, C. W. 2003. "Das Archontat des Philokrates und die Chronologie der Hellenistischen Akademie," *Rheinisches Museum für Philologie* 146, 1–9.

Müller, C. W. 1975. *Die Kurzdialoge der Appendix Platonica*. Munich: W. Fink.

Nails, D. 2002. *The People of Plato*. Indianapolis: Hackett Publishing Company.

Neuhausen, H. 2010. *Der Zweite Alkibiades: Untersuchungen zu einem pseudoplatonischen Dialog*. Berlin: Walter de Gruyter.

Neuhausen, H. 2007. "Der Pseudo-platonische *Alkibiades II* und die sokratischen Alkibiadesdialoge," in K. Döring, M. Erler, S. Schorn (eds.), *Pseudoplatonica*. Stuttgart: Franz Steiner Verlag, 175–184.

Ramsey, R. 2012. "Plato's Oblique Response to Issues of Socrates' Influence on Alcibiades: an Examination of the *Protagoras* and the *Gorgias*," in M. Johnson and H. Tarrant (eds.), *Alcibiades and the Socratic Lover-Educator*. London: Bristol Classical Press, 61–76.

Reale, G. 2015. *Platone: Dialoghi Socratici. Alcibiade Secondo, Sulla Preghiera*. Milan: Bompiani.

Renaud, F. and Tarrant, H. 2015. *The Platonic Alcibiades I: the Dialogue and its Ancient Reception*. Cambridge: Cambridge University Press.

Rosenthal, F. and Walzer, R. 1943. *Plato Arabus III: Alfarabius de Platonis Philosophia*. London: In aedibus Instituti Warburgiani.

Scrofani, G. 2009. "La preghiera del poeta nell'Alcibiade Secondo: un modello filosofico e cultuale," *Kernos* 22, 159–167.

Sedley, D. 2009. "A Thrasyllan Interpretation of Plato's *Theaetetus*," *The Oxyrhynchus Papyri* 73, 65–71.

Sharpe, M. 2012. "Revaluing *Megalopsuchia*: Reflections on the *Alcibiades II*," in M. Johnson and H. Tarrant (eds.), *Alcibiades and the Socratic Lover-Educator*. London: Bristol Classical Press, 134–146.

Sommerstein, A. H. (ed.) 1987. Aristophanes: Birds. Warminster: Aris & Phillips.

Stover, J. A. 2016. *A New Text of Apuleius: The Lost Third Book of the De Platone*. Oxford: Oxford University Press.

Tarrant, H. 2020. "One Academy? The Transition from Polemo and Crates to Arcesilaus," in P. Kalligas, C. Balla, E. Baziotopoulou-Valavani, V. Karasmanis (eds.), *Plato's Academy: Insights into its Workings and its History*. Cambridge: Cambridge University Press, 200–219.

Tarrant, H. 2019. "*Philebus*, *Laws* and Self-Ignorance," in A. German, J. Ambury (eds.), *Knowledge and Ignorance of Self in Platonic Philosophy*. Cambridge: Cambridge University Press, 223–236.

Tarrant, H. 2018. "The Socratic Dubia," in A. Stavru and C. Moore (eds.), *Socrates and the Socratic Dialogue*. Leiden: Brill, 386–411.

Tarrant, H. 2017. Review of *Platonic Theories of Prayer*, by John Dillon and Andrei Timotin, *International Journal of the Platonic Tradition* 11, 91–93.

Tarrant, H. 2015. "Dangerous Sailing: [Plato] Second Alcibiades 147a1–4," in Debra Nails and Harold Tarrant (eds.), *Second Sailing: Alternative Perspectives on Plato. Commentationes Humanarum Litterarum* 132. Helsinki: Societas Scientiarum Fennica, 59–71.

Tarrant, H. 2013. "Tetralogies IV and VII: Key to the Thrasyllan Reading-Order," in A. Balansard and I. Koch (eds.), *Lire les dialogues, mais lesquels et en quel ordre: Définitions du corpus et interprétations de Platon*. Sankt Augustin: Academia, 1–24.

Tarrant, H. 2012. "The Origins and Shape of Plato's Six-Book *Republic*," *Antichthon* 46, 52–78.

Tarrant, H. 2008. "The Dramatic Setting of the Arguments with Callicles, Euripides' Antiope, and the Date of an Athenian Anti-Intellectual Argument," *Antichthon* 42, 20–39.

Tarrant, H. 1993. *Thrasyllan Platonism*. Ithaca and London: Cornell University Press.

Tarrant, H., Layne, D. A., Baltzly, D., and Renaud F. (eds.) 2018. *Brill's Companion to the Reception of Plato in Antiquity*. Leiden: Brill.

Thesleff, H. 2017. "Pivotal Play and Irony in Plato's Dialogues," *Arctos* 51, 179–218.

Versnel, H. 2015. "Prayer and Curse," in E. Eidinow and J. Kindt (eds.), *The Oxford Handbook of Ancient Greek Religion*. Oxford: Oxford University Press, 447–461.

Wilson, C. H. (ed., trans.) 1996. Homer: *Iliad Books VIII and IX*. Warminster: Aris & Phillips.

Zeller, D. 2002. "La prière dans le Second Alcibiade," *Kernos* 15, 53–59, https://doi.org/10.4000/kernos.1364.

Zeyl, D. 1987. *Plato: Gorgias*. Indianapolis: Hackett Publishing Company.

Index Locorum

Index of Names

Index of Selected Topics

ARISTOTLE

Aristotle's Empiricism: Experience and Mechanics in the Fourth Century B.C. by Jean De Groot

One and Many in Aristotle's Metaphysics—*Volume I: Books Alpha-Delta* by Edward C. Halper

One and Many in Aristotle's Metaphysics—*Volume 2: The Central Books* by Edward C. Halper

Reading Aristotle: Physics VII.3 "What is Alteration?" *Proceedings of the International ESAP-HYELE Conference* edited by Stefano Maso, Carlo Natali, and Gerhard Seel

HELLENISTIC PHILOSOPHY

A Life Worthy of the Gods: *The Materialist Psychology of Epicurus* by David Konstan

THE *ENNEADS* OF PLOTINUS

Translations with Introductions & Philosophical Commentaries
Series edited by John M. Dillon and Andrew Smith

Ennead* I.1: *What Is the Living Thing? What Is Man? by Gerard O'Daly

Ennead I.6: On Beauty by Andrew Smith

Ennead II.4: On Matter by A.A. Long

Ennead II.5: On What Is Potentially and What Actually by Cinzia Arruzza

Ennead II.9: Against the Gnostics by Sebastian Ramon Philipp Gertz

Ennead III.4: On Our Allotted Guardian Spirit by Wiebke-Marie Stock

Ennead IV.3–IV.4.29: Problems concerning the Soul by John M. Dillon and H. J. Blumenthal

Ennead IV.4.30–45 & IV.5: Problems concerning the Soul by Gary M. Gurtler

Ennead IV.7: On the Immortality of the Soul by Barrie Fleet

Ennead IV.8: On the Descent of the Soul into Bodies by Barrie Fleet

Ennead V.1: On the Three Primary Levels of Reality by Eric D. Perl

Ennead V.5: That the Intelligibles are not External to the Intellect, and on the Good by Lloyd P. Gerson

Ennead V.8: On Intelligible Beauty by Andrew Smith

Ennead VI.4 & VI.5: On the Presence of Being, One and the Same, Everywhere as a Whole by Eyjólfur Emilsson and Steven Strange

Ennead VI.8: On the Voluntary and on the Free Will of the One by Kevin Corrigan and John D. Turner

Ennead* VI.9: *On the Good or the One by Stephen R. L. Clark

ETHICS

Sentience and Sensibility: *A Conversation about Moral Philosophy*
by Matthew R. Silliman

PHILOSOPHICAL FICTION

Pythagorean Crimes by Tefcros Michaelides

The Aristotle Quest: A Dana McCarter Trilogy. Book 1: Black Market Truth
by Sharon M. Kaye

AUDIOBOOKS

The Iliad (unabridged) by Stanley Lombardo

The Odyssey (unabridged) by Stanley Lombardo

The Essential Homer by Stanley Lombardo

The Essential Iliad by Stanley Lombardo

FORTHCOMING

Ennead **I.2:** ***On Virtues*** by Suzanne Stern-Gillet

Ennead **I.3:** ***On Dialectic*** by Pauliina Remes

Ennead **I.4:** ***On Well-Being*** by Kieran McGroarty

Ennead **I.5:** ***On Whether Well Being Increases With Time*** by Danielle A. Layne

Ennead **I.8:** ***On the Nature and Source of Evil*** by Anne Sheppard

Ennead **I.9:** ***On Going Out of the Body*** by Suzanne Stern-Gilet

Ennead **II.1:** ***On the Heavens*** by Andrew Smith

Ennead **II.6:** ***On Substance, or On Quality*** by Damien Caluori

Ennead **II.7:** ***On Complete Blending*** by Robert Goulding

Ennead **II.8:** ***On Sight*** by Robert Goulding

Ennead **III.5:** ***On Love*** by Sara Magrin

Ennead **III.6:** ***On Impassibility*** by Eleni Perdikouri

Ennead **III.7:** ***On Eternity and Time*** by László Bene

Ennead **III.8:** ***On Nature and Contemplation*** by George Karamanolis

Ennead **IV.6:** ***On Sense-Perception and Memory*** by Peter Lautner

Ennead **IV.9:** ***If All Souls are One*** by Eyjólfur Emilsson

Ennead **V.2, V.4, and V.6:** ***On the One and Intellect*** by Eleni Perdikouri

Ennead **V.3:** ***On the Knowing Hypostases*** by Marie-Élise Zovko

Ennead **V.9:** ***On Intellect, Ideas, and Being*** by Matthias Vorwerk

Ennead **VI.1-2:** ***On the Genera of Being (I+II)*** by Damien Caluori and Regina Füchslin

Ennead **VI.3:** ***On the Genera of Being (III)*** by Riccardo Chiaradonna

Ennead **VI.7:** ***The Forms and the Good*** by Nicholas Banner